INDEPENDENCE

AND POLITICS

PERSPECTIVES ON ISRAEL STUDIES

S. Ilan Troen, Natan Aridan, Donna Divine, David Ellenson,
Arieh Saposnik, and Jonathan Sarna, *editors*

INDEPENDENCE

AND POLITICS

CROSSROADS IN THE SHAPING OF
ISRAEL'S POLITICAL SYSTEM

MEIR CHAZAN

Translated by MERAV DATAN

INDIANA UNIVERSITY PRESS

This book is a publication of

Indiana University Press
Office of Scholarly Publishing
Herman B Wells Library 350
1320 East 10th Street
Bloomington, Indiana 47405 USA

iupress.org
Originally published in Hebrew by Magnes Press 2020
English translation © 2024 by Meir Chazan

Manufactured in the United States of America

First Printing 2024

Cataloging information is available from the Library of Congress.

ISBN 978-0-253-06867-5 (hardcover)
ISBN 978-0-253-06868-2 (paperback)
ISBN 978-0-253-06869-9 (ebook)

To my brother-in-law, David Shainok, and family
And to my sister-in-law, Ariella Shainok, and family

CONTENTS

ACKNOWLEDGMENTS

I would like to thank the Hebrew University Magnes Press for its support in publishing the Hebrew version of this book (2020). Tel Aviv University, my academic house, supported the research. I am grateful to the Harry S. Truman Library Institute, which awarded me a generous grant that helped me to conduct the research behind this project. Thanks to the Koret Center for Jewish Civilization at TAU for its help in financing the publication of this book. My heartfelt thanks to Prof. Ilan Troen, the editor of the series *Perspectives on Israel Studies*, who guided me with a great deal of wisdom and sensitivity in the process of publication. I would like to send my dedicated thanks to the book's translator to English, Merav Datan. A previous version of some of the material in chapter 5 was translated by David Ben-Nahum and published in *Israel Studies Review*—thanks. As always in my academic career, this book could not have been written without the kindness and love of my private family: my wife, Yael, and the smiles and bites of our lovely children—Ore, Saar, and Rotem.

INDEPENDENCE

AND POLITICS

INTRODUCTION

"The State of Israel was founded in a revolutionary manner, without elections or democracy, and it could not have been otherwise. It was more important to establish the state than to adhere meticulously to democratic procedures." This is how David Ben-Gurion described the state of governance and the legal reality that had prevailed in the country over the preceding year, as it prepared for the Constituent Assembly elections of January 25, 1949. He added that this was a "temporary arrangement" and "at the first opportunity, the power assumed by the government and the Provisional Council will be transferred to the people, who will elect its representatives through democratic elections, and they in turn will determine the legal foundations of the state."[1]

The salient revolutionary act that took place in 1948 was the Declaration of the Establishment of the State of Israel, issued on May 14. At Ben-Gurion's initiative, the declaration stipulated that an "elected Constituent Assembly" would begin operating no later than October 1.[2] The date was not arbitrary. It was based on United Nations General Assembly Resolution 181, adopted November 29, 1947, and it reflected a desire to abide by the spirit of the resolution without adhering strictly to its timetable. The resolution called for Palestine's partition into two independent states, Arab and Jewish, in the framework of an economic union, and for the establishment of a special international regime to govern Jerusalem. Its timetable specified that two months after the withdrawal of British armed forces and termination of the British Mandate, events that were to take place no later than August 1, 1948, the two independent states and international regime would come into existence, "not later than 1 October 1948." Resolution 181 further stipulated that each state's Provisional Council of Government was to hold elections to a Constituent Assembly, to be conducted "on democratic lines" and no later than two months after withdrawal of the Mandatory armed forces; that is, on December 1.[3] It was this timetable that determined the initially scheduled date of elections to the Constituent Assembly. Not only was this a democratic act and a natural part of the process of establishing a new state, it also constituted a significant step toward Israel's inclusion among the sovereign, legitimate states that form the family of nations.

The aim of adhering to the steps set by the UN, inasmuch as the Jewish side could do so, was, for the members of Mapai (Mifleget Poalei Eretz Yisrael, "Workers' Party of the Land of Israel"—the dominant political party at the time), both an important step toward establishing an independent Jewish state and part of a struggle on two fronts: the domestic arena of the Yishuv (prestate Jewish community), with actors who sought to undermine Mapai's political standing and its ability to lead the Jews toward independence, and the international arena, with actors who sought to torpedo the Partition Plan. Yet once the date of Israel's statehood was moved forward, from October 1 to May 14, and the process itself was delinked somewhat from the other provisions of Resolution 181 because of the war, Ben-Gurion decided to move the date of Constituent Assembly elections forward as well, to October 1, 1948. In practice, however, the ongoing hostilities, political upheavals, and pace of internal political-organizational maturation delayed the elections by almost four months. These elections marked the beginning of the end of the revolutionary chapter in the story of Israel's establishment.

Israel's establishment and early statehood were grounded in a series of important factors and developments. These included the UN General Assembly resolution of November 29, 1947; battlefield successes between 1947 and 1949; the departure and expulsion of the Palestinian population from the territory of the Jewish state; accelerated immigration of the remaining refugees in Europe and a significant portion of the Jewish population of Islamic states; the institutional consolidation and solidarity of the Yishuv in times of crisis and hardship; worldwide Jewish support for and identification with the Zionist struggle for independence; the major powers' positions on the quandary posed by Palestine; the armistice agreements signed with Arab countries; and the division of responsibilities among various authorities in the new state, including between the senior representative officeholder (the president) and the principal executive officeholder (the prime minister). Also worth noting are the navigational skills Ben-Gurion demonstrated under circumstances of prolonged uncertainty, his decision-making capabilities and decisiveness amid the turbulence of war as illuminated by Shlomo Avineri, and the critical backing he enjoyed from his party, Mapai.[4] Given the centrality of Mapai and its leading figures in the transition from Yishuv to state, I highlight throughout our discussion the party perspective of its members, including as reflected in their deliberations over a range of issues relating to the founding of the state, the structure of its government, and its first elections. Appreciation of the close link between a leader's standing within a party and that leader's standing within the political leadership is essential to understanding the relative power of the political personality and comprehending the latter's relative influence in public life. This is particularly evident in times of elections, as illustrated in a series of historical events that *Independence and Politics* will explore.[5]

Historical accounts of this period often and understandably devote most of their attention to military issues, political aspects surrounding the Palestinian Nakba (expulsion from Palestine), and the clashing narratives developed by the warring parties. As noted by Yoav Gelber, however, recent years have seen a trend to shift attention toward various aspects of civilian life in the transition from Yishuv to state, thereby building on and further developing historiographical scholarship in contexts arising from an expansion of the historical panorama to encompass the founding of the state and the consequences thereof. My study, which centers on internal political dimensions related to the Yishuv and Zionism in those days, accords with this historiographical trend.[6] It also adopts Zeev Tzahor's conclusion that Israel's establishment was, to a large extent, facilitated by the existence of a multipronged system that earned the label of "a state in the making" and was led by figures from the Second Aliya (the 1904–1914 wave of Jewish immigration). The transition from the voluntary structure that characterized the Yishuv era to an agreed-upon, binding institutional framework of sovereign statehood—as methodically described by Israel's first cabinet secretary, Ze'ev Sharef, in his pioneering work, *Three Days*—occurred without pronounced turbulence. In the course of this shift, the nontransparent governing style of the Yishuv made way for a new system based on the authority of the state.[7]

The present study explores Israeli political life at the inception of sovereignty by highlighting a number of key issues: the upheavals that shaped governmental frameworks during the transition from a voluntary society to state structures; decisive moments in the establishment of the State of Israel; the struggle for support from the United States and, particularly, its de facto and de jure recognition of Israel; and Chaim Weizmann's tenure as president of the State Council and election as president of the country.[8] These developments were sometimes interwoven as in a tapestry, and only by identifying the various threads spanning its length and breadth can we form a reasonable picture of events that took place in different arenas, according to different time frames, and sometimes with only the appearance of being independent of one another.

The crossroads at which the issues addressed in this book converge, and from which they variously reemerge, meet around May 12, 1948—the date of two crucial political discussions in Washington and Tel Aviv about the establishment of Israel, and the date on which the high commissioner of the British government in Palestine announced the pending expiration—in two days—of the Mandate.[9] Nor should one "deny the credit due" for the act of proclaiming independence two days later, an act that required "no small amount of wisdom, courage, and foresight," in the words of Ben-Gurion, on one occasion when he allowed himself to claim historical credit. He added, "It would have been easy to overlook and squander this historical opportunity—whether because of excessive caution and apprehension, as advocated by visionless realists, or because of a maximalism that lacks any sense of reality, as demanded by those who demand everything from others."[10] The "maximalist" in this case was the American Zionist leader Abba Hillel Silver, and the "realists" will cross our path later.

No less significant was Weizmann's involvement during this period in laying the foundation for a long-term, multifaceted relationship with the United States. The political partnership forged between the Zionist Movement—or, later, the State of Israel—and the United States would reach maturation only in the 1970s, but its actual inception took place during the period covered in this book. In any event, US involvement under the leadership of President Harry Truman in determining the fate and future of the Jewish community in Palestine was, for a variety of reasons, a vital aspect of the portrait we plan to paint of this period.[11] The basic foundation of this alliance formed part of a political vision that Weizmann presented to Truman at their first meeting, on December 4, 1945, and subsequently described in a letter to the president: "We have planned our work and our institutions in Palestine on the most modern and progressive lines." In using the term "Jewish state," Weizmann clarified that "we place no stress on the religion of the individuals who will form the majority of its inhabitants, but we have in mind a secular state based on sound democratic foundations with political machinery and institutions on the pattern of those in the United States and in Western Europe."[12] Had the vision of the Jewish state taken a different form, it is doubtful that Truman would have helped bring it to fruition.

An important factor in the realization of this vision was the intensive activity of American Jews, Zionists as well as non-Zionists, in the struggle to shift the balance in Israel's favor in 1948. US Jewry's embrace of the Jewish state at the time was perhaps most authentically and poetically captured by Ezriel Carlebach, whom historical memory customarily regards as the leading Israeli journalist of the time. On May 9, 1951, he covered the first visit of an Israeli prime minister to the United States. New York welcomed Ben-Gurion with a festive parade, admittedly a smaller and less boisterous one than the parade held for the ousted General Douglas MacArthur a few days earlier, according to Carlebach, "but all agreed that no foreign leader had ever received . . . such a reception." The Jews in the crowd vigorously waved the flags of both states (while the Gentiles shouted, "Hi Ben," believing this to be his first name), devotedly sang "*od lo avdah*" (Israel's national anthem), and mumbled the words of the US national anthem, which they did not quite know by heart. When the parade ended, they dispersed "with hearts full of pride and spirits soaring" and with a sense of dignity and joy. "For half an hour, they too had known independence. One half-hour in 2000 years."[13] For the purposes of our discussion, we will consider the contribution made by one of these groups, a semiofficial entity within the multilayered American Jewish community. One might recognize its partially concealed imprint behind the scenes of a few dramatic developments that occurred the year Israel attained independence, in parallel to the US presidential elections. The loyalty of this group to Weizmann and the institution that would eventually bear his name was, in certain contexts, most fateful.

The combination of a democratic vision, formation of functional democratic institutions despite fierce internal divisions, and faith in a leadership despite not always agreeing with its approach—all amid an existential war necessitating weighty decision-making—are the cornerstones for describing and analyzing the issues addressed in *Independence and Politics*. The time span covered in this book saw a dual pendular movement, as Mapai, whose political status was ascending, and Weizmann, whose twilight was approaching, crossed paths and joined efforts. Their encounter provided an anchor for Israel's establishment and continued existence. Admittedly, the party and its leadership accounted for a much larger portion of this relationship. Nevertheless, in my view, even in the days of Weizmann's public and personal decline, his greatness of leadership and his outlook on the Jewish, Zionist, and Israeli course of life as it approached the crossroads of sovereignty and state independence left their unique mark.

1

THE PATH TO SOVEREIGNTY
From Administration to Government

On December 27, 1946, British prime minister Clement Attlee and Foreign Secretary Ernest Bevin made a strategic decision to withdraw from Palestine as part of the process of dismantling the British Empire. The following day, in a completely unrelated event, the Zionist General Council (HaVa'ad HaPoel HaTzioni, the supreme institution of the World Zionist Organization between the Zionist Congresses) decided not to reelect Chaim Weizmann as president of the Zionist Organization.[1] These two decisions mark the starting point for the historical chapter explored in this book. Attlee and Bevin's decision was part of an ongoing internal review by the British Cabinet regarding the future of the British Mandate. (Britain ruled Palestine from 1918 to 1948, after conquering the country from the Ottoman Empire during World War I. Britain got international legitimacy to its rule by obtaining a Mandate from the League of Nations in June 1922.) On the eve of the Mandate's conclusion, David Ben-Gurion, chairman of the Jewish Agency Executive (the operative branch of the World Zionist Organization) and foremost political figure in the Zionist Movement at the time, agreed to postpone it. He was ready to examine a postponement of the anticipated date for the resolution of the question of Palestine in exchange for British support in transforming the Jews into a majority in the land within a few years. After British talks with Palestinian and Jewish representatives failed, however, the cabinet adopted Attlee and Bevin's position. In line with the foreign secretary's proposal, on February 14, 1947, the cabinet decided to refer the question of Palestine's future to the UN General Assembly. On the following day, Ben-Gurion noted in his diary that "the major [historical chapter] of the Mandate has come to an end. . . . We now face a great, difficult, and decisive battle."[2] The British Parliament's affirmation several days later marked the opening round of this battle, which continued until the UN adopted its Partition Plan resolution in late November. During the intervening months, the United Nations Special

Committee on Palestine (UNSCOP), established by the General Assembly, examined various alternatives for the future of Palestine.[3]

The essence of UNSCOP's report, completed on August 31, 1947, was that the Mandate was no longer workable and should therefore be terminated "at the earliest practicable date," and, likewise, Palestine should be granted independence "at the earliest practicable date." A majority of the committee recommended that on September 1, 1949, Palestine be constituted into two independent states, Arab and Jewish, within the framework of an economic union and with Jerusalem placed under international trusteeship. The recommendations further stipulated that the inhabitants of both states elect constituent assemblies with voting rights granted to men and women over twenty years of age, and that during the two-year transitional period, 150,000 Jewish immigrants be admitted within the borders of the proposed Jewish state. Thus the foundation was laid for "the battle over Palestine" and its future.[4] From the perspective of political decision-makers in the Yishuv, the concrete dilemmas stemming from UNSCOP's proposal were threefold: Would there be a transitional period? How long would it last in practice? And what would transpire in Palestine in the interim? In effect, the adoption of UNSCOP's report gave the signal, as of September 1947, for political, organizational, security, and legal preparations for a sovereign Jewish state in Palestine to commence.

On the Road to Partition: Internal Conflicts in the Yishuv

While the Zionist political establishment and public opinion in the Yishuv were preoccupied with the fate of the *SS Exodus* (a passenger ship carrying forty-five hundred Jewish refugees whose entry the British had barred), the implications of UNSCOP's recommendations regarding Jerusalem, the feasibility of an economic union, and the state of security, the leadership of the Jewish National Council (Va'ad Le'umi, the Yishuv's internal executive body) was preoccupied with another issue altogether: elections. At a meeting on September 11, 1947, Yitzhak Ben-Zvi, National Council president and prominent Mapai (Zionist, democratic, and socialist political party of workers) member, stated that any measures taken in regard to UN discussions in New York clearly fell within the purview of the Jewish Agency Executive, but "there is one matter for which the initiative and the responsibility fall to the National Council, and that is what will happen after the two-year transitional period, or what will happen in the event that the question arises, without a transitional period, of jumping into statehood." He asserted that the

National Council must be the initiator "regarding a proposed constitution, [whether] for a lengthy or a brief transitional period, and we cannot assign all the responsibility and action in this matter as well to the Agency." He was joined by council chairman, David Remez, another leading Mapai member, who explained that "for the time being we will not have any authority in this matter other than the authority to initiate, and authority to initiate does not require permission." On the basis of their recommendation, the council approved the establishment of a committee to formulate "a proposal that will include the contours and bases of a constitution for a Jewish state." The committee members were Ben-Zvi, Remez, Mordechai Eliash (legal adviser of the National Council), and Zorach Warhaftig of HaPoel HaMizrachi (Mizrachi Workers, a religious Zionist and socialist political party). As part of this process, Warhaftig was assigned the task of establishing a legal department within the National Council. Remez then added another step: elections to the Assembly of Representatives.[5] He invoked Jewish folklore to provide a metaphorical explanation of the need for such elections: How does one make spirits? Distill various chemicals for seven days and then go to the store and buy spirits. His analogy went as follows: "For thirty years we have been building democracy in the Yishuv and educating it for self-government," and it was inconceivable that at precisely this point, democracy should be discarded as if it were worthless scaffolding.[6]

The role of the Assembly of Representatives in the history of the Yishuv was of secondary importance. It operated within the framework of a vague entity known as "the Knesset of Israel" (Assembly of Representatives), whose authority derived not from the force of law or tradition but rather from the voluntary participation of diverse bodies.[7] The Assembly of Representatives served as the supreme public body of the Yishuv during the British Mandate years, although it convened on an irregular basis at intervals of several months. The quasiexecutive arm of the Assembly of Representatives was the National Council, which, during the latter days of the Mandate era, had responsibility in the areas of education, welfare, healthcare, and religious affairs. Matters of policy, security, finances, and relations with the Jewish world and international entities fell within the purview of the Jewish Agency Executive. Mapai, the dominant party in the Jewish Agency Executive, was also the dominant political force in the Assembly of Representatives and the National Council.

Democratic tradition and loyalty to democratic principles as the means of cultivating ever-evolving and branching systems of government, organization, and society routinely guided the elected political bodies of the Zionist Organization, the Yishuv, and the Histadrut (General Association of Workers, the national trade union) as well as civic life among a decisive portion of the public that sought to realize Zionist aspirations. These factors laid the foundation for the gradual development of prestate national governance. Avi Bareli and Yosef Gorny rightly argue that establishing the authority of "national institutions"—in the form of the Jewish Agency Executive and the National Council Executive—was the most important political act undertaken by Mapai in the 1930s and 1940s. Mapai's hegemony in these quasigovernmental systems was based on repeated victories in democratic elections. The election results and Mapai's continuous work as a hegemonic body in the political Zionist arena established its status as the leading force in the Jewish struggle for national independence.[8]

At a Mapai Secretariat meeting on September 18, 1947, Remez commented, "We now need to prepare a transition plan of our own and proceed on the assumption that we must carry out the work ourselves."[9] Notwithstanding the vagueness of Remez's wording, the message was no doubt clear to Ben-Gurion: Remez was seeking to use the institution he headed to guide the political process in a direction that might detract from the authority and seniority of the Jewish Agency's chairman, while at the same time directing decision-makers on the Jewish side toward a course of action in which war against the Arabs would not be considered inevitable. Ben-Gurion, however, made it clear on two occasions during August 1947—before the Mapai Council and before the Zionist General Council at a gathering in Zurich—that although public opinion and the Zionist political system were preoccupied with a range of issues (such as Jewish terrorism and illegal immigration), in his view, there was one vital, central, and decisive issue on the agenda: the question of "the physical existence of the Yishuv" in the face of Adolf Hitler's disciples, "who know one way, and one way only, to solve the Jewish problem—complete annihilation."[10] When speaking publicly, he chose flowery language to make this point: "States are not handed to a people on a golden platter. And let us not entertain the delusion that a miracle will befall us." In institutional terms, Ben-Gurion's response to the lacuna in governance and the future political vacuum expected to result from the declared British intention of not implementing whatever plan the UN might adopt is summed up in his assertion: "Let a provisional Jewish government be established immediately."[11] This was the political principle underpinning his efforts until May 14, 1948—namely, a ruling executive decision-making body rather than a platform for deliberations along the lines of the Assembly of Representatives.

The other side of the Yishuv's ideological divide was characterized by lackadaisical right-wing efforts to organize civic life. The General Zionists

Party, joined in 1947 by leaders of the HaIhud HaEzrahi (Civic Union) and headed by Tel Aviv mayor Israel Rokach and Petah Tikva mayor Yosef Sapir, relied on the power bases of local governing authorities, members of the business sector, and financial organizations as they demanded a role in the decision-making process leading to independence. Backed by their newspaper, *HaBoker*, the General Zionists strove to take part by means of an "Emergency Jewish Higher Committee" (recalling the Arab Higher Committee)— at the expense of the Jewish Agency Executive and the National Council Executive—which would include leading figures from the (economic or political) right. However, the practicability of their demand for representation, regardless of whether the will to implement it existed, was doubtful given that those who had been considered strong figures from their ranks, such as Pinhas Rutenberg or Menachem Ussishkin, had long since passed away. Even though the Revisionists viewed him as a Garibaldi of sorts, Rokach was not seen as a figure of political significance or an authoritative personality in the Yishuv community. Golda Myerson (Meir) mocked civic groups that, according to her, sought to create a governmental structure in the form of "a fantasy suited to their spirit," and Ben-Gurion charged, "A higher committee is what the Arabs have; we have elected bodies."[12] Even the other decidedly right-wing liberal newspaper, *Haaretz*, refrained from aligning itself with the General Zionist party and in fact supported elections in the spirit advocated by Remez and Ben-Zvi.[13]

The report from UNSCOP did not specify when elections to the Constituent Assembly should take place. In a memorandum of October 9, 1947, to the National Council, Warhaftig stated that it was imperative these elections take place only after the arrival of an additional 150,000 Jews. This would have ensured a Jewish majority in the Jewish state, given that at the time of his writing, there were only 500,000 Jews as opposed to 506,000 Arabs, and under those circumstances, any constitution adopted by a Constituent Assembly might "turn out to be monstrous."[14] Despite the lack of clarity surrounding elections to a constituent assembly, as they still depended on resolutions to be adopted by the UN General Assembly, a debate raged within Mapai between Ben-Gurion and Remez over the body that would henceforth make critical decisions about Zionist policy.

At a Mapai Secretariat meeting on October 11, 1947, Remez warned against "amputating" one of the legs of the twin democratic institutions of the Yishuv and the Jewish Agency "through emergency measures"—meaning that the impending state of emergency in Yishuv life must not be exploited by any entity (ostensibly the Jewish Agency Executive, though Remez, without naming him directly, was actually referring to Ben-Gurion)—in order to claim the sole decision-making role in policy and military matters at the expense of the Zionist Organization and Yishuv institutions. Ben-Gurion, who would have preferred to keep this dispute out of the party's top forum, was forced to make his position clear to his colleagues. He asserted that if the British government came to an abrupt end, a new government would have to be formed immediately to prevent a vacuum. To dispel any doubt, he noted that he was not referring to the Jewish Agency or the National Council, or a merger of the two: "This will be a body of an entirely different nature, the likes of which has never existed in the Yishuv or among the Jewish people." In a spirit similar to Ben-Gurion's remarks at the start of this book, Eliezer Kaplan, head of the Jewish Agency's Finance Department and a Mapai leader, stated that if the British evacuated the country, a state of revolution would follow. He concluded, therefore, that pursuing democratic measures such as those sought by his moderate associate Remez would not be enough, and that when the time came, it would be necessary to establish an ad hoc institution that might be called a "provisional government or some other name . . . to which we will have to turn over management for decision-making when the time is right."[15]

At the November 25, 1947, National Council plenary meeting, in a laconic style comprehensible only to those in the know, Ben-Gurion and Remez concisely captured the nature of their dispute. The National Council chairman stressed that the main issue on the agenda was the democratic task of establishing a state, which fell to the "two democracies"—that is, the democratic institutions of Zionism and the Yishuv. In contrast, the Jewish Agency chairman predicted that the founding of the state was a matter for "the day after tomorrow," whereas "tomorrow" necessitated immediate preparation to ensure implementation of the "legal, political, and moral" decision adopted by the UN, and "tomorrow's questions are two that are [actually] one: security and peace!" Ben-Gurion warned, "If we don't resolve them immediately and successfully, we will not get to see the day after tomorrow."[16]

On November 30, 1947, the day after the UN General Assembly adopted its Partition Plan, Ben-Gurion did not even bother to make an entry in his diary along the lines of *Davar*'s main headline: "The State of the Jews Is Established." Instead, he opted to record the results of elections to the printing press trade union, which had taken place on the same day: "Mapai Party 376 (68%), HaShomer HaTza'ir 109 (19.7%), Poalei Tzion Smol 67 (12%)."[17] He saw this outcome as an indication of both Mapai's and (in particular) his own solid standing moving forward. These would be the only elections to preoccupy him during the coming year. In selecting the new state's name, however, he was less successful. "New Judea" was the name he gave in an announcement issued the day after the UN's Partition Plan resolution. But it was the pure logic voiced by Ben-Zvi, his fellow companion from the outset of his own political journey, that prevailed: "Eretz Israel" (the Land of Israel) is a geographical term; "Judea" was indeed the last state to exist, but to call its citizens "Judaists" would be grating, whereas most parts of the biblical state of Israel were currently within the jurisdiction of the state in the making.[18] Ben-Gurion would adopt the name proposed by his colleague within a few weeks. The proposal to name the new state Israel passed by a majority of seven votes in the People's Administration (Minhelet HaAm, a provisional cabinet) on May 12, 1948, and was approved at a meeting of the People's Council (Moetzet HaAm, a provisional legislative body) on May 14, shortly before the public declaration of independence.

In a rare display of satisfaction, Ben-Gurion stated at the start of a Jewish Agency Executive meeting on the day after the UN adopted the Partition Plan that "the Jewish people deserve a *mazel tov* [congratulations]," adding that this was the greatest one-time feat of the Jewish people since it had become a people. Regarding the role of Moshe Shertok (Sharett), head of the Jewish Agency's Political Department and delegate to UN meetings, in reaching this moment, Ben-Gurion voiced the opinion that "if the only thing he did in his life was what he did in Lake Success, he would still be promised a place in the historical afterlife of our people."[19] While the National Council Executive considered a proposal to hold annual "Resurrection Day" celebrations on the first day of Hanukkah and sought to summon Ben-Gurion to praise him for "launching the war for the Jewish state and unhesitatingly summoning all of us," Ben-Gurion absconded from this forum, focusing instead on more prosaic concerns.[20] A few days later, he openly shared his views with members of the Histadrut Executive Committee, observing that the designated borders of the Jewish state "are very strange" and expressing doubt that any state had ever had such borders. On this occasion, he shared his concerns that it would be extremely difficult to achieve statehood "because who knows whether the Jews are capable of self-governance." In a lecture he delivered that day at the Mapai Central Committee, Ben-Gurion spoke about long-term challenges that had to be sidelined for the moment in light of the security imperative: "The Jewish state is missing quite a few things: a name, a capital, a government, an anthem, a constitution, a budget, a currency, an army, police—and on and on. . . . All these voids are easy to fill, and do not require much time. . . . But the state is missing one fundamental thing, which is its most serious and acute shortcoming: *It is lacking in Jews*. . . . As long as this shortcoming is not minimally addressed, there can be no surety of the state's existence, even after its establishment."[21] In line with his lifelong fondness for numeric data and a tendency to set absolute numerical objectives, Ben-Gurion posited that the immigration of 1.5 million Jews during the state's formative period, within a decade would represent "not the purpose of building a state, but the start of and preparation for statehood." He viewed the promotion of Jewish immigration as "not only the central role of the Jewish state, but the main justification for its establishment and existence."[22]

Statistically, Ben-Gurion's objective would only be achieved in 1973, the year of his death.[23] In early 1948, a leading economist of the emerging state, David Horowitz, drew a comparison between 1917 and 1947 and, with independence around the corner, observed, "Had we invested just a small portion of the self-sacrifice, vast amounts of money, talent, and will of world Jewry in building Eretz Israel, then we would long ago have had a Jewish state throughout all of [Western] Eretz Israel [from the sea to the Jordan River]." Not being a politician, Horowitz could allow himself to express such views. He added, "Had the [Jewish] people made available for the Zionist enterprise just one-tenth of what Hitler took, the issue would have been resolved. We did not take advantage of that chance. A miracle happened, and now we have a second chance. Such a chance will not recur a third time."[24] Ben-Gurion, in his previously cited speech, refrained from addressing the realities of war, but in a subsequently published version of that speech, he added the following remarks: "Only a self-styled genius or total idiot would dare, at this point, to offer absolute and definitive answers to the questions arising from the establishment of the state. In the course of this new undertaking, we will have to adapt our thoughts and deeds to shifting situations and changing circumstances internally and externally, yet we are not free from [the duties of] general planning, which should herald developments to come, not merely be dragged along by them."[25]

These succinct observations encapsulated Ben-Gurion's sense of the nonbinding nature of the road map laid out by the UN for the implementation of its Partition Plan. They reflect his lack of commitment to the plan's provisions and his assessment of the low likelihood of their implementation, as specified, if the Jews wished to establish an independent, sovereign state at that time and place. His position, frequently voiced in the subsequent weeks and months, was that war would inevitably play a part in shaping the fate of Eretz Israel and in determining the political status of its Jewish inhabitants. In the course of celebrations on the day after the victory at the UN, he voiced the views his associates wanted to hear, without masquerading as a "genius" or as an "idiot." On that occasion, he opted to refrain from voicing his assessment of what was around the corner. However, for the purposes of historical documentation, which required an honest assessment of reality as he saw it,

Ben-Gurion made no secret of how much his thinking deviated from the UN's plan. He preferred to think in terms of "shifting situations and changing circumstances" when the facts of the situation still seemed vague and there was no certainty that they would lead to a life-and-death war. United States president Harry Truman, however, saw things very differently. In a December 2, 1947, letter to Henry Morgenthau Jr., US secretary of the treasury under President Franklin Delano Roosevelt from 1934 to Roosevelt's death in 1945 and therefore the highest-ranking Jew in the American political establishment at that time, Truman wrote, "Now is the time for restraint and caution. . . . The Jews must now display tolerance and consideration for the other people in Palestine with whom they will necessarily have to be neighbors."[26]

At a Jewish Agency Executive meeting on December 7, 1947, the first time this forum addressed preparedness for the establishment of a state in light of the UN Partition Plan, Ben-Gurion noted that "on paper there are dates" stipulated by Resolution 181, but if violence broke out in the country, it would not be possible to hold elections. In that case, there would be a long period of provisional rule, which would require "a government with maximal authority."[27] On December 30, 1947, members of Etzel (the Jewish underground paramilitary Irgun Zva'i Le'umi, "National Military Organization," also known as "the Irgun") launched several improvised bombs at Arab laborers gathered outside the gates of an oil refinery in Haifa where more than one thousand Arabs and several hundred Jews worked side by side. The attack resulted in six deaths and dozens of injuries. Arab workers then began attacking Jews, killing thirty-nine and injuring dozens. In response, the Haganah (the main Jewish paramilitary) attacked the Arab villages of Balad al-Sheikh and Hawassa, where many of the refinery's Arab workers lived, resulting in the deaths of approximately twenty residents, including women and children. Given the large number of casualties, Ben-Gurion published a statement in the Hebrew press on January 2, 1948, asserting that this was not another round of rioting along the lines of the earlier Arab revolt but a war that represented some of the "labor pains of the State of Israel."[28] This marked Ben-Gurion's first public act of leadership in the context of Israel's war of independence. From this point forward, the military situation would often dictate the pace and substance of political developments.

THE POLITICAL SCENE ON THE EVE OF THE CONVOY OF 35 BATTLE

About two hundred Jews (and at least twice as many Arabs) were killed in the six weeks that followed the adoption of the UN resolution. Even some of the

Yishuv's leading experts in Arab affairs viewed the steadily prevailing state of war as a revolution, and despite the ever-growing number of casualties, the Yishuv community had great difficulty accepting the reality of war.[29] On January 8, 1948, the eighteenth anniversary of Mapai's founding, its central committee convened not to celebrate but to address the urgency of the moment. Ben-Gurion presented a chronology of eight fateful dates arising from the UN Partition Plan and British policy for which it was necessary to prepare in the coming year: the arrival of the UN Palestine Commission established by Resolution 181 to implement the Partition Plan on an unspecified date; the opening up of Haifa Port to unrestricted Jewish immigration on February 1; the establishment of a Provisional Council of Government on April 1; the termination of the British Mandate on May 15; the withdrawal of British forces on August 1; the establishment of two states on October 1; elections to the Constituent Assembly on December 1; and, on an unspecified date, the convening of the Constituent Assembly and its election of a provisional government. Of all these dates, there was one he singled out: "One can never foresee complicated things, and things in the country are very complicated. But if the date of May 15 happens, and England ends the Mandate, then we must assume that war will break out or intensify and perhaps even reach its peak. . . . And then we will be put to the test, *a test we have not faced in thousands of years.*"[30] His ability to predict the critically decisive moment so precisely amid the confusion, and to prepare for it successfully, is what solidified his place in history at the time and in subsequent years. In retrospect, Ze'ev Sharef, first cabinet secretary and the official closest to Ben-Gurion and the decision-making process at the time, captured this fundamental characteristic of Ben-Gurion's conduct during 1947–1952 with the seemingly trivial observation: "He suddenly saw."[31]

Speaking on January 13, 1948, at the Security Committee (a body created by the Jewish Agency Executive and the National Council Executive to oversee security matters on their behalf during the transitional phase until the establishment of state institutions), Ben-Gurion cautioned, "It will get much worse here. We are about to face collective suffering, hardships we have not yet known, because a war of annihilation has been declared against us, and we must have no illusions."[32] Two days later, responding to complaints about the slow pace of military preparedness, he told members of security committees in the south that since the Zionist Congress of December 22, 1946, he had been trying to "make our Republic see the security problem in a new light, and insisting on a new approach to the mission of defense, and I have found almost no receptive ears." This did not result from the absence of visible danger: "It is not enough to see danger; one has to feel it—otherwise one cannot make a supreme effort; otherwise one lives life as usual, not lying awake at night, not sharing one's food with one's friends." He stunned the recruits who had enlisted for security missions in remote Negev communities when he told them, "You are expecting us to bring you concrete and iron to build fortified positions. Dig trenches! And where the land is rocky, create ramparts." To those who complained about the heavy burden, he replied, "So far we have been spoiled" and cautioned, "This burden is child's play compared to what will befall us in two months."[33]

At the end of the week, on Sabbath Eve, January 16, 1948, members of the Mapai Secretariat convened in the assembly hall of the Histadrut Executive Committee to discuss the functions and schedule the inauguration of Beit Berl, the Mapai educational institution.[34] Zalman Rubashov (Shazar), the editor-in-chief of *Davar* and known for demonstrating his impressive, flowery rhetorical flair at Mapai gatherings, stated at the outset of the meeting, "The wisdom of Israel now is the wisdom of redemption." Ben-Gurion disagreed, asserting that "the wisdom of Israel now is the wisdom of war." He assessed that the coming seven or eight months, "until the establishment of the state"—on the date determined by the UN resolution—"enfold all three thousand years of Jewish history, and will perhaps determine the entire course of our history in the coming hundreds or thousands of years."[35] His remarks were intended to make clear to members of the Mapai Secretariat and invited guests why he "very much wants" the party's main intellectual and educational institution, named after his close political ally and fellow Mapai leader Berl Katznelson, to start operating within two to three months at the latest. An edited version of his speech was reprinted in Ben-Gurion's writings on security affairs under the heading "War and Vision." The thrust of his argument provides a good justification for today's readers to describe him as something of a warmongering militarist.[36]

At the time of their delivery, however, Ben-Gurion's words were intended to promote precisely the reverse in terms of educational and intellectual values. Ben-Gurion was pointing out to his audience that war is a unique phenomenon in human history because it subjugates everything, and whoever does not know how to subjugate everything for wartime needs is doomed to moral, national, and physical extinction. This is a supreme test, which may also be a last test, not of power but of the will to live. All of one's body, senses, and desires must be subordinated to the test posed by war. Jewish life to date had had such tests—during the Crusades, in the time of Zynoviy Bohdan Khmelnytsky (a Cossack leader), and under Hitler—observed Ben-Gurion. The decisive verdict, however, was now approaching, and it would be determined in the coming months not "over there," in hinterland settlements such as Kfar Etzion and Kfar Szold, but "here," at the front that forms part of the soul of every Jew in the country. His conclusion: "Everything—for the war effort!" The state, immigration, settlement, and culture are important, but without a victory in this war, "there's nothing!" Therefore, Ben-Gurion continued, as the soul was about to be subjugated completely to war, it would be imperative to create an institution "that symbolizes our true being," and it would be necessary "to establish a cultural enterprise whose essence is peacemaking and human fraternity—this is the enterprise and this is its name"—Beit Berl.

Inaugurating this enterprise at this time does not detract from the war effort but rather reinforces it "because it underscores why we are fighting and who our fighters are." Ben-Gurion concluded that those entrusted with founding Beit Berl "precisely now, during these terrible months . . . will, I know full well, be doing a tremendous service for the warfront and the cause of the war we are called upon to wage."[37]

On the following morning, January 17, Ben-Gurion made a diary entry about the "harsh news" brought to him by his military aide, Nehemia Argov: "A convoy dispatched in the evening the day before yesterday to Kfar Etzion by way of Hartuv—has gone missing. They were going to the mountains."[38] This was the Lamed Heh (thirty-five soldiers) convoy commanded by Danny Mas. As Sharef observed, "he suddenly saw," having spoken on the previous evening about war as the all-encompassing cause, only a few hours after the final shot was fired on that "hilltop battle" without his knowledge. The arrogance evident in Davar's front-page story of January 16, under the headline "Decisive Defeat for Gush Etzion Attackers," alongside another headline asserting "Arab Losses Outnumber Ours Tenfold," was somewhat moderated by a warning penned by the newspaper's military correspondent that appeared on the last page: "Only the Pope is never wrong (and only in the eyes of his followers). Flesh and blood make mistakes and fail every day, all the more so in war. There is no army that never makes mistakes. Nor do we have a contract with God ensuring we always win." These words of warning turned out, on that very day, to be horrifyingly true, and Davar's arrogance instantly turned to lament: "Thirty-five fell. In all their glory. In the promise of their future, in the sanctity of their sacrifice, in the sanctity of their families' sacrifice."[39]

Ben-Gurion's vociferous warnings of impending war over the previous months had apparently been valid. His speeches at Mapai gatherings on January 8 and 16, in combination with the growing numbers of casualties—and the massacre of an entire convoy of elite fighters, resulting in the highest number of losses to date—tipped the balance in the struggle to shape public consciousness and the public agenda in the Yishuv community as it proceeded toward independence. A January 23 editorial in *Davar* voiced concern about the need to complete this shift: "A decisive majority of the Yishuv is living life as if we are not in the midst of an existential war."[40] Conversely, in a letter to all the editorial boards of the Hebrew press, Hebrew University president Judah Leib Magnes, philosopher Martin Buber, and the university's chief administrator, David Werner Senator, criticized the prevailing "psychosis of war" and "psychosis of fear" that caused people to view every foreigner or apparent foreigner as "a criminal and murderer, attacker and enemy" whose murder is permissible.[41] On the same day, January 27, in a speech before invited guests from across the political spectrum at the Ohel Shem Cultural Center in Tel Aviv, Ben-Gurion stated that since the beginning of hostilities, 480 Jews had been killed (in addition to 950 Arabs and 47 British), and 749 injured. He opened his remarks by declaring, "I won't be revealing anything new if I say that security is at the center of our lives."[42] The widespread acceptance of this outlook had concrete political implications.

In February 1948, Ben-Gurion reviewed the "first round" of hostilities against the Arabs and ruled it "in our favor." At the request of Mapai's youth newspaper, he sketched the desired profile of the soldier whom the Labor Movement ought to cultivate: "The young Jewish fighter should know that for us the war is a bitter necessity imposed on us from outside, not a yearning for battle, and that we view the Arabs fighting against us as victims of incitement and bitterness, not as a historical enemy; and that we know how to be both undeterrable fighters who will not be stopped and pure of will and thought, preserving the image of God in our hearts even in battle."[43] This moral idealism would fail the test of battlefield reality in a number of well-known instances, but it indicated that from the perspective of the political system that had brought the "state in the making" to the point of fruition, the "purity of arms" was and remained the guiding principle and code of standards, to be instilled in recruits and preserved in times of war despite frequent violations. As to the commencement of the second round, Ben-Gurion's security assessment, which invariably also had far-reaching internal political implications, was that foreseeability did not extend beyond the next two months, during which, he warned his colleagues on the Security Committee, "it is not out of the question that we might receive severe blows." Accordingly, there was no room for planning actions aimed at achieving a decisive victory in the coming month, "nor is there any need to strive for this. What we seek is to remain steadfast for two months." The purpose of buying time centered on the expected arrival of military equipment purchased abroad. Then, Ben-Gurion hoped, "the situation might change radically" and "we will be able to deliver a victorious blow."[44] This agenda dictated the pace of political developments in anticipation of the target date—May 15, 1948.

The Efforts to Form a Governing Structure

During February–April 1948, there were six weighty, and interrelated, political questions on the agenda of the Jewish community in Palestine: first, the extent of the Jewish commitment to implementing the provisions of UN Resolution 181; second, the political party composition of the Provisional Council of Government; third, the mandate of this council; fourth, the fate of the National Council and the Jewish Agency Executive after the establishment of the Provisional Council of Government; fifth, the relationship between the emerging political system and the war effort; sixth, the responsibility for decision-making in conducting the war and for issuing orders and instructions to the military apparatus. Of this mix, we will focus on those aspects that relate directly to the issues examined in the present study.[45] Retrospectively, one might, with due caution, argue that from a historical perspective, the events of those three months and the conduct of the Jewish leadership during that period shaped Israel's future for the coming decades. The main political dilemma they posed was whether the Zionist Movement and the Yishuv would be able to produce a legitimate, reliable, and purposeful system of governance capable of making realistic decisions suited to the concrete circumstances of an ongoing war and uncertainty in the international arena, with the aim of reaching the threshold of independence.

Any plans to hold elections to the Assembly of Representatives were dashed by late February 1948 as a result of the intercommunity war and the US State Department's inclination to replace the Partition Plan with a "trusteeship" as a means of resolving the conflict. The die was cast following a plea from Shertok, the envoy to New York in charge of diplomatic contacts at the UN, to the Jewish Agency Executive and the National Council on January 30. In light of growing uncertainty about the American commitment to promoting the Partition Plan, he urged them to send him, without delay, the list of names for the Provisional Council of Government indicated in the Partition Plan so he could pass it along to the UN-appointed Palestine Commission.[46] The commission, which met for the first time on January 9, 1948, was intended to serve as the international institutional body overseeing the implementation of the Partition Plan. Its most prominent figure was American decolonization expert Ralph Bunche, a UN undersecretary-general and head of the Trusteeship Department. The Arab Higher Committee refused to cooperate with the commission, whereas the Zionist side urged it to move forward with full force in implementing the Partition Plan. David Horowitz, liaison officer to the commission, described its conduct as "completely disconnected from the bloodshed-ridden country."[47]

The attentive focus on contacts at the UN around the issue of the Provisional Council of Government, including its composition, powers, and responsibilities, was intended to satisfy the administrative demands arising from the UN Partition Plan, but in effect, it made elections to the Assembly of Representatives redundant. The personal power struggle between Ben-Gurion and Remez and the friction between the executive bodies of the National Council and the Jewish Agency over their relative degrees of influence in the transition to statehood appeared, over the course of the following two and a half months, to be determinative. Hostilities escalated across Palestine during February–April, 1948, resulting in chaos and making Remez's outlook increasingly irrelevant to the Jewish struggle for independence. As death notices in the press listing the names of the previous day's casualties became a matter of daily routine, Remez's political ally in Mapai, Kaplan, declared at the opening of a February 9 fundraising event—"A Tax for Our Defense"—that the international community should not expect "to find 'moderate' Jews who would agree to negotiate a compromise under pressure of threats and intense sacrifice."[48]

The shift—that is, the tipping of the political scale in favor of Ben-Gurion's approach—took place in two stages. On February 2, 1948, the National Council Executive agreed to subordinate its role to Shertok, the Jewish Agency representative in Lake Success, New York, recognizing him as the agreed-upon representative of the Jewish side in negotiations with the Palestine Commission on the composition of the Provisional Council of Government. The heads of the National Council Executive also agreed to join in efforts to persuade the ultraorthodox party Agudat Israel and the Sephardic Community Committee, which lacked any representation in national institutions, to send letters to New York affirming their recognition of Shertok, thus allowing him to be considered an authorized delegate representing nearly all of the Yishuv's political spectrum. In its letter, the National Council Executive stipulated that its subordination was subject to the condition that ultimately the National Council plenum and the Zionist General Council be the ones to determine the composition of the Provisional Council of Government.[49] It would eventually turn out that this condition was what effectively determined the identity of the two bodies tasked with ratifying the provisional political structure established to manage the affairs of the future Jewish state. Another consequence was the nullification of the need for elections to the Assembly of Representatives.

The shift was completed with a multipartisan move initiated by Meir Grabovsky (Argov), a second-tier Mapai leader. At a National Council plenary meeting on February 16, 1948, Grabovsky drew a direct connection between the two issues. He noted that "the bloodshed and the plot to violate and sabotage the UN resolution demand[s] a speedy response on our part," pointing out that under the circumstances, the path to consolidating a governing structure for the future Jewish state had changed course.[50] Grabovsky submitted a proposal, which the National Council Executive had approved two days earlier, whereby the Jewish Agency Executive and the National Council Executive would constitute the Provisional Council of Government, which could be further expanded with the addition of representatives from Agudat Israel, the Sephardic Community, HaIhud HaEzrahi, the Communist Party (one each), and two Revisionist representatives. The Provisional Council of Government would, if necessary, create an executive body comprising a subset of its membership and subordinate to it. "The Council will function as the authoritative and decision-making organ in all major and important questions that arise during the period of the Yishuv's existential war. It will also be able to appoint a smaller organ [within itself] to conduct the war, if it decides to do so."[51]

Ben-Gurion advocated the formation of an executive body comprising five members who would meet "if necessary, every day, not for major theoretical discussions; they need to act, to activate institutions and people," and a second body "that would fill the position of a parliament." It would be composed of members of the National Council Executive and the Jewish Agency Executive, alongside a few dozen geographical representatives from various parts of the country—"an institution of 40–50 people, not representatives of divisions [political parties] and opinions" that would meet biweekly or so. He admitted that he was "afraid to propose this because it will spark such an argument that it will eat up all our time."[52] His decision to adopt a course of action based on the existing political system reflected an understanding that the complex circumstances of political life at the time contained a dynamism and a vitality sufficiently suited to the needs of the hour, both in terms of security and the desire to shape the regime of the emerging Jewish state based on democratic systems developed by the Zionist Movement and Yishuv society.

Though politically defeated, Remez did not change his mind. In light of the internal dispute among decision-makers at the February 16 National Council plenary meeting, he tried one last time to make his case that "we have the option of announcing immediate elections [to the Assembly of Representatives], amidst the shooting, amidst the fighting. I'll tell you: I would not be deterred. If we all wanted it—it could happen."[53] The words "amidst the shooting" were meant literally. In a letter to his daughter composed during the meeting ("for lack of time"), Yosef Sprinzak wrote, "The deliberations are accompanied by the unrelenting echo of explosions and gunfire reaching us from the front, at the boundaries of the city [Tel Aviv] and the suburbs; it is sometimes hard to suppress awareness of the contrast between our discussions and the harsh reality."[54] Free from any illusions that foreign intervention would change the reality on the ground, Ben-Gurion stated at Jewish Agency meetings during the first half of February that the key question was: What is the starting point for discussions on the Provisional Council of Government? He argued that any "juridical constitution" formulated by the Assembly of Representatives, the Zionist Congress, or the United Nations was of no relevance, nor was there any basis for expecting that the UN, United States, or the Soviet Union could have a political impact on developments in the country. "To the extent that any political decision can be made, it has already been decided" at the UN "and perhaps there will not be" another political decision. "This is the most we can hope for. The matter will now be decided by force—and only by force, and the key to all of this is the question of security or lack of security, will we stand [firm] or will we not." Political activism in the United States would not, in his view, be determinative, but the political situation could affect the extent of suffering and losses because "if another ten thousand Jews fall [in battle] it will make a great difference. It will be the best of the Jewish people who fall."[55] Thus he unintentionally gave his assessment of the expected losses resulting from the war of independence. Sprinzak, whose three sons were serving in the Haganah, believed it was important to find a way to negotiate and compromise with the Arabs. Yet even though his outlook differed fundamentally from Ben-Gurion's, his words to his daughter reveal that he came to the same conclusion: "I see no wise man or prophet who can predict what is to come. There remains only the principle—to stand [firm] in battle."[56]

Remaining steadfast in battle required—foremost in Ben-Gurion's view—money to purchase armored vehicles, aircraft, ships, and heavy weapons. Toward this end, Myerson traveled to the United States on January 23 and soon managed to raise fifteen million dollars.[57] Concurrently, a delegation of the United Jewish Appeal arrived in Palestine. In their travels around the country, its members were exposed to the war atmosphere and scale of mobilization for the war effort in the Yishuv. With some measure of satisfaction, an editorial in *Davar* stated that "in terms of the risk involved in following along the precarious roads of Eretz Israel, the delegation members have already become citizens of the country."[58] A similar sense of pride is evident in the words of poet Natan Alterman, in his regular "Seventh Column" in the same newspaper:

> They now saw the picture from every side.
> They saw the real (not just lyrical) scene
> How Sa'adia responded to fire with fire
> And they praised his displaying
> "The right spirit" indeed . . .
> Which for Sa'adia went without saying.
>
> When suddenly there came a young volunteer
> A woman whose belt was strung with grenades
> Her task to protect them as they made their way
> They said: Son of David, Messiah, is nigh
> And this the messiah did not deny.
>
> As the evening descended on them from on high
> Slowly finding its way through the metal and cracks
> Of the armored vehicle in which they sat
> Immobile and gazing in each other's eyes
> Two tribes of Jews
> On one front united.
>
> As Saa'dia's teeth shone in the dark,
> And the kibbutz girl with them
> Her eyes were a spark . . .
> The Yankees spoke not . . . for this was a stage
> In the resurrection of Jewry
> In the United States.[59]

Another illustration of how Jewish community activists in the United States gradually adapted to the war reality "over there in the land of our forefathers" involves a fundraising event in New York, where Mapai member Avraham Herzfeld (who oversaw the establishment of new kibbutz or moshav settlements on behalf of the Histadrut) captivated his audience by describing how, despite the abundance of sand in the Negev, they lacked the sacks to make sandbag fortifications. A member of the audience then queried, "Did they not hang the person responsible for the sacks?"[60]

The question of correspondence between the political campaign in the United States and the military campaign in Palestine revived a latent dispute between Ben-Gurion and Shertok regarding the path to realizing the aim and interests of Zionism. This dispute would fuel countless debates, with varying focal points, for years to come. Ben-Gurion's faith in Jewish military capabilities reached a low point in the first half of February, leading him to insist that Shertok "demand an international force, or at least a delivery of [military] equipment from the UN or the United States."[61] In response, Shertok requested that Ben-Gurion come to New York and participate in diplomatic talks on the international force. In his view, the assistance of such a force was necessary to secure the Jews' control over the territory allocated to them under the Partition Plan. He believed that Jewish military capabilities were only adequate for defending existing settlements against "efforts to destroy them," but not for repelling groups of Arab volunteers seeking to "establish fortifications in parts of the country within the territory of the Jewish state in order to uproot [the Jews]."[62] From the outset, however, Shertok was aware that the likelihood of Truman sending American troops to the country was slim, notwithstanding his need for the Jewish vote during this election year, because "just as the Republican Party will attack him on the matter of a Jewish state [if it does not come to be], so too it will attack him on the matter of sending American boys to Eretz Israel." Added to this, of course, was the lack of American willingness to "create an opening" for the deployment of Soviet troops to the Middle East under the auspices of a multinational UN force.[63]

Given the military situation at that time, Ben-Gurion, who at one point had considered undertaking the fundraising mission on which he eventually sent Myerson, was no longer entertaining thoughts about leaving the country. A few days later, however, he revised his assessment of the situation. Intelligence information that he had received about an invasion by Arab armies on February 15, 1948, turned out to be false, and after meeting with experts on Arab affairs, he concluded that only a "small number" of Palestinians were participating in the hostilities, whereas "most of our sons and most of members of the Arab people in the country refused to join the military campaign." In a February 17 speech at a conference of the Yishuv's Mobilization Fund, he noted, "One prediction that was intended to alarm the United Nations—an uprising among the Arabs of Eretz Israel—turned out to be false. . . . The Arab village for the most part remains quiet." He drew satisfaction from learning about the battle at Tirat Zvi on February 16, where forty of the attackers were killed, and from the strong impression this incident left "in the surrounding areas—both Jewish and Arab. And rightly so! Good for them!" He was undoubtedly further encouraged by another report received that day, informing him that Fawzi al-Qawuqji, commander of the Arab Salvation Army (a volunteer force from Arab countries), had told a group of fighters about to depart for Palestine, "You are entering a battle against a strong and well-organized enemy, numbering 42,000 daring young men armed with sophisticated weapons."[64] Despite the overstatement—for who knew better than Ben-Gurion the true state of the Haganah—the extent of Jewish power as perceived on the other side contributed to a shift in his stance, as reflected in his response to Shertok's invitation. In a letter of February 27, Ben-Gurion wrote that if the purchased military equipment arrived in time, the Jews would seize territorial control and come face-to-face with Arab armed forces, "and therefore the only thing preoccupying me is not various power plays in Washington and Downing Street, and not even official UN resolutions—but rather equipment, in sufficient quantities, of the necessary quality, and at the right time (before May 15). Everything, in my view, depends on this!"[65]

Throughout the decades of Ben-Gurion's political career, no other cause led him to apply such focused, vehement pressure on his colleagues as did this aim of purchasing military equipment during the six months preceding statehood, which prompted him to urge senior and junior officials alike to intensify their efforts in this regard, insisting that they view it as their top priority. His focus on military acquisitions began on July 1, 1945, the day he met with seventeen Jewish millionaires from across the United States. That meeting, held at the residence of Rudolf Sonneborn in New York, was in Ben-Gurion's view one of the three most important events of his life, alongside his immigration to Palestine in September 1906 and Israel's declaration of independence on May 14, 1948.[66] The meeting led to the formation of a group known as the Sonneborn Institute, which engaged in the clandestine purchase of machinery and raw materials for the Jewish military industry, taking advantage of the availability and low cost of equipment for the manufacture of weapons and ammunition following World War II. The institute also engaged in smuggling civil technological equipment into Palestine. In December 1947, Ben-Gurion wrote to Kaplan (who was in New York at the time) that he did not wish to overburden him, "but the difference between security needs and other needs is that everything [else] can be postponed a week, a month, without dangerous harm, [but] security needs cannot be postponed even one hour, and if we miss the right moment—[our cause] may be lost." In February 1948, he informed Myerson, who was visiting the United States to raise funds and purchase weapons and supplies, that in the near future, parts of the Yishuv would be cut off and under siege—particularly in the Negev, the Upper Galilee, and Jerusalem. He added, "The difficult question in my view is whether we can remain steadfast for these two months, until we are likely to receive the equipment from Europe and America." In April, he chastised Saul Meyerov (Shaul Avigur), head of the Mossad LeAliyah Bet (Institution for Immigration B, a branch of the Haganah that facilitated Jewish immigration), who was also in charge of weapons acquisition in Europe, warning him against transporting weapons and illegal immigrants on the same ship. He emphasized that "equipment is a matter of *life*," which took priority over immigrants, adding, "I'm nearly exhausted by these demands—but I do not have the right to exhaustion." He also wrote immediately to Meyerov's brother-in-law, Shertok, in the United States: "The situation is incomparably severe. If we do not receive the rest of the equipment (to date we have received less than 20%), especially heavy equipment and large numbers of aircraft—both bombers and fighter jets, and if we cannot ensure large supplies of fuel—our situation could be desperate." A few days later he reminded him, "As I wrote to you—many times, I believe—our fate depends not so much on what happens in Lake Success, but on acquiring equipment. This acquisition depends on us—and is [only] slightly in God's hands."[67]

During this time, Shertok was focusing his efforts on the diplomatic arena and particularly on adhering to the timetable stipulated in the Partition Plan inasmuch as it depended on the Jewish side. Ben-Gurion and Shertok saw eye to eye on the importance of establishing a Provisional Council of Government as an immediate response to American reluctance surrounding the Partition Plan and as an expression of the Jewish intention to proceed, no matter what, toward political independence.[68] Throughout February 1948, Shertok sent frequent telegrams to his associates in Palestine, imploring—or, more precisely, begging—them to send him the composition of the Provisional Council of Government as well as authorizations from the relevant political bodies in the Yishuv for talks with the Palestine Commission. His appeals reached a fever pitch on February 29, when he laconically asserted, "It is now more urgent than ever."[69] Ben-Gurion was, as noted, ostensibly staying out of the political bargaining on the grounds that he was entirely preoccupied with security matters, which required him to focus on unifying and mobilizing the Yishuv for the war effort, leaving no room for quarrels and disagreements. On February 27, however, he had tried and once again failed to persuade his associates in the Jewish Agency Executive to establish an "Executive Council for the Territory of the Jewish State." The positions were split among three options: first—the Provisional Council of Government would elect an executive body; second—the council, once approved by the Palestine Commission, would elect an executive body; third—once the council was formed, "if an agreement can be reached within a few days regarding the composition of a smaller executive body," then this would be the course followed. On the face of it, these were subtle and insignificant nuances, but in practice, they embodied clashing perspectives over the urgency of establishing an executive body, which Ben-Gurion had identified as a matter of supreme importance back in October 1947.[70]

Into this governance vacuum stepped the National Council Executive, with full force.

At its plenary meeting of March 1, 1948, the National Council decided that the Provisional Council of Government should be composed of the executive bodies of the National Council and the Jewish Agency, alongside public bodies that neither of them represented (Agudat Israel, HaIhud HaEzrahi, the Sephardic Community, the Revisionists, and the Communists). The language of this decision, which was widely and prominently disseminated, made no mention of the fact that the decision had initially been taken by both executive bodies or that the Jewish Agency Executive was effectively an equal partner in determining the structure of this new body. An agreement reached by the two executive bodies—that the issue would be submitted for approval by the National Council plenum as well as the Zionist General Council—had seemingly evaporated. Avraham Katznelson, Mapai representative to the National Council Executive, commented on the nature of this new body: "At the moment it is neither a parliament nor a cabinet, but rather a transitional framework with a six-month lifespan that will have to fulfill both parliamentary functions and executive functions," which included making preparations for elections to the Constituent Assembly and establishing the election bylaws.[71]

The National Council's decision was seen as posing a challenge, at a critical time, to the supremacy of the Jewish Agency Executive and its head in leading the political processes being pursued by the Yishuv and the Zionist Movement. On March 3, Remez sent a formal letter to Ben-Gurion—one chairman to another—justifying the National Council's decision and its public announcement. He argued that because the Palestine Commission had officially approached twenty-one Jewish bodies, seeking their approval for the composition of the Provisional Council of Government, "there was no logic in delaying the public announcement." Remez added that the decisions offer encouragement to the public at a time of "emotional distress in the Yishuv" resulting from the Mandate government's announcement that "British military personnel will find it difficult to view Jews as entitled to protection" following the death of twenty-nine British soldiers on a train to Rehovot in an attack launched by Lehi (Lohamei Herut Israel, "Fighters for the Freedom of Israel," a militant Zionist paramilitary outfit that split from the Irgun in 1940). In closing, he commented, somewhat provocatively, "The National Council Executive, for its part, wishes to emphasize the need for the

Jewish Agency Executive to avoid any further delay in reaching a final decision on this matter, and to bring it to a complete close by implementing the final measures decided upon."[72] By presenting the Jewish Agency Executive as tasked with implementing "final measures" and ignoring the complexity of bringing Zionist General Council members from around the world to Palestine (and by implication demanding that the requirement of convening this body be waived, thereby entrusting the National Council plenum with the authority for granting the final seal of approval in determining the governing structure), Remez was in effect denigrating the status of the Jewish Agency Executive and its leader.[73]

In response, Ben-Gurion scrambled to thwart the National Council's move for dominance in political leadership just months before the target date for statehood. Meeting on March 3, the Jewish Agency Executive resolved: "In addition to determining the Provisional Council of Government—a government comprising thirteen portfolios has been decided upon." The basic framework for "the structure of the Jewish government" consisting of thirteen ministers was not something politicians had formulated after balancing their respective interests. Rather, it stemmed from an earlier proposal initiated by the Secretariat of the Emergency Committee (a body established in October 1947 by the Yishuv leadership to prepare for the establishment of a state apparatus) and submitted to Ben-Gurion on December 17, 1947. This proposed format was to survive all the upsets and crises in the formation of a government and assignment of portfolios over the following six months.[74] The format accepted by the Jewish Agency Executive on March 3, 1948, was approved by the Mapai Secretariat that evening. In his diary, Ben-Gurion noted with satisfaction, "Our friends in the National Council waged an astonishingly bitter and harsh attack against the Agency's decision on this matter [the government]. The Secretariat approved the Agency's position."[75]

The dispute erupted when Mapai's Central Committee convened on March 6. Remez decided not to attend "for health reasons," as was announced at the start of the meeting, which discussed the establishment of the Provisional Council of Government, the establishment of a provisional government, and the election of Mapai members to this body. Ben-Gurion strongly insisted that Myerson be appointed instead of Remez as one of Mapai's four representatives to a provisional government. In true form, he threatened not to join this body if his demand was not met. Although he suddenly "remembered" the vital "historical" importance of having a woman in the future first government, even if it were to be short-lived and temporary, it was clear that the gender aspect was a hollow claim coming from him—so hollow that in his letter to Myerson on the matter, he wrote that Myerson "would deserve the position even if she were a man." In none of the eight governments of Israel that he later headed (and that only ever had one woman minister—Myerson) would he advocate the appointment of a woman, neither as a "moral and political necessity" nor as "a signal to the Near East"—as he bitterly and disappointedly noted in his diary at the time—nor as a "signal of man's liberty and equality"—as he responded to women's organizations that decried the apparently all-male composition of the emerging government. Ben-Gurion's only motive was to override the position advocated by Remez in determining the decision-making apparatus of the Yishuv and the Zionist Movement in advance of statehood, which would inevitably also affect the substance of decisions on political and security matters. By a majority of 21 to 10, the Mapai Central Committee chose Ben-Gurion, Remez, Kaplan, and Shertok as its representatives to the provisional government.[76]

Soon thereafter, the other political parties also decided on their representatives to the People's Administration (Minhelet HaAm) and the People's Council (Moetzet HaAm). Ezriel Carlebach, editor-in-chief of *Maariv*, supplemented the grandeur of the event with comic commentary: "As at Zionist congresses, the executive body is chosen at the final moment, when the ship is about to sail, or when the Swiss visa is about to expire, or [because] the assembly hall has already been leased for the Basel Fire Brigade's Christmas ball." On a more serious note, he then commented on the significance of the circumstances: "The appointment of a government transforms us—by necessity—into a people. Henceforth we must regard our government as 'all the gentiles [nations]' do. First, discipline (then: criticism and elections and change of government depending on its earned credits and deeds, and no longer can we act as before: first criticism and then obedience and discipline as it suits the critic). This is essential for us."[77] But neither a government nor a council had yet been formed. As Ben-Gurion reported to Shertok and Myerson, then in New York, "What I feared—has occurred. The effort to establish a Provisional Council of Government has exacerbated clashes within the Yishuv at this time."[78]

In the meantime, a shift in US policy, which came to light on March 19, 1948, meant that the prospects for Jewish statehood were diminishing. Instead of supporting partition, the United States began advocating a UN trusteeship over the course of several years, during which efforts would be made to reach an understanding between Arabs and Jews. Given these circumstances, the American section of the Jewish Agency Executive, led by Abba Hillel Silver, advised Ben-Gurion that the best course of action would be to immediately declare the establishment of the Provisional Council of Government, even if its powers would only take effect on May 15.[79] While this would have been a hasty decision, Ben-Gurion's nerves did appear to be fraying, and his skills in identifying the significance of a given action and its timing, with simultaneously cautious and critical insight (that quality whereby "he suddenly saw," in Sharef's words), seemed momentarily dulled. In reaction to the US shift, Ben-Gurion wrote in his diary, "We must announce the establishment of the Jewish state and declare that a Jewish government has been formed."[80] By the following day, he had calmed down, as was indicated in an announcement by the Jewish Agency and the National Council that appeared in the Hebrew press on March 24: "Immediately upon termination of the Mandate government, and no later than May 16 of this year, a provisional Jewish government will be instituted." It would be a mistake to presume that this was the intended target date for Jewish statehood. The headline accompanying the announcement—"A Jewish Government"—reflects the actual intent. The Jewish Agency Executive had reached this decision at a March 23 meeting, and the National Council Executive was compelled to adopt it.[81] Ben-Gurion informed Shertok of the decision "to announce the establishment of a provisional government on May 16" (assuming the Mandate government was terminated on May 15, a Saturday)—rather than on April 1, as stipulated in the November 1947 Partition Plan, "because it is not possible to seize power in practice as long as the Mandatory government is in the country, and it is not desirable at this time, I emphasize at this time, to make an announcement that would be interpreted as opposing the UN at a time when talks are still taking place there."[82]

His avoidance of any talk about statehood attested to the excessive caution and extreme sensitivity that Ben-Gurion preferred to employ at that time. This manifested as adherence, to the extent possible, to the UN plan as a way of camouflaging the timing of a declaration of statehood, without producing premature public expectations or speculations in the Yishuv as to any announcement, or absence of announcement, about statehood, as these would inevitably spark what he considered an unnecessary and dangerous public debate. In contrast to the longings, ideals, and slogans he voiced, which were of great import, any declaration about the establishment of a state remained an aspiration at the decision-making level and in concrete political discourse. It was conditional on future developments and subsequent conduct amid a fog of uncertainty that might ultimately take the course of history in any number of directions. Given this situation, as it relates to Ben-Gurion's leadership style during the two months preceding statehood, historian Yigal Eilam rightly observed that the Jewish Agency Executive was trying to be extracautious in dealing with foreign entities—the UN, the United States, Britain—as it recognized the Zionists' limited power relative to these entities; accordingly, it strove not to commit to a process to which it could not adhere, and to leave all options for the course of Zionist conduct open.[83] To ignore this fundamental dimension—particularly concerning Ben-Gurion, whose greatness as a leader at the decisive moment is most evident here—is to overlook the historical reality on the ground. Only by appreciating the actual situation is it possible to understand the seemingly meandering trail that led to an unequivocal outcome—an independent Jewish state upon termination of the Mandate. Ben-Gurion would arrive at the moment of certainty only on May 9, as we shall see later. It is mentioned here solely as a signpost to mark the pace at which historical events unfolded from the perspective of decision-makers, and in order not to present the historical narrative as a myth with a foretold conclusion from which all preceding events are deduced.

The changing political situation had not yet prompted Ben-Gurion to amend the strategic directive guiding the Haganah since December 1947: to contain the fighting on the ground to the extent possible. "The approach," he informed the Mapai Secretariat, "must be the same approach—not to fight the Arabs. . . . We will fight those who fight us, and by effective means." He did not deny that "admittedly they had a very important diplomatic victory" with the shift in US policy on March 19, 1948, "but is this a reason to kill Arabs? There is no need to kill Arabs. . . . There are changes in the political arena, which is the arena of talk. Politics is a matter of talk, which I do not disparage, but on the field it is concrete issues that are determinative—immigration, settlement, and defense."[84] Instead of taking measures that had not received due consideration, the Jewish Agency Executive decided, on March 25, to convene the Zionist General Council on April 4 to establish a thirteen-member executive body and a larger representative body. It also decided to establish an executive committee that would operate until the Zionist General Council convened to approve the previously mentioned proposal. This committee, acting instead of the government, would address issues of human resources, supplies, transportation, and financing. The committee comprised four members of the Jewish Agency Executive—Ben-Gurion, Kaplan, Moshe Shapira, and Peretz Bernstein—as well as Remez, in an advisory capacity, as a representative of the National Council.[85]

The appointment of this committee sparked the next substantive crisis between the two executive bodies. It coincided with the direst security situation since the hostilities had begun: on March 26, 1948, the Old City of Jerusalem came under siege and Haganah chief of staff Yaakov Dostrovsky (Dori) was hospitalized for surgery; on March 27, forty-six Haganah fighters on a supply and reinforcement convoy from Nahariya to Kibbutz Yehiam were killed; and over the course of that day and the next, the Nebi Daniel convoy, returning from Gush Etzion to Jerusalem, suffered fifteen deaths and dozens of injuries. On March 28, even before learning of the fate of the Nebi Daniel convoy, Ben-Gurion wrote to Shertok, "This is the worst day since the war began. The convoy from Gush Etzion is still wrestling with a network of barricades and the fierce Arab attack—while the British army that set out today to meet them continues to play its diabolical games." With deep sorrow he added, "By the time these words reach you—the fate of our boys will be known."[86] It was under these circumstances that the committee of five convened, on that day, for its first meeting. On the following day, March 29, the National Council Executive prohibited Remez from attending meetings of this committee because it interpreted the latter's existence as preparations for taking over "all matters relating to the state of emergency and period of transition leading up to the establishment of the state on May 16."[87] In a scathing letter to the Mapai Bureau, Ben-Gurion responded with razor-sharp sarcasm: "I must present a simple question to our party: Are there two *yishuvs* in the country—one [affiliated with] the [Jewish] Agency and one with the National Council?" And are there two parties—one represented at the Agency and one at the National Council? He warned that "time is short, things are pressing, and any delay—by one week, one day, in some cases even one hour—could be fatal," resulting in "disaster that could turn into destruction." Accordingly, he demanded that "the party reach a clear decision—*immediately*, because any delay is an unforgivable crime that will lead to disaster and destruction!—to assign Agency members responsibility only for matters that do not relate to the state of emergency, such as establishing Jewish federations in all countries, disseminating the shekel, and expediting fundraising abroad." Responsibility for the war and preparations for the founding of the state should immediately be transferred to the National Council Executive, declared Ben-Gurion.[88]

Remez, offended, replied, "The National Council Executive has committed a grave sin: it remains loyal to the supreme leadership of the Zionist movement. It will persist in committing this sin, even in the absence of reciprocal loyalty, but in times of emergency and war, when the Jewish Agency Executive is handling the affairs of the Yishuv and the Jewish people, there is no escaping the choice: either cooperate fairly or let go fairly."[89] Remez's crocodile tears were a response to Jewish Agency members' increasing control over areas of responsibility that had hitherto been within the purview of the British authorities or had emerged as wartime necessities. Yet they did not obscure his feelings about the political balance of power being decidedly counter to his outlook.

During this period, Ben-Gurion became embroiled in another difficult confrontation, this time with a fellow member of the Jewish Agency Executive, Yitzhak Gruenbaum. At an Agency meeting on March 23, 1948, Gruenbaum accused Ben-Gurion of deliberately delaying the approval of an agreement to join forces with Etzel and Lehi and, raising his fist, charged, "You know what? You're just a cheater!" According to Gruenbaum, Ben-Gurion had refrained from issuing instructions to send an official letter to the Jewish Agency Executive section in the United States to solicit members' views about an agreement with Etzel and Lehi, as had been decided two weeks earlier, because he opposed giving a stamp of approval for their activities before they agreed to accept the authority of the Haganah and elected governing bodies. In an emotional outburst, Gruenbaum announced his resignation from the Jewish Agency Executive and stopped participating in its discussions. Ben-Gurion opted "not to describe what Mr. Gruenbaum had done or to assess his action" and denied the charges against him, describing them as "a malicious and baseless accusation." Although a special committee, formed under the auspices of the Zionist General Council conference in April, cleared him of any wrongdoing, Gruenbaum refused to retract the accusation.[90]

Gruenbaum's resignation impeded the proper functioning of the Jewish Agency Executive specifically and preparedness for the war in Jerusalem generally. In light of the siege of Jerusalem and the needs of the hour, Ben-Gurion was spending most of his time in Tel Aviv, while Gruenbaum, alongside National Council president Yitzhak Ben-Zvi, had been the leading public figure in charge of political and organizational affairs in Jerusalem. On March 28, following the losses of the Nebi Daniel convoy, senior officials at the Jewish Agency's Political Department sent a frantic telegram to Shertok warning that "the authority of the Jewish Agency in Jerusalem is completely gone" and urgently calling for cease-fire talks because "Jerusalem is in mortal danger." On the following day, an executive official informed Ben-Gurion by telegram that "the shortage in food supplies and oil have caused panic," with milk supplies depleted and bread on the verge of depletion, "and rioting is expected in the poor neighborhoods."[91] Gruenbaum, however, was focused on other concerns. His resignation remained in effect until May 10, 1948, and throughout this time, a position was reserved for him on the Jewish Agency Executive and the future People's Administration.

Operation Nachshon, a Haganah operation aimed at breaking through the blockade on the road to Jerusalem, was launched on April 3, 1948, against the background of "the Convoy Crisis" and its heavy toll. The Khulda convoy, which had added twenty-three deaths to this toll on March 31, 1948, became the first one not to reach the besieged Jerusalem. The operation signaled a strategic shift in the Yishuv's approach to the war and marked the initial implementation of Plan Dalet (Plan D), intended to capture Arab-controlled territories that were designated for the Jewish state under the Partition Plan. In historian Motti Golani's view, the convoys reflected the Yishuv's steadily growing autonomy, conveying not only physical supplies but also signs of Jewish sovereignty. In this sense, Plan Dalet was another stage in the evolution of Jewish sovereignty in the tangible sense. The concentration of military and logistical efforts on an unprecedented scale was intended to deliver a decisive outcome within a geographical area of vital importance in the war effort. The ultimate overseer of the operation was Ben-Gurion, who imposed it on the General Staff of the Haganah against the latter's will on March 31. In retrospect, the head of operations, Yigael Yadin, then acting chief of staff, commented that "this was Ben-Gurion's most positive, most decisive intervention, in the pre-state period."[92]

A document prepared by the Operations Directorate of the Haganah in early April grounded the new war-fighting strategy: "It must be recognized that all stages of the campaign, to date, have been dictated to us by the enemy, and we have not been able to determine the strategic and operative course of the campaign as the character of the struggle is evolving from incidents into a war between two semi-regular forces." To cope with this state of affairs, the document stipulated, "the only solution is to take operational control ourselves, with the aim of achieving a decisive military outcome, for our side, against the enemy." This required the urgent formation of a "national combat force that is concentrated and released from defense and security duties, organized into large units (battalions, brigades), with mobility, maneuverability, and firepower."[93] The subsequent success in the field—on the road to Jerusalem and later in April at Mishmar HaEmek and in Haifa and nearby—is attributable to a shift in thinking, from a spatial, militia-style approach to one aimed at concentrating efforts to achieve a decisive outcome at a specific locus determined by the changing military, civilian, and political reality.[94] Those successes also had a powerful political impact, as they dramatically reinforced the growing recognition of Ben-Gurion's skills as a victorious wartime leader throughout the public and political arenas of the Yishuv.

THE ZIONIST GENERAL COUNCIL'S APRIL DECISION

Two days before the April 6 gathering of the Zionist General Council, Ben-Gurion and Israel Galili, head of the Haganah National Command, held preparatory talks with Jewish Agency Executive members Emanuel Neumann, president of the Zionist Organization of America (ZOA) and Silver's partner in its leadership, and Selig Brodetsky, a senior member of the British section of the Jewish Agency Executive. The Zionist Movement rested largely on the Zionist federations in the Diaspora. Brodetsky and Neumann, who belonged to the General Zionists Party, were considered key figures whose support was necessary to establish a new governing structure. In this respect, Galili, a leader within HaKibbutz HaMeuchad (a kibbutz movement), served as Ben-Gurion's close ally. His remarks at their meeting added a professional, objective dimension to Ben-Gurion's political agenda and reinforced the urgency of its implementation in light of pressing security concerns. First, Galili laid out the military agenda, explaining that "we must prepare forces so that on May 15 we can fill the following roles": first, defense for each separate locality and for the Yishuv as a whole; second, "the elimination of Arab localities within our enclaves, for example so that Jaffa does not cause harm"; third, seizing positions that the British evacuate, such as key junctions, police stations, trains, water sources, and ports; fourth, defense of "the borders of the Jewish state as delineated by the UN, which will be impossible unless we strike at enemy concentrations beyond the boundaries of the Jewish state as well." Galili was adamant and explicit about the implications for the interface of security, politics, and governmental structure: "This cannot occur under a regime [that combines] the Jewish Agency Executive and the National Council Executive and entails clarifying which issues relate to which body. We need to establish a government with authority over all the concentrated power of the Yishuv. . . . The Yishuv must establish its norms in accordance with the needs of war."[95]

Presumably, Ben-Gurion was fully aware that without Neumann and Brodetsky's support, the formation of the new governing institutions—the People's Administration and the People's Council—could be delayed for procedural reasons, for fear of developments on the warfront or because of changes in policy on the part of British and American officials and leaders. Moreover, Ben-Gurion was aware that decisions reached by the Zionist General Council could easily be diverted to other, seemingly "fateful" issues, such as the question of "dual loyalty" that preoccupied delegates from abroad or the various bargaining processes underway with Gruenbaum, HaIhud HaEzrahi, Mapam (Mifleget HaPoalim HaMeuhedet, "United Workers Party"—a new Zionist-Marxist party at the time), and Etzel and Lehi. After Galili, Ben-Gurion spoke: "During war, one people cannot have two governing authorities conducting the war. . . . There will be a body that for now, for the sake of convenience, I call Yud-Gimel [Hebrew letters with the numeric value of thirteen], which will be the executive, and a body [termed] Lamed-Vav [thirty-six, which later turned into thirty-seven, Lamed-Zayin], which will be the parliament, and after May 15 they will be called the government and the council."[96] Viewing the events and political upheavals surveyed from October 1947 to April 1948 reductively, one might say that from a historical perspective, this was the decisive meeting that determined and enabled the transition from Yishuv to state.

At two meetings of the Security Committee in early April, Ben-Gurion made it unequivocally clear that he intended to disband this body as well as the Haganah National Command, as their roles were redundant. On a personal note, he attested that when he was placed in charge of the security desk at the Jewish Agency, he realized the absurdity of having multiple bodies engaged in the issue, but he "decided not to address that. I said: let the anomaly remain. I learned in England that in public affairs there doesn't have to be logic; if it meets a need, even if the need is not important, if it prevents new conflicts, then it should remain." But this English wisdom regarding public life no longer held sway. Sapir and Rokach, heads of HaIhud HaEzrahi (which since the 1930s had partnered with the Histadrut in managing the Yishuv's security affairs) protested that without the consent of the civilian public, they would not accept any change in the composition or authority of security bodies. Ben-Gurion unhesitatingly rejected their claim: "It would be better if we had military experts among us, if we had a Napoleon or Montgomery sitting here; if we don't, then why have a security committee rather than Yud-Gimel?"[97]

A day before the April 6, 1948, gathering of the Zionist General Council in Tel Aviv, Ben-Zvi called on the Jewish Agency Executive to pursue a cease-fire in Jerusalem, otherwise there would be "a fatal outcome for us, an outcome heralding annihilation and destruction of the Jewish community in Jerusalem."[98] The palpable echoes of the war fighting were the dominant factor throughout the seven days of political talks at the Zionist General Council conference. Ben-Gurion's opening remarks weighed heavily in the air: "During the past four months, since the attack against us was launched on November 30, more than 900 Jews have been killed."[99] Casualties included Yitzhak and Rachel Yanait Ben-Zvi's son Eli, who was killed near Kibbutz Beit Keshet on March 6, and the son of Shlomo Lavi (Ben-Gurion's close friend from his city of birth, Plonsk, in Tsarist Russia, now Poland), Yerubaal, one of the founders of Kibbutz Ein Harod and HaKibbutz HaMeuchad, who was killed on Mount Gilboa on March 19.

At this critical moment in the intercommunity war, a speech delivered by Kaplan, head of the Jewish Agency's Finance Department, was particularly pertinent in terms of Yishuv unity and its relevance for overseas delegates. Kaplan, a senior Mapai member who had been handling the Yishuv's economic affairs since 1933, was known for his moderate views on security and political matters throughout those years. His judgment served as a compass for many in both the domestic political and the external Zionist arenas. "No one knows how the war will develop," Kaplan surmised in April 1948, adding, "I deliberately use the word war, and it is important that when members go back abroad, when they leave the country, they convey this to the Diaspora, that war surrounds us and the problems are hard. And this might endanger the lives of each and every one of us, as well as the economy as a whole." Four months earlier, he recalled, "When I was in America and trying to imagine how things would develop, . . . I thought that if the United Nations and their governments remain true to the principles and charter of the UN, there will be clashes in Eretz Israel, but there won't be war." However, "circumstances have now changed" and "we are now facing war." His message to the Zionist delegates from the Diaspora was direct and free of any false hope:

> It's good that you're in Tel Aviv, but there is also a big disadvantage in this because you're not getting the right picture of Eretz Israel. Ben-Gurion told you that Eretz Israel does not have a warfront and home front, because it is all a warfront, but psychologically Tel Aviv might be the hinterland where things are not so bad. Life goes on, the shops are full, the theaters are full, schools are in session. Where's the great danger? If it's possible, and for some of you it might be, to take you to Jerusalem, to Haifa, to the Negev, and to the north—then you will see that the word war is not a poetic term, nor is the word danger.[100]

At this juncture, there was no going back politically, and for our purposes in *Independence and Politics*, that is the thrust of the issue. The Zionist General Council conference concluded on April 12. *Davar's* headline that day was fictitious: "Declaration of Jewish Independence before the Zionist General Council." Shertok's emotional pleas of the day before, which only reached Palestine two or three days later—not to wage a coup d'état and to refrain from "any demonstrative measure until May 15"—had gone unheeded.[101] The first sentences of the story in *Davar*, however, explained that on that day, the Zionist General Council had "announced its decision to establish the supreme authority for our political independence in the country." This was the essence of what had been achieved in the Zionist General Council talks. It was accompanied by lofty lyrical musings that masqueraded as a declaration of independence, and which *Davar* took to the extreme. At the conference itself, *Davar's* editor-in-chief, Rubashov, who was also in charge of the committee that formulated the flowery text and who no doubt infused it with his own spirit and outlook, ceremoniously read out the statement.[102] The Revisionist *Hamashkif* astutely observed that Rubashov's pathetic statement did not mention "what it lacks, the spirit of sanctity, the Word of the Nation enfolded in a few lines."[103] Perhaps there was a lesson for the future here—in the sense of how not to do things properly.

Only on the following day, in an announcement relegated to page 2, did *Davar* describe the real achievement—the composition of the Provisional Council of Government (Lamed-Zayin) and its smaller executive body (Yud-Gimel). The Provisional Council of Government: Mapai—10, the General Zionists—6, HaMizrachi and HaPoel HaMizrachi—5, Mapam—5, Agudat Israel and Poalei Agudat Israel—3, Revisionists—3, Communists—1, Women's International Zionist Organization (WIZO)—1, Aliya Hadasha—1, Yemenites—1, Sephardim—1. The executive body: Mapai—4, the General Zionists—2, Mapam—2, HaMizrachi—1, HaPoel HaMizrachi—1, Sephardim—1, Aliya Hadasha—1, Agudat Israel—1. The final agreement regarding the composition of Yud-Gimel followed stormy discussions at two meetings of the Jewish Agency Executive on April 11, which in turn came immediately after it approved (without discussing) the publication of a statement condemning the massacre committed by Etzel and Lehi in the Arab village of Deir Yassin two days earlier. Agudat Israel's delayed acceptance of membership in the Yud-Gimel left an opening for numerous efforts to exert pressure at the last minute. While the General Zionists demanded that membership be increased to fourteen so as to include a representative from HaIhud HaEzrahi (presumably Sapir or Rokach rather than Ben-Gurion's preference, Aryeh Shenkar), HaPoel HaMizrachi insisted, for the sake of "Yishuv cohesion," on including a Revisionist among the thirteen representatives or, if that proved impossible, expanding the membership to fourteen. This position received backing from *Haaretz*, which called for HaIhud HaEzrahi to be included in the cabinet, arguing that it represented financially influential and resourceful circles, that the question of thirteen or fifteen cabinet members was "not a holy writ!" and that failure to include the Revisionists "does not seem like a smart political move in our view." Mapai and Mapam, however, threatened to not join the Yud-Gimel if the Revisionists were included, and this was the deciding factor. Regarding the Revisionists, Ben-Gurion stated, "If I felt that they were capable of even a smidgen of loyalty, I wouldn't object to their inclusion, but in my view they are organically incapable of this." Under the influence of Mapai representatives, the two votes held during these meetings concluded that the executive body would have thirteen members. Despite talk about a "flag for the [Middle] East," and in contrast to the spirit of a decision reached by Mapai's political committee on March 24 (which created an opening for the inclusion of Myerson and for increasing the executive body to fifteen members), Ben-Gurion did not take advantage of the opportunity for his party to enjoy representation commensurate with its relative power in the Yishuv, which would have granted it five members, because, from his perspective, it was more important to keep the Revisionists out.[104]

On April 11, just before the Zionist General Council conference concluded, Nahum Goldmann, a Jewish Agency Executive member in New York whose political views were moderate, made a last-minute maneuver. He proposed that the political committee of the Jewish Agency Executive's American section be authorized to make political decisions based on developments at the UN. In practice, he was seeking to seize the authority to decide whether to establish a state a month later rather than leave it to the executive body about to be formed in Palestine. Alarmed, Ben-Gurion hastened to explain that Goldmann's proposal might, on the face of it, seem understandable, but the formation of the Yud-Gimel created "a new Jewish governmental reality in Eretz Israel," and "I cannot imagine that they would make a decision over there [in the United States] without it." In this spirit, he pointed out that while "we must trust our associates over there, the issue depends not only on what they say, but on what we do here." This appears to be an incidental, preliminary version of his famous 1955 statement: "It doesn't matter what the Gentiles say; it matters what the Jews do." In this case, however, the point was that while it matters what the Zionist delegates in New York say, the decision will be made in Palestine because in the "political game" underway at the UN regarding the question of loyalty, the key factor was "the extent of the Jews' strength and their ability to demonstrate their strength."[105]

The parties submitted the names of their representatives to the Yud-Gimel at a Jewish Agency Executive meeting on April 14: Mapai—David Ben-Gurion, Eliezer Kaplan, David Remez, and Moshe Shertok; the General Zionists—Yitzhak Gruenbaum and Peretz Bernstein; Mapam—Aharon Zisling and Mordechai Bentov; HaMizrachi—Yehuda Leib Fishman; HaPoel HaMizrachi—Moshe Shapira; Aliya Hadasha—Pinhas Rosenblit; Sephardim—Bechor Sheetrit. Officially, Fishman was chosen over David-Zvi Pinkas only at HaMizrachi's international conference on April 17. The identity of Agudat Israel's representative remained unknown, as the party was engaged in a struggle to receive some of the United Jewish Appeal's funding, although its official position was that it would announce its representative only on the condition that the Palestine Commission granted it legal recognition. Ashkenazi Chief Rabbi Yitzhak (Isaac) Halevi Herzog ridiculed this stance: "I haven't found a requirement anywhere in Maimonides or in any other source that a UN commission approve a Jewish government." On April 22, Agudat Israel announced that its representative would be its leader, Yitzhak-Meir Levin, who remained in the United States for the time being.[106]

The organizational and institutional developments that took place between October 1947 and April 1948 had tremendous political significance and far-reaching implications. Most salient throughout this process was the practice of consensual politics, which, notwithstanding crises and exceptions, had been part of the customary political culture in Yishuv society and the Zionist Movement for decades.[107] Its impact, reflected in repeated efforts to resolve internal power dynamics with restraint, is fully evident in its mature implementation throughout the period addressed here. The ability to overcome countless personal and internal party obstacles relating to the questions of the day attests, above all, to the principled and moral force of a fundamental understanding that had to be present in any dispute. That is, in the concluding words of Chaim Weizmann's speech on the political situation at the Twentieth Zionist Congress in 1937, which focused on the debate over the partition of the country: "I pray that sacred strength may be given to us all, to find a way, and that, in advancing we may preserve intact our national unity, for it is all we have."[108]

The names of the new bodies—in place of the letters Yud-Gimel and Lamed-Zayin—were preliminarily selected by Mapai's political committee on April 17 and affirmed on the following day at the Yud-Gimel's first session, following a proposal by Remez: "Minhelet HaAm [the People's Administration]; its members—administrators; the larger body—Moetzet HaAm [the People's Council]."[109] This decision drew blatant ridicule from the right side of the political map: "What should have been a government—will be called the People's Administration; what should have been a parliament will be called—the People's Council. Let's hope that the state, at least, will be called a state rather than ... Beit HaAm [the People's House—the term used for cultural centers]."[110] A reluctance to use the explicit and accepted terminology of governance typified the Zionist Movement from the time of its first congress in 1897 through the developments surrounding the 1917 Balfour Declaration and the 1942 Biltmore Program. This reflected the leadership's consistent discretion in decision-making, which remained sensitive to timing and proportionality and was able to separate the wheat from the chaff at the critical moment. At the same time, this reluctance also pointed to the sense of awareness, responsibility, and caution necessary for overseeing complex political processes whose purpose was not to issue formal declarations but to secure concrete political achievements in delicate situations. The adoption of this informed political position also attested to consideration of Shertok's previously mentioned entreaties about avoiding premature demonstrative gestures and visibly adhering to the UN Partition Plan to the extent possible.[111]

At its first session, the People's Administration decided to convene the first assembly of the People's Council on April 27, 1948, but because of the war and the difficulty for members from Jerusalem to attend, it was postponed to May 4. An editorial in *Davar* sought to mark the day as a celebratory occasion: "Let this day be recorded in the annals of our people as the first day of operations of the Jewish government."[112] Several important upcoming dates would, however, soon overshadow this one and sideline it in collective memory. Ben-Gurion, the only speaker at the May 4 People's Council gathering, presented the gradual construction of state institutions as a consequence of the needs of the hour, while also warning against false preconceptions as to the nature of these institutions and the sovereign regime in the making:

> The People's Council and People's Administration—the one is not a parliament and the other is not a government. Soon, we believe, a free parliament will be established in the State of Israel on the basis of democratic elections by all its citizens—all its Jewish citizens as well as all those Arab citizens who wish to remain. At that time an elected government will also be formed, with a responsibility to the democracy of the State of Israel. The People's Administration and the People's Council—they are an emergency headquarters for the purpose of standing at the gate and preventing the chaos that the Mandate government has maliciously inflicted on the country, in contravention of the United Nations' stated intention.[113]

Not only was this no "Beit HaAm" as the right had feared; Ben-Gurion was in fact already framing it as a state, albeit not yet officially. The threat of gunfire along the Jerusalem-Tel Aviv Road prevented Jerusalem delegates from attending on the next day as well, as a result of which the People's Council's second meeting adjourned shortly after it had convened. The subsequent meeting convened on May 14, 1948, only hours before Israel declared independence, in order to approve the text of that declaration. Under Mapai's direction, the institutional chaos gradually evolved into an agreed-upon structure comprising both an executive body and a body entrusted with deliberations, legislation, and regulation. These were formed with attention to the political situation, wartime needs, political party interests, and personal power dynamics, which coexisted with the continuing state of uncertainty, the administrative void resulting from the departure of Mandatory government personnel, the complications of delegating authority among governing bodies, and the aspiration "to find the right way of ensuring maximal defensive capability and the maximal utility of our political system."[114]

On the morning of April 18, 1948, just before the Yud-Gimel's first meeting, Ben-Gurion wrote to the Mapai Bureau proposing that the security portfolio be assigned to Levi Shkolnik (Eshkol). He further noted that he was convening the meeting solely as a member of the Jewish Agency Executive, adding that even though his March 6 proposal to the Mapai Central Committee to elect Myerson "among the four [representatives] of our party" had not been accepted, his announcement at that meeting that he did not view himself as a member of the Yud-Gimel "remains in effect."[115] Myerson and Shkolnik, both future prime ministers, were among Ben-Gurion's strongest supporters, and in this instance, their names were serving only as window dressing—a fact that was self-evident to all involved in the decision-making process on the eve of statehood. The struggle over the management and decision-making process surrounding security affairs would continue for many weeks to come, eventually reaching a resolution only in July 1948, in the spirit of Ben-Gurion's stance that no barrier should be established between the official in charge of the defense portfolio and the chief of staff.[116] By placing this issue center stage in the political arena, Ben-Gurion was signaling the end of the struggle with the National Council and its various branches. The institutions of the "state in the making" had served their purpose and reached their expiration date, after having purposefully and wisely guided the Yishuv and the Zionist Movement through countless obstacles to the threshold of independence. Crossing this threshold now required Chaim Weizmann's involvement.

On March 6, 1948, toward the end of the Mapai Central Committee's deliberations regarding its representatives to the People's Administration, Chaim Ben-Asher and Aryeh Bahir, two of Ben-Gurion's noted allies in the party, suggested excluding Remez and instead appointing him president of the People's Council. A reservation in this spirit—"If it turns out that there is a possibility of having a Council presidency, then the issue will be discussed with Remez"—was appended to the committee's decision. All those present knew full well, of course, that Remez would not dare to follow up on the proposal, as the negative reaction of Meir Grabovsky and Eliyahu Dobkin, members of the National Council and Jewish Agency Executives, respectively, carried more weight than the appended (and approved) reservation. These two, appointed by Mapai to conduct sensitive, behind-the-scenes talks on administrative and governing arrangements, as well as the assignment of positions within the new bodies, pronounced decisively: "The presidency of the Council can only go to *Weizmann*."[117]

2

THE "RED SHADOW" AND WEIZMANN'S INVOLVEMENT

In December 1946, Chaim Weizmann was ousted from his position as president of the Zionist Organization. About a year and a half later, on May 16, 1948, he was elected as president of Israel's Provisional State Council. David Ben-Gurion, the provisional prime minister, explained his choice: "It is inconceivable that Chaim Weizmann not serve as head of our state. It may not be necessary for Weizmann, but it seems to me that it's a moral imperative for the Yishuv and the people."[1] This is a somewhat bewildering statement, considering that Ben-Gurion had been responsible for ousting Weizmann earlier and that political considerations outweighed moral doctrine in determining the course of public affairs. Later, he would remark that Weizmann did not interfere with those who had chosen a new path even if he had long doubted its necessity, adding that Weizmann rediscovered himself upon the founding of the state.[2] This statement embodies a riddle, which we will ponder in the present and coming chapters. In doing so, we will trace the circumstances of Weizmann's reappointment as president, examining who planned this process, what considerations guided them, and how it was implemented in practice. The search for answers to these questions, which will usually feature only in the background of our discussion, may shed light on one of the major missing links in the early chronicles of the formation of Israeli statehood.

The initial premise of this chapter is that Weizmann's appointment should not be viewed as morally driven nor as purely a reward for his stance during the months preceding the proclamation of statehood, and not even as a gesture of recognition for his long years of service during the early days of the Zionist Movement. In my view, the selection of Weizmann was a political move of the highest order, intrinsically linked to the internal debate among US decision-makers surrounding the Palestine crisis in 1948, American fears about the future state aligning itself with the Soviet Union, and President Harry Truman's decision to adhere to the principle of partition and recognize the State of Israel. Reciprocally, and no less importantly, it was linked to Truman's refraining from taking active measures to thwart the state's establishment. The cases of Hiroshima, Berlin, and Korea—to name just a few—demonstrate that as far as Truman was concerned, issuing such orders was neither inconceivable nor exceptional. The assumption underpinning our discussion is that Weizmann's appointment as president of Israel's Provisional State Council on May 16 embodies both a decision and a declaration, at the very outset of independence, regarding several matters of state—namely, its political identity, the nature of its regime, and its place in the Cold War world. Nothing could match Weizmann's appointment in conveying a clear, decisive, unequivocal message regarding these questions of principle: Israel would be a Western-style democracy identified with the liberal mindset. At the same time, his appointment was intended to deliver this message with caution and restraint, as necessitated by the delicate situation and limited maneuverability that characterized the Zionist leadership's decision-making in the chaotic aftermath of the British Mandate in Palestine.

From the Anecdotal to the Political

In the minds of Weizmann's contemporaries, his name was inextricably linked with the presidency in part because of his long-term leadership as president of the Zionist Organization, from 1920 to 1931 and from 1935 to 1946—twenty-two years in all, a substantial period on the résumé of any leader, in Israel or elsewhere. His removal from the presidency in December 1946, during the Twenty-Second Zionist Congress, was compounded by his own physical weakness and Ben-Gurion's political achievements as leader of the Zionist Movement and the Yishuv throughout 1947. These factors cast genuine doubt on whether Weizmann would reassume any sort of official position in the Zionist arena. He himself shared these doubts, noting soon thereafter in his autobiography: "I believed then that my task was ended and that the long—perhaps too long—record was complete."[3] However, any doubts surrounding Weizmann and his public status dissipated immediately with the establishment of Israel.

The literature of the time describes Weizmann as suffering from poor health in February and March of 1948. He spent those months at the Waldorf Astoria in New York, which served as his base of operations.[4] That description is credible but incomplete. His health issues—physical fatigue and severe vision problems—were undoubtedly very burdensome, but those circumstances would have also played in his favor. They freed him from the obligation to attend perfunctory meetings with Jewish and other personalities or to interact with the general public, and they allowed him to engage in political matters discreetly and behind the scenes, as he favored, without clashing with Zionist figures or anti-Zionists who opposed his views.

Weizmann's participation in the decision to proclaim independence on May 14, 1948, and his appointment as Provisional State Council president two days later were, in my view, the final significant political contribution of his public life. Yet collective memory and Israeli political folklore have downplayed his role at the actual moment of Israel's establishment, focusing instead on a marginal episode that prevented him from signing the declaration of independence. At the time, he was in the United States, without any official position in the Zionist leadership and far from the events underway in Palestine.[5] Weizmann himself was not averse to dwelling repeatedly on the matter of his signature. On one occasion, when David Horowitz, director general of the Ministry of Finance and later the first governor of the Bank of Israel, was visiting him at his "Palace" in Rehovot (as his home was known), Weizmann complained, "I would have preferred that Ben-Gurion leave room for my signature after his long *nun* [final letter in Ben-Gurion's name], which takes up the whole sheet."[6] Supposing Weizmann had signed the declaration, would his political standing or his status in collective memory be different? In any event, this is a classic example of a Weizmann anecdote, one that focuses on the chapter of his life that began with his arrival in Israel on September 30, 1948.

The years 1947–1952 are rife with such anecdotes surrounding Weizmann. Another one from this period, which over time has been increasingly attributed to him, relates to his dropping a handkerchief. When his aide picked it up and returned it to him, Weizmann thanked him warmly, adding that this was the only place into which he could still stick his nose—a bitterly humorous reference to his exclusion from affairs of the state by Shertok and Ben-Gurion. Norman Rose deftly dispersed his biography of Weizmann with countless illustrative anecdotes from the tapestry of the leader's life, creating a delightful atmosphere that reflects the character and breadth of activities of this "historical hero."[7] The anecdotes about Weizmann's signature and his handkerchief, the most famous from his final years, reveal his frustration over having a political position that was effectively designated as "symbolic" (as president of the Provisional State Council and later of the state). The tone of personal distress they convey indicates that his steadily deteriorating health did not allow him to extract himself from the political strait into which he had been forced. In our context, it is best not to let later developments overshadow the relevant historical chapter—namely, the weeks preceding Israel's founding and the days immediately following it. Determining the extent of Weizmann's political weight on the eve of statehood requires careful examination, and it is therefore appropriate to refrain from embracing either of these popular anecdotes as clues to the answers we seek.

It was common knowledge that over the preceding decade or so, Weizmann had supported the partition of western Palestine as a means of realizing the political aspirations of Zionism. Since 1937, he had been a prominent advocate of territorial partition, which became a keystone of his political approach. He backed his stance with an allegory about a Jew in czarist Russia who was conversing amicably with a Russian officer during a train ride. When mealtime arrived, the officer produced a piece of pork and invited the Jew to partake. The latter explained that Jews were forbidden to eat pork. "Under any circumstances?" asked the officer. "Unless it's a matter of saving a life," replied the Jew. The officer then drew his pistol and ordered the Jew, "Eat, and I won't shoot you!" "In that case," said the Jew, "give me a nice slice."[8]

Another anecdote that deserves mention, indicative of its subject's tact and temperament, appears in the autobiography of Meyer Weisgal, Weizmann's most noted and loyal assistant and future president of the Weizmann Institute (1954–1969). According to Weisgal, just a few days before May 14, 1948, he was summoned by Ben-Gurion, who instructed him to fly to Europe right away so that he could speak with Weizmann directly by telephone, without fear of the British eavesdropping, and clarify his position on the immediate declaration of independence. Weizmann responded in flavorful Yiddish: "What are they waiting for, the idiots?" Weizmann's wife, Vera, explained in her autobiography that the reason Weisgal had to travel to Europe was that Shertok, who could have confirmed Weizmann's position, was still in New York because his flight had been delayed. Immediately after speaking with Weizmann, Weisgal sent a telegram to Ben-Gurion, stating that the answer was yes (as Shertok confirmed when he reached Palestine shortly thereafter).[9] The proper presentation of this anecdote in its precise context will be a cornerstone of our later discussion surrounding the decision to proclaim independence.

Weizmann's support for the decision to establish the State of Israel on May 14 was a necessary condition for his appointment as president of the Provisional State Council. It would be a mistake to present his position on such a critical and sensitive issue as part of a political bargain or quid pro quo involving his support in exchange for the appointment. Rather, it should be viewed as a stage in an ongoing political struggle, both within the Zionist leadership and among decision-makers in the United States, surrounding the possibility of establishing an independent Jewish state and the link between its establishment and the war against Arab states.[10] Had Weizmann been indecisive or hesitant on the critical issue of supporting the state's establishment in May, it is highly unlikely that his appointment to this prominent official position would have been possible or constructive. Historian Yoram Nimrod drew a link between Weizmann's stance and future Foreign Minister Shertok's conduct, arguing that "perhaps Weizmann, precisely because of his political astuteness, observed that Sharett's struggle was a lost cause and preferred not to identify with it and not to be inscribed in collective memory as someone who 'opposed the state.'"[11]

In examining this issue, I draw on a broad base of knowledge comprising two types of sources. The first consists of academic as well as nonacademic historiographical writings on President Truman's involvement in the process that led to Israel's founding. This is an exceptional body of work in terms of both quantity and detail.[12] The second category derives from the fact that during Weizmann's final years and after his death in November 1952, his closest supporters rallied to defend his legacy, including, foremost, his unique contribution on the eve of statehood. Their efforts to dispel the fog surrounding Weizmann's activities during this period were based on fragments of information gleaned from their own experiences at the time and on a small assortment of documents found in his and his loyalists' possession.

It was Weizmann who fired the opening shot in this struggle. Nine months after completing his autobiography, *Trial and Error*, which concludes with the UN Partition Plan resolution of November 1947, and a month before arriving in Israel in September 1948, he documented some of the events in which he had been involved during 1948 and included them as an epilogue to his book just before it went to print.[13] During the final year of his life, when in practical terms he had almost completely ceased functioning as president and it was clear to his close associates that his days were numbered, five figures were asked to provide reminiscences of his activities on the eve of statehood for inclusion in what would become the Weizmann Archives. Two of the five, Edward Jacobson and Josef Cohn, complied, while the remaining three, Samuel I. Rosenman, David Ginsburg, and David Niles, declined.[14] The purpose of this documentation effort was not only to immortalize this important chapter of Israel's establishment but also to ensure Weizmann's inclusion among the state's "founding fathers." Concurrently, the documentation was intended to help ward off any vilification of Weizmann for his absence from the country at the critical moment, whether due to alleged cowardice or to political irrelevance, as well as any attempts to malign his name by accusing him of having opposed statehood. Indirectly, the endeavor also attested to advance preparations for a confrontation with those seeking to downplay Weizmann's scientific enterprise by denigrating his memory vis-à-vis the sensitive issue of statehood in order to impede the establishment of a scientific institution in his name and thwart external investment in it.[15] The historical chapter presented here relates to the final phase of Weizmann's personal biography, but it also provides a key to understanding the formation of one of Israel's sovereign institutions—the presidency—by shedding light on a hidden dimension of the decision-making process that, amid internal dispute, led to statehood on May 14. The path to this final destination required that two senior leaders of the Zionist Movement first pass through the intermediate station of partition—that is, the geographic partition of the country.

Weizmann's Ouster and His Efforts to Return to the Political Arena

Upon conclusion of the Twentieth Zionist Congress, which discussed the Partition Plan proposed by the Peel Commission in 1937, and after achieving a temporary internal political victory in advancing the partition approach, Jewish Agency Executive chairman David Ben-Gurion wrote an effusive letter to Zionist Organization president Chaim Weizmann, declaring: "I have always loved you." As is customary in politics, this love was conditional. Ben-Gurion, who had neither voiced regret over Weizmann's removal in 1931 nor joined the efforts to reinstate him, continued, "Your 'exile' lasted four years, and during these four years I (and many of my associates) felt bad: as if we had participated in the cruel trick played on you. Your return to the movement's leadership was in my view not only a *political* need, but also, above all, a *moral* imperative." This was precisely the phrase he would invoke in 1948. "The Zionist Organization was blemished as long as it was overshadowed by sin of '*rabban dakru*' [they stabbed their rabbi, a reference to the 1931 ouster of Weizmann]," added Ben-Gurion, as if fearing the revenge of ancient gods, and comparing Weizmann to Rabbi Yohanan Ben-Zakkai, who had escaped from Jerusalem to Yavne during the Great Jewish Revolt against the Romans and from there to Bror Hayil. "I never was, and will never be, one of your blind devotees," wrote Ben-Gurion, distinguishing himself from Weizmann's supporters in Mapai, such as Yosef Sprinzak, David Remez, and Shmuel Dayan, and foreshadowing disputes that would erupt between them in the future. "But even amidst the storm of war, my love and admiration for you will not diminish in the slightest, because I know that you are a messenger of the people, not by virtue of a majority vote but by virtue of your having been created for this purpose. The Divine Spirit of the people of Israel flows over you. You are fulfilling a historical calling that no Jew has fulfilled for 2000 years." Ben-Gurion stressed the importance of standing by Weizmann "so that you succeed in carrying out the grand and awesome task assigned to you by the historical Providence of our people—the revival of the Kingdom of Israel."[16] In October 1946, two months before Weizmann was ousted for the second time from the role of Zionist Organization president, with Ben-Gurion's active participation, the latter wrote in a similar spirit: "For me (and I'm sure not only me), you remain a prominent figure in Jewish history, symbolizing, like none other, Jewish suffering and genius, and wherever you go you will have love and loyal admiration from me and from members of the generation after you, who may have known harder and crueler experiences and therefore (sometimes) view things differently from you."[17]

The different view of things in those days centered on activities of the Jewish Resistance Movement (an alliance of the Zionist paramilitaries the Haganah, Etzel, and Lehi). In particular, it was the "Night of the Bridges" (an operation to destroy the bridges linking Mandatory Palestine to its neighboring Arab countries) on June 16, 1946, that prompted Weizmann to threaten that he would resign as president of the Zionist Organization unless the Haganah refrain from military action against the British. His ultimatum, followed immediately by "Operation Agatha," which the British launched on June 29 (also known as "Black Shabbat"—a massive crackdown involving curfews, arrests, and searches), led to the dissolution of the Jewish Resistance Movement. Its fate was sealed following Etzel's bombing of the King David Hotel in Jerusalem on July 22, 1946.[18] On December 16, speaking at the Twenty-Second Zionist Congress, Weizmann praised the course of the Zionist Movement to date—"of building, of laying brick upon brick and stone upon stone." He declared that the inauguration just a few months earlier of eleven new settlements in the Negev, whose political contribution outweighs "a hundred speeches about resistance, especially when the speeches are made in Washington and New York, while it is intended that the resistance shall take place in Jerusalem or Tel Aviv." Emanuel Neumann, one of the Zionist Organization leaders in the United States, called out, "This is demagoguery!" Later in his speech, Weizmann replied, "Every farm-house and every stable in Nahalal and every building down to the tiniest workshop in Tel Aviv or Haifa contains a drop of my life's blood." He cautioned against taking shortcuts, falling for false prophecies or historical fabrication, or employing violence, and concluded by asserting that "Zion will be redeemed through righteousness" (Isaiah 1:27) and not by any other means.[19]

During the Congress, Ben-Gurion's harsh ultimatum of December 20, 1946—"I will not be in the Executive if Weizmann is serving or will serve as president"—was the decisive factor in a series of manipulation-laden votes led by Ben-Gurion, Abba Hillel Silver, and Moshe Sneh regarding dialogue with the British, active struggle, and the composition of the coalition. They ended with the Congress deciding to delegate authority for the selection of a president to the Zionist General Council, which convened immediately thereafter and decided by open vote to refrain from electing a president to the Zionist Organization "this time."[20] On December 29, Ben-Gurion was re-elected as chairman of the Jewish Agency Executive. "Personally I am happy to have acquired a friend and associate, for whom I have acquired respect," Ben-Gurion stated enthusiastically, referring to Rabbi Yehuda Leib Fishman (Maimon), representative for HaMizrachi. In so doing, he was reaffirming the "historical alliance" between the Labor Movement and religious Zionism, which began in the 1930s, lasted until May 1977, and drew on a shared activist worldview. It also came at the expense of an alliance with Weizmann. As to the latter, Ben-Gurion limited himself to a somewhat minor observation: "I think that he [Weizmann] will serve the movement in any capacity, and I am certain that he will be able to help a great deal, and we will ask his help, because he is the foremost figure in Zionism."[21] These remarks were purely a matter of courtesy, in the spirit of the already well-established practice of viewing Weizmann as an elder statesman of sorts, respected but lacking in standing, even when he was no older than sixty.[22] The full import of this comment would, however, become evident only later.

After the Congress, Weizmann decided to form a small group of influential individuals with moderate and liberal views who would serve as a base for deliberation, support, and action. He intended to include close, longtime associates from Britain, such as Simon Marks, Harry Sacher, and Leon Stein, alongside several devotees (with different areas of focus), such as Meyer Weisgal, Abba Eban, David Ginsburg, and Isaiah Berlin. He also hoped to add political figures from Mapai, such as Sprinzak, Eliezer Kaplan, and Berl Locker, as well as figures from HaIhud HaEzrahi, such as Yosef Sapir and Israel Rokach.[23] In some ways, which we will consider when we discuss the second half of 1948, one of the most significant figures whom Weizmann identified as key to forming the progressive group of loyalists he was trying to establish within American Zionist circles was former US secretary of the treasury Henry Morgenthau Jr. A non-Zionist, Morgenthau had since late 1946 been increasingly involved in American Jewish life after becoming chairman of the United Jewish Appeal (UJA), which allocated a third of the funds it raised to the Jewish community in Palestine. Weizmann instructed Weisgal to contact Morgenthau and ensure that Neumann did not latch onto him. He also wrote to Morgenthau directly, warning him about the "rabbi from Cleveland" (Silver) and other Zionist extremists who were refusing to adopt the concept of partition as a means to establishing a Jewish state. As an initial step, this move was successful, and Morgenthau invited Weizmann to speak at a celebratory UJA event that eventually took place in Boston in October.[24]

At the immediate political level, Weizmann's efforts seemed hopeless. They would gradually come to fruition during the course of 1948, but at the time, they did not yield the outcome he had expected—namely, a rapid erosion of the role of the Jewish Agency Executive, which relied on cooperation between Mapai under Ben-Gurion, the General Zionists under Silver, and HaMizrachi under Fishman. Weizmann's appeals to Kaplan, arguing that he and other loyalists, such as Nahum Goldmann and Selig Brodetsky, ought to refrain from joining the Jewish Agency Executive, were flatly rejected because Kaplan's loyalty to Mapai and Goldmann's to himself were what determined their conduct at the time and generally. Concurrently, Weizmann began (on his friends' advice) to fear for his physical safety—without dwelling on it, the clear impression that emerges is that he was concerned about attacks by Jews, whether from activist circles or Etzel and Lehi—and he discreetly asked Kaplan, in the latter's capacity, to provide security arrangements for him.[25] He admitted to his close political associate Sprinzak that he could not shed the feeling that Ben-Gurion had achieved some form of personal victory over him. In a letter to Kaplan, and a déjà vu of sorts, he reiterated accusations he had leveled at Ben-Gurion during the debate on the implementation of the Biltmore Program in 1942, charging that his opponents had planned to "politically assassinate" him and successfully did so at the Congress. In his despair, he went so far as to warn Morgenthau, after Weisgal established contact between them as requested, that "soon we will all be helpless to prevent the destruction of the Third Temple."[26]

If in the past it went without saying that every time Weizmann visited Palestine he was met with the warmth and spontaneous enthusiasm due his eminence and graciousness, in early 1947, Sprinzak had to scramble, artificially summoning Weizmann's close associates and loyalists in the Labor Movement in order to receive him with "the appropriate warmth and respect."[27] Relations between Weizmann and some of the Mapai leaders remained murky for several long months. He refused to meet with Shertok, whose conduct at the Zionist Congress he interpreted as a personal betrayal, and he regarded Ben-Gurion's invitation to meet as no more than a perfunctory obligation. With hyperbole that attested primarily to his despondency, he warned Kaplan that his and his moderate colleagues' fate would be akin to that "of German Social-Democrats upon the advent of Hitler." To illustrate the depth of the rift and fend off any attempts to repair it, Weizmann paraphrased the well-known English nursery rhyme: "All the king's horses and all the kings men can't put it together again."[28] For the time being, he concentrated on completing his autobiography and expediting preparations for the inauguration of the scientific research institute that would bear his name following the expansion of the existing Daniel Sieff Research Institute in Rehovot. In this context, he instructed Weisgal that "meanwhile"–until Sprinzak made good on his promise to allocate $40,000 from the Histadrut, which he headed, for the completion of the institute's construction–"all the deliveries of cigars will be withheld."[29] Of course, this delay was not the reason for Sprinzak's outburst at a Mapai Central Committee meeting a month later when he challenged Ben-Gurion on Weizmann's continuing involvement in the Zionist enterprise: "When you speak about the 'great Jew' sitting in Rehovot, be consistent." The latter countered, slightly mockingly, that he had tremendous respect for Sprinzak's feelings toward Weizmann but did not share them and never had, adding that while some of their members view Weizmann as their symbol, there are others who do not, and their feelings, too, must be respected. Ben-Gurion continued, if only to point out that the issue at hand did not turn on questions of respect: "I consider Weizmann a great Jew; I consider Professor Einstein, for example, an even greater Jew, but I would not appoint Einstein as president of the Zionist Organization."[30]

Following the National Council Executive's decision to designate Weizmann as one of the Zionist Movement speakers to appear before the United Nations Special Committee on Palestine (UNSCOP), Peretz Bernstein and Fishman spoke out against his selection at a Jewish Agency Executive meeting on June 8, 1947. Ben-Gurion, while fully aware that Weizmann's views differed from his own, was also mindful of the value of Weizmann's appearance before the committee given his unmatched global prominence as a Zionist figure. He therefore announced that he preferred not to express a view on the matter. In the vote that followed, the remaining Mapai members unequivocally supported Weizmann as speaker (Locker, Kaplan, Shertok, Eliyahu Dobkin, and Golda Myerson, joined by Goldmann). Bernstein, Fishman, Sneh, Ben-Gurion, and Yitzhak Gruenbaum chose to abstain, leaving HaPoel HaMizrachi's delegate, Shlomo Zalman Shragai, to cast the sole negative vote.[31] The opponents were aware that the Jewish public—in the Yishuv and the Zionist Movement generally—would view a decision by the Jewish Agency Executive to prevent Weizmann's appearance before UNSCOP as a blow to the legitimacy of the body to which they belonged, aside from the fact that such a decision would undermine the best possible presentation of the Zionist cause. When Weizmann did appear before the committee on July 8, 1947, it was as a "simple soldier" in the words of *Davar*.[32]

It was not as a "simple soldier," however, that Weizmann met clandestinely with Truman on November 19, 1947, and managed to persuade him that the United States should support the designated Jewish state's retention of the Negev. Weizmann later marveled that this was the first time he saw a president able to read a map.[33]

A month earlier, Neumann and Silver had been compelled to accept Locker, Goldmann, and Weizmann's proposal that Weizmann, alongside Shertok, would deliver the closing speeches on behalf of the Zionist Movement upon conclusion of the Palestine Commission's deliberations. Silver's claim, that Weizmann would not be able to make any substantive historical contribution, was of course refuted.[34] In the interim between Weizmann's speech before the Palestine Commission and his meeting with Truman, Neumann found an opportunity to pay Weizmann back for his remarks at the Twenty-Second Zionist Congress. He opted not to invite the Jewish figure whose name was linked with the Balfour Declaration to speak at a large celebratory dinner organized by the Zionist Organization of America and to be held at the Waldorf Astoria on November 2, 1947, the thirtieth anniversary of the Balfour Declaration. With the UN General Assembly vote around the corner, Neumann noted in his invitation to Morgenthau (UJA chairman at the time) that "the celebration of this anniversary takes on special meaning." When Neumann's deliberate slight became known, sparking the ire of Jewish Agency Executive members (Shertok, Locker, Gruenbaum, and Goldmann), he was compelled to send an invitation by telegram to the Savoy Plaza Hotel, where Weizmann was staying, just hours before the gathering. Sprinzak regarded the incident as illustrative of the ill-mannered treatment of Weizmann, and in reaction, he and his associates decided not to attend the event.[35]

At the same time, during these stressful weeks of anticipation in advance of the decisive UN vote of November 29, 1947, the personal tension between Weizmann and Shertok, head of the Zionist delegation to the UN, lessened slightly, perhaps thanks to mediation efforts by Kaplan and Sprinzak, who numbered among the delegates from Palestine who contributed to the political success. Upon his return to Palestine following the UN General Assembly deliberations, Jewish Agency Executive legal adviser Dov Joseph (Yosef) briefed the Mapai Central Committee on political developments, adding that he would be committing an "injustice" if he did not mention Weizmann's work. "He was dedicated, met with the president, worked with all his might, and was also effective. I want you to know this, and also that relations between him and our members were largely repaired."[36] The committee members could easily surmise that by "members," he meant Shertok. This calmer atmosphere became evident three months later in the position adopted by

Dobkin and Meir Grabovsky—decidedly not "Weizmannists"—when the Mapai Central Committee turned its attention to the Provisional State Council presidency. At the same time, Weizmann's political views were still a focus of suspicion, and a patronizing regard for him in public arenas continued without repercussions. Following the adoption of the Partition Plan, Reuters quoted Weizmann as cautioning against unrestricted immigration, warning that the country's stability should not be endangered during its first two or three years, and asking for a measure of caution for the sake of those still waiting in refugee camps. An editorial in *Davar* qualified its criticism by noting that it did not have the precise wording of Weizmann's speech, but it still concluded decisively: "The state to be established will be a state of immigration and for immigration. That is its destiny, that is its purpose, that is the essence of its being, that is the justification for its establishment. This is the difference between it and the waning [Mandatory] Palestinian state—it will be concerned not with restricting immigration but with increasing it."[37]

The limited relevance of this fervent, belligerent rhetoric, in concrete terms, became evident in January 1948. Silver arrived in the country with a political mission, to survey the situation and assess the viability of his US colleagues' presumptive aspirations for him to lead the Zionist Movement in implementing the Partition Plan. He devoted part of his time to caring for his dying mother. He also found that the state of war was far more acute than people in the United States believed. He quickly realized that his eminent standing, demonstrated in his skillfully persuading US Jews to pressure decision-makers in Washington and in the decisive contribution he made to the Partition Plan resolution, was not seen as particularly valuable in the country's present circumstances. All that was left for him was to serve as a low-ranking external adviser of limited influence amid a struggle for survival. His impressive philosophical writings about the value of liberal ideology in shaping diaspora-state relations, which had earned Silver admiration among his Reform Jewish followers, never became a popular issue in the local discourse. As an alternative, he sought to employ techniques of public pressure that had proved themselves in the past in the political arena, but it soon became evident that when it came to strategic military matters, these techniques did not provide the leverage necessary to tip the scales once again in support of Zionism. Drawing on tested practices, Silver sent a telegram to his colleagues in New York, urging them to launch a campaign of pressure on Truman and US Secretary of State George Marshall to lift the embargo on arms shipments to the Middle East, particularly on privately purchased shipments. The American embargo had been imposed a month earlier at the initiative of Loy Henderson, director of the Office of Near Eastern and African

Affairs in the State Department, who had also led the opposition to partition, and more generally to Zionism, within the US establishment. At a meeting of the Jewish Agency Executive in Jerusalem on January 25, Silver admitted that the two-thirds majority vote at the UN was achieved "thanks to President Truman" but that Truman had acted "as if the devil made him do it." On this point, Silver's account is somewhat dubious, as relations between him and the president had long been fraught. Indeed, Truman had barred him from entering the White House. Silver's solution was to "flood the White House" once again with telegrams of protest and fiery letters.[38]

At the start of this meeting, Kaplan noted that according to the grapevine, concerns about the new state's relations with the Soviet Union were prompting Britain and the United States to consider changing the contours of the Partition Plan "in order to secure bases in the country for the British army."[39] Three days earlier, British Foreign Secretary Ernest Bevin had stated in the House of Commons that the Soviet policy was "to use every means in their power to get Communist control in Eastern Europe, and, as it now appears, in the West as well" and that any effort "to dominate Europe by whatever means, direct or indirect . . . will inevitably lead again to another world war."[40] Concurrently, various actors in the US administration were increasingly calling for a reassessment of American support for the Partition Plan. Under these circumstances, the practical approach available to Zionist leaders in the United States for addressing any threat to the foundational pillars of partition—namely, superpower cooperation, cultivation of Jewish-Arab understanding, and international legitimacy—was embodied by the figure of Chaim Weizmann.[41]

THE "PANS" AND COMMUNIST REVERBERATIONS FROM THE ZIONIST STRUGGLE

Assessing the importance of Weizmann's role in 1948 Zionist politics necessitates that we consider the position of Zionism and the emerging state along the East–West axis in light of escalating interbloc tensions. A meeting between Ben-Gurion and British Foreign Secretary Bevin on February 12, 1947, shortly before Britain announced that it was referring the question of Palestine to the UN, illustrates this point. At the meeting—held about a month and a half after the Twenty-Second Zionist Congress, which had placed Ben-Gurion at the head of the Zionist political pyramid—the Jewish Agency Executive chairman spoke as if his political outlook were fully aligned with the ousted Weizmann's fundamental belief that the Zionist Movement's affiliation with Britain was vital. He explained to Bevin that the Zionist Movement perceived its ties with Britain as stemming from shared interests and ideals. In light of the impending Cold War between East and West, Ben-Gurion pointed out that there were many Russian Jews in Palestine, that he himself was born in Russia, and that of course Weizmann was a Russian Jew. "Many aspects of Russian culture are still dear to us. But we find ourselves in a situation where, if a dispute erupts, we will have no choice" but to support the Western bloc. Under the Russian regime, he added, Jews were not discriminated against, but "under such a regime, the Jewish people will disappear. Our existence and survival depend on the presence in the world of the Anglo-Saxon ideals of liberalism—tolerance, respect for human liberty and dignity, freedom of expression of political opinion." He concluded that if a clash were to emerge between these two ways of life, "we will not have a choice" because "we belong" to the Western world "and our interest is that England and America preserve their place in the world."[42] How far was Ben-Gurion willing to go? Evidently, in a last-ditch effort to pacify Bevin two days later, when the British Cabinet was scheduled to decide on referring the question of Palestine to the UN, Ben-Gurion promised him that his Labor Movement shared most of the British Labour Party's ideals and that a Jewish state, if it emerged, would "for our own sake, regard your interests—economic and political—as our own."[43]

This political approach was presumably informed by a series of events in 1947, including, in particular, Soviet Deputy Foreign Minister Andrei Gromyko's statement at the UN on May 14. Gromyko asserted that the Soviet Union was maintaining its official position in favor of one binational state in Palestine, but if that proved impossible, then the appropriate solution would be partition. A few weeks later, Soviet Foreign Minister Vyacheslav Molotov explained to his deputy, "We were driven by tactical considerations in proposing the establishment of a binational state as the first option to resolving the question of Palestine. We did not want to take the initiative for establishing a Jewish state, but the second option . . . —the establishment of an independent Jewish state—better reflects our position."[44] The remarks of several senior Mapai members are indicative of the extent of suspicion toward the Soviets among Zionist policymakers. At a Jewish Agency Executive meeting a few days before Gromyko's statement, Ben-Zvi complained that the Soviet Union had not "shown any understanding regarding the matter of the Jewish state in Eretz Israel," and Myerson commented, "I've never thought that Gromyko's appearance would mean support for Zionism; clearly the three Russian votes [counting Ukraine and Belarus] will not be in our favor." Deliberations over the correct interpretation of Gromyko's speech lasted for several weeks. About three months later, Shertok still held that the Zionists were interpreting Soviet intentions based on their own wishes, as if they believed that if it turned out a binational state was not viable, then "they would decide on two states. But another interpretation, the right one in my view, is also possible: they will *establish* a binational state and if it later becomes evident that it is not working properly—they will partition [it]."[45]

According to Yaacov Ro'i, the leading scholar on Soviet-Israeli relations in the transition from Yishuv to state, Mapam's pro-Soviet orientation was mainly in the conceptual and educational sphere. The attempts by a few of its leaders to establish political and organizational ties with the Soviet "world of tomorrow" were bound to fail. "The USSR seems to have accepted *a priori* the fact that Israel belonged to the capitalist world."[46] Herzl Berger, an up-and-coming Mapai thinker at the time, rightly identified the concurrently conceptual and practical dilemma that framed the Israeli left's political discourse surrounding events on the ground, as distinct from the ideological discourse surrounding the Soviet Union. He assessed that "we in the workers' movement have divided the tasks: we [Mapai] know the truth and keep quiet, and others [Mapam] know the truth and lie. We hear how they lie while knowing the truth, and still keep quiet, because we [both Mapai and Mapam] live in the hope that there is still some spark of hope that Jews can be saved."[47]

In any event, the future state's essential approach to foreign policy, as Ben-Gurion presented it to the Mapai Central Committee, was "world peace and the unification of humanity." In his view, the "salient fact" was that about two-thirds of the Jewish people were scattered across Western countries while one-third lived in the East, and the Zionist Movement aspired to bring a large portion of them to the emerging state while fearing for the safety of the others. Later, the nonoverlapping terms *neutrality* and *nonalignment* would be used to describe Israeli foreign policy during the early years of statehood.[48] In 1948, however, Ben-Gurion was content with identifying the overlap between the ideal guiding the United Nations and the ideal of a Jewish state's existence, although he admitted, "Perhaps, this may sound rather chauvinistic."[49]

Israel's international affiliation at the time of its establishment remained deliberately vague in light of the escalating East–West confrontation, concrete examples of which included the communist takeover of Czechoslovakia and the Soviet blockade of Berlin. According to Uri Bialer, given the circumstances of its founding and the conditions facing Diaspora Jewry around the world, Israel could not align itself with any particular bloc of countries or form a strategic alliance with either superpower and, to some extent, did not wish to do so either.[50] With her characteristic affinity for speaking plainly, Myerson pointed to the crux of the international, historical issue as it related to realizing Zionist aspirations at that time and place: "I am certain that if a representative of Soviet Russia, a good friend of ours, and an American representative, also a good Zionist friend of ours, were seated here now, most would agree that the greatest folly Jews and Zionists could commit now would be to fight among themselves about an orientation with one bloc or the other."[51] Two clusters of reasons shaped this reality. The first was the constellation of interests in the Middle East maintained by the United States' Cold War ally, Britain, and the deep distrust that overshadowed political relations between the British and the Zionist leadership. These were compounded by certain weighty factors the United States had to consider in implementing the Marshall Plan for Europe's rehabilitation using low-cost Middle Eastern Arab oil. Such considerations reinforced the view among Pentagon personnel that there was a reciprocity between the question of Palestine and dilemmas in Central Europe that were forcing the "free world" into a confrontation with communism and "Soviet aggression."[52] The second cluster was the Jewish dependence on preserving close ties with the Soviet Union for the sake of four existential objectives: the purchase of arms from Czechoslovakia (which necessitated Soviet authorization), preventing the blockade of smuggling routes for Jews from Eastern Europe to Mediterranean ports en route to Palestine; the hope that the Soviets would relax the prohibition against Zionist activities in the Soviet Union and perhaps even allow Jewish emigration or at least subdue antisemitic fervor throughout Eastern Europe, and the guarantee of Soviet backing during confrontations in international forums over the status and sovereign powers of the Jewish state during its first eighteen months of statehood.[53]

On the other side of the superpower divide, a fierce debate was raging within the American administration regarding the implementation of the UN Partition Plan resolution. The backdrop to this was a growing unease in the Democratic Party surrounding Truman as its candidate in the upcoming November 1948 presidential elections. That unease provided a measure of legitimacy in questioning his policy on the quandary of Palestine. It was further compounded by the efforts of two senior administrative officials whose integrity and capabilities gave them much sway in Washington—Marshall and Secretary of Defense James Forrestal. The conceptual foundation for the debate among American decision-makers appeared in two documents formulated by George Kennan and Clark Clifford. Kennan, head of the State Department's Policy Planning Staff, was known as the architect of the doctrine of Soviet "containment" in Europe. In contrast, Clifford, senior political adviser to President Truman on domestic affairs, was depicted on the cover of the popular *Time* magazine during the election year as a covert, sophisticated, mysterious adviser. His detractors in government circles described him as a "political accident" (like Truman, who had entered office following Roosevelt's death), as someone who had "accidentally" acquired his position by being in the vicinity when an administrative vacuum presented an opportunity.[54]

Kennan began drafting his memorandum in early December 1947 in close cooperation with Henderson, director of the State Department's Office of Near Eastern and African Affairs, and completed it on January 19, 1948. The memorandum concluded that without foreign assistance in weapons, funding, and personnel, the Zionists would not be able to implement the Partition Plan because "the partition of Palestine cannot be implemented without the use of force." In this regard, he saw things eye to eye with Ben-Gurion and in line with a Central Intelligence Agency (CIA) assessment completed two days before the Partition Plan resolution. However, Kennan believed that US assistance, whether governmental or of another form, would harm American interests in the Arab world. He also assessed that the Soviet Union was interested in the implementation of the Partition Plan because this would allow it to assist in "maintaining order" by deploying forces to Palestine as part of an international force. As a result, "Communist agents would have an excellent base from which to extend their subversive activities." At the same time, with a professional integrity informed by his expertise in Soviet affairs, Kennan noted that the Soviets might refrain from deploying forces to the region because, alternatively, they might be interested in the United States entangling itself in the question of Palestine, thereby allowing the Soviets to gain support in the Muslim world. He advised against taking any action to advance the implementation of the Partition Plan because doing so would be "to the detriment of overall US security interests." His recommendation was to refer the issue back to the UN General Assembly to consider other alternatives, such as a federal state or trusteeship. While Marshall did not respond to the memorandum, his deputy, Robert Lovett, tersely observed that he had expected the Policy Planning Staff to come up with a different plan that would survey various alternatives and consider their advantages and disadvantages. The Policy Planning Staff, accordingly, produced a memorandum that was presented on February 22, 1948, pointing to three alternatives: (1) full support for partition including a willingness to use military force, (2) a passive stance, not taking any measures to implement partition, and (3) rejection of partition and referral to UN bodies to formulate an alternative based on a federal state or international trusteeship. The decision about which alternative to adopt fell to the political level, namely, Marshall and Truman. However, Kennan's original memorandum provided the conceptual foundation for opponents of partition in the American administration, and Defense Secretary Forrestal in particular. He regarded the memorandum as proof of the impossibility of implementing partition without the use of force and agreed that the United States had no interest in providing arms to either side and that it should therefore refrain from supporting partition.[55] Forrestal had his own solution to the Jewish problem, reminiscent of Theodor Herzl's long-forgotten musings: "The best place for Jews is Kenya."[56]

Ultimately, however, the cold, unempathetic analysis Kennan recorded in his personal diary is actually quite instructive in the way it captures the approach to Palestine among many US officials at the time and ever since:

> I have come to doubt that any arrangement for Palestine worked out by outside powers and enforced either physically or morally by the international community can ever prove satisfactory. Unless the inhabitants of Palestine, both Jews and Arabs, and the international elements which stand behind them, are finally compelled to face each other eye to eye, without outside interference, and to weigh, with a sense of immediate and direct responsibility, the consequences of agreement or disagreement, I think they will continue to react irresponsibly in the face of the proposed solutions, and there will be no one that can command their loyalty and cooperation. It may be that there will be bloodshed in the wake of a negative American policy. But we Americans must realize that we cannot be the keepers and moral guardians of all the peoples in this world. We must become more modest, and recognize the necessary limits to the responsibility we can assume.[57]

Clifford, a liberal lawyer from St. Louis, Missouri, was of a different temperament. In the past he had not hesitated to urge Truman to clash with trade unions, and, like Kennan, he took an anticommunist stance. In Washington's senior decision-making circles, Clifford represented the pro-Zionist position, which he laid out for Truman in a March 8 memorandum. Taking the Balfour Declaration as his starting point, Clifford presented testaments in support of its objective from all US presidents since 1917. Although the individual who personified its validity was, of course, Weizmann, the memorandum did not mention his name. Clifford described partition as "the only course of action with respect to Palestine that will strengthen our position vis-à-vis Russia." In his assessment, "Jewish Palestine is strongly oriented to the United States, and away from Russia, and will remain so unless a military vacuum in Palestine caused by collapse of UN authority brings Russian unilateral intervention into Palestine."[58]

On January 30, 1948, in the intervening period between these two memoranda, the Jewish Agency office in New York produced a memorandum intended for Forrestal. The interesting timing of this document suggests that information about Kennan's memorandum, and possibly its main points, had reached Zionist sources, compelling them to reply. The agency's memorandum focused primarily on alleviating concerns that the Jewish state would be a Soviet puppet. Employing the customary American terminology and concepts, the memorandum pointed out that the practices of collective agriculture and cooperative industrial management prevalent among Jews in Palestine were the products of free choice relating to economic activity rather than political coercion as practiced under Soviet communism. Moreover, stated the memorandum, a substantial portion of the settlers were refugees who fled communist countries and came to Palestine because they did not wish to live in accordance with the current practices in Eastern Europe. Democracy and free enterprise expressed not only the aspirations of Palestine's Jews, the memorandum added, hinting at the American way of life, but also the lifestyle prevalent throughout the Jewish world. Certain Jewish individuals might adopt the communist approach, admitted the memorandum's drafters, but the Jewish community as a whole knew that it could not exist in a totalitarian atmosphere; there could be no doubt, therefore, that the new Jewish state would be decisively affiliated with the Western democratic world.[59]

This "memoranda war" offers a window into the political chaos surrounding the Zionist struggle in the United States, in parallel with the escalating hostilities in Palestine, and indicates how shaky the political situation was from the Zionist perspective. Concerns about the possibility of a shift in US policy, as conceptualized and indicated in Kennan's memorandum, were the main reason that, on February 4, 1948, Weizmann returned from England to the United States (which he had left in mid-December 1947) even though he had already begun preparing to move to Palestine permanently. He decided to acquiesce to the appeals of several leading Zionist activists in New York, who insisted that he join them immediately to address the State and Defense Departments' apparent inclinations to reject the Partition Plan. Shertok informed Ben-Gurion about Weizmann's invitation, expressing the hope that Ben-Gurion did not object. The latter merely noted the fact in his diary, adding that the invitation had been Goldmann's suggestion, approved by the Jewish Agency Executive's American section. Abba Eban, a member of the agency's delegation to the United States and one of Weizmann's close associates, took credit for initiating the invitation. Yet it would appear that the credit for actually persuading Weizmann to come belongs to his loyal private secretary, Josef Cohn, who knew how to strike the right notes, implying ominously that "if we don't establish the state there will be chaos or worse in Palestine, and you won't have an institute (to be named after Weizmann)."[60]

On the day the Weizmanns arrived in New York, Weizmann's wife, Vera, wrote in her diary that "Washington is a desert . . . whispering malicious rumors: Jews are Bolsheviks, bringing communists to Palestine; threat of Bolshevism to the Middle East; Americans fear for their oil interests . . . Americans regret their support for partition, fearing Russian participation in the international force."[61] This was the reality the Weizmanns encountered upon arriving. In the background was information leaked by British Foreign Office officials to the *New York Times*, according to which many of the fifteen thousand Jewish refugees from Romania who had set sail aboard two large illegal immigrant ships—the *Pan York* and *Pan Crescent*—were communist Jewish spies in the service of the Soviet Union (the refugees had surrendered to the British without struggle in late December 1947 and were then transferred to detention camps in Cyprus). Shertok responded that the British government was trying to incite American public opinion against the establishment of a Jewish state through the manipulative exploitation of widespread American suspicions regarding communism. He described the British information about Soviet attempts to smuggle spies into Palestine under the camouflage of clandestine immigration as "a cruel joke."[62]

The British allegations were based on a report by the Joint Intelligence Committee of the British secret services submitted to the War Office on January 23, 1948. It was based in large part on a report by Alan Cunningham, the British High Commissioner to Palestine. The document's authors did not confirm British naval sources' claim that the Soviets had allowed the *Pan Crescent* to set sail only after one thousand communist Jews had boarded, and even noted that there was no direct evidence of Soviet spies among the passengers. It was sufficient for their purposes that a thousand of them spoke Russian. In light of the assistance provided by Eastern European Soviet satellite states in preparing for these voyages, the authors concluded that such illegal immigration accorded with Soviet policy in the Middle East.[63] The presumably conclusive evidence of communists among the passengers, according to British naval officers, included the fact that many of them had cosmetic mirrors with a picture of Joseph Stalin on the back. They forgot to note that this was the only type of mirror available in Romania at the time.[64] When Sir Godfrey Collins, the commissioner of Jewish camps in Cyprus, contested the credibility of information about communists having infiltrated the passengers on the two ships, a British Foreign Office spokesman responded that Collins was not involved in the details. To dispel internal tension, the secretary of state for the colonies, Arthur Creech-Jones, informed his subordinate Collins on February 3, in circuitous diplomatic terms, that "there is evidence to show that the Russians were not entirely disinterested in these ships." He went on to admit, "I am in any case anxious not to discourage the belief now current in the United States that illegal immigration into Palestine may aggravate the communist danger in the Middle East," adding that "publicity here [in London] is being conducted on the above line."[65]

Some in Washington bought into the British manipulation, as intended, because among other reasons it accorded with the political agenda they sought to advance; that is, replacing partition with trusteeship. For some years, the British had been feeding information to American sources in the State Department and Pentagon about the Soviets' supposed use of Zionism and Jewish refugees from Eastern Europe seeking to immigrate to Palestine as a way to infiltrate loyalists into the area. On February 4, 1948, Marshall reported that his office had received information about two illegal immigrant ships on which about 150–200 passengers had been identified as communists.[66] In response to these recurring allegations, Silver, who had returned from Palestine, convened a press conference on February 6 at which he accused the *New York Times* of publishing "these faked stories." Shertok, who attended the press conference, added that all the adults on board both ships had been carefully screened by Zionist organizations in Europe, and he noted cynically that no communist organization had ever asked to join the Zionist Movement. Marshall, who did not find the information about communist infiltration into Palestine to be compelling, presumed that it was British propaganda. Nevertheless, the State Department opted not to present concrete information on the matter to the Jewish Agency Executive, noting only that about a thousand passengers on the two *"Pans"* were Russian speakers and referring the agency directly to the British government.[67]

Arthur Hays Sulzberger, publisher of the *New York Times*, complained that the stories about "Russian agents" among illegal immigrants had caused the newspaper's circulation to drop by ten thousand, presumably because of Jewish anger over the blow to the Zionist struggle.[68] Liberal Jewish journalist I. F. Stone ridiculed the exploitation of the "red scarecrow" by various State Department officials, claiming that it would soon require immigrant Jewish refugees from Europe to Palestine to refrain from wearing red underwear, and the observant ones among them would have to shave their beards for fear of bearing any resemblance to bushy-bearded Karl Marx.[69]

In retrospect, one might view the story, which the Yishuv press also angrily contested, as one of many examples of disinformation circulated and subsequently refuted during the final days of the Mandate.[70] In this case, however, Forrestal claimed that American sources confirmed the British allegations. The British Joint Intelligence Committee also continued to advance the charge that communist Jewish would-be immigrants were trying to infiltrate Palestine and transform the future state into part of the Soviet bloc.[71] As we shall see, this was precisely the claim that Deputy Secretary of State Lovett presented as his final and presumably winning argument in his arsenal of rationales during the decisive May 12, 1948, White House debate on the recognition of a Jewish state.[72]

Time and again, the certain threat of communist infiltration into Palestine, under the auspices of the clandestine immigration enterprise, emerged from the dark depths of intelligence sources as a recurring pattern. It surfaced once again just before the UN vote on partition. At a meeting with Secretary of State Marshall on November 24, 1947, British Foreign Secretary Bevin stated that according to their sources, illegal Jewish immigrants from the Balkans to Palestine included among their ranks "many indoctrinated Communists which presented a serious threat to Middle East stability."[73] In reaction to these charges, Weizmann wrote to Truman on the day before the vote:

> Fears are . . . expressed that our project in Palestine may in some way be used as a channel for the infiltration of Communist ideas in the Middle East. Nothing is further from the truth. Our immigrants from Eastern Europe are precisely those who are leaving the Communist scene with which they do not wish to be integrated, otherwise they would not leave at all. Had there been a serious attempt by the Soviets to introduce Communist influences through our immigration they could easily have done so in previous decades. Every election and all observation in Palestine testify to the trivial hold which Communism has achieved in our community. An educated peasantry and a skilled industrial class living on high standards will never accept Communism. The danger lies amongst illiterate and impoverished communities bearing no resemblance to our own.[74]

While Weizmann was fervently denying any hint of a claim of communist involvement in the Zionist enterprise, along came the *Pans* affair, which granted a tangible, physical dimension, in quantitative terms, to the vague, sporadic fear of communist inclinations among remaining refugees and the Yishuv generally. The passengers on board these ships were portrayed as representative of the ideational trends prevalent among illegal immigrants whose arrival in Palestine was intended to transform the notion of a Jewish state into a reality. By ascribing a communist image to the passengers of the *Pans* and ostensibly backing the claim with confirmed sources drawn from a morass of intelligence information, the recurring threat of communist influence met the minimum threshold to inscribe itself in the consciousness of the time and become a significant factor in the deliberations of State Department officials.

By February 11, 1948, Shertok had not yet calmed down from the "vicious propaganda campaign" waged by the British a few months earlier in the context of the *Pans* when they alleged "a communist infiltration into Palestine and the Middle East . . . that poisoned the State Department in this regard from its foundation to its rafters." In a letter to Ben-Gurion, he pondered whether it would be the "smartest move," at that time to authorize the transit of two additional illegal immigrant ships from communist-controlled Bulgaria.[75] It is not surprising in this context that, as the end of the British Mandate drew near, the fear of the Soviets gaining a foothold in the Middle East with the assistance of the Jewish state enterprise was foremost on the minds of decision-makers in Washington. The Zionist Movement was caught in a dilemma between East and West, as described by Shertok: "In closed-door conversation it's okay to say that the Jews are escaping Sovietization. It's not so easy to say this publicly," as that would have undermined any Soviet willingness to support Zionism.[76] Eliahu Epstein (Eilat), the Jewish Agency representative in Washington and later Israel's first ambassador to the United States, summarized this dilemma succinctly in a review of the American position for the Mapai Secretariat in early April 1948: "Just as Russia openly lends its support with every additional speech—this only reinforces the fear [in Washington], that here [in Palestine] there is not only the danger of the Russian army entering [the country], but also the fear that the Yishuv is proceeding toward some form of identification with Russia. It does not matter if the Yishuv is communist or not, it is enough that there is a pro-Soviet orientation, and England only contributed to the situation with all its provocation about ships bringing communist agents to Palestine."[77]

Under these circumstances, the only leader who somewhat balanced the situation, by advancing the view of the Zionist Movement as allied with the West, was Weizmann. A rare indication that the Soviets understood Weizmann's approach in the struggle over Palestine's fate during the first half of 1948 appeared in *Maariv* on April 9. According to the newspaper, "In its Yiddish radio broadcast last night, Radio Moscow fiercely attacked Dr. Weizmann, saying, 'Weizmann is a Jewish advocate of the Marshall-Bevin plan for Palestine. From time to time he tries to persuade the Jewish masses to forget the bloody terror of English imperialism and forge an alliance with England in order to extend its rule over Palestine.'"[78] Even if this description of Weizmann's position on England was baseless, the statement reflects Radio Moscow's awareness of Weizmann's identification with the Anglo-Saxon world and its interests in the Middle East, alongside implied reservations about Weizmann stemming from the pro-Western position he represented in Zionist politics.

From February to April of 1948, tensions increased between East and West, which reduced the US administration's willingness to consider having American troops participate in a UN mobilization force tasked with implementing the Partition Plan by force if necessary. Meanwhile, the fighting in Palestine was intensifying, which was a source of disappointment for Marshall, who voiced concern about the Haganah's ability to repel Arab attacks.[79] The impression in the State Department was, increasingly, that partition was not viable and should be replaced with trusteeship. At a February 18 meeting at the White House, Truman, Marshall, and Forrestal were briefed by the Joint Chiefs of Staff, who assessed that implementation of the UN Partition Plan would require 80,000–160,000 troops, some of whom would have to remain in the area indefinitely to repel terrorist and guerrilla attacks (they did not say by whom), on top of the 57,000 British troops in Palestine at the time.[80]

It was this assessment that prompted Marshall and Lovett to adopt on the following day the position that it was time to abandon the Partition Plan and adopt the trusteeship approach. There is no documentation of their conversation, but this is the approach they advanced over the coming months through statements by the US ambassador to the UN, Warren Austin.[81] In practice, Marshall delegated the authority to Lovett to formulate the State Department's position and determine its conduct on Palestine throughout 1948. The worldview that guided Lovett in this regard centered on improving its ties and influence in Europe and avoiding hostilities or friction with the Arab world linked to the establishment of a Jewish state. In seeking to balance the State Department's resources and commitments, he regarded this confrontation as one burden too many, and his intellectual and bureaucratic lack of sympathy for the Zionist cause reinforced that view. His lukewarm attitude toward Zionism stood in stark contrast with the emotional turbulence that, in his words, characterized the conduct of the other participants in discussions about the future of Palestine.[82]

The United States made the shift in its policy publicly known on March 19, 1948, when Austin, speaking before the Security Council, announced that his country would support the establishment of a UN trusteeship regime headed by a representative appointed by the Security Council and backed by an international mobilization force, as an alternative to partition.[83] *Time* concluded: "The U.S. no longer supported Partition." Joseph and Stewart Alsop, in their influential opinion column in the *New York Herald Tribune*, explained that the main reason behind the US adoption of a trusteeship approach was its fear that partition provided the Soviets with an opportunity to gain a foothold in the Middle East and that the move was premised on the assumption that a guaranteed majority in support of American positions in the UN Trusteeship Council would put an end to this opportunity. The brothers, conservative Republicans, strongly criticized the government's position, arguing that it would necessitate the deployment of American forces instead of British troops, if only to prevent the slaughter of Jews by Arabs.[84]

The shock waves in the Yishuv following the declared shift in US policy are evident in the following editorial:

> The abrupt shift in the American position will be recorded in the history books as one of the most contemptible acts committed by a superpower, a superpower seeking the scepter of leadership in the civilized world. In many respects this act is worse than the Munich Betrayal [the Munich Agreement between Adolf Hitler and Neville Chamberlain in 1938].... No one in the world should delude themselves about the nature of the Jews' response. It is short and clear, and may be summed up in one word: No! No and no! ... [The Jews], like any mature people, are entitled to demand national independence. They do not rank below the shepherds of Transjordan or the peasants of Iraq and Egypt.

From a contemporary perspective, these words deserve a second reading because of where the editorial appeared: in the newspaper *Haaretz*.[85] It represented a clear statement of the consensus in the Yishuv. Ben-Gurion announced that the shift in American policy "does not fundamentally change the situation in the country and does not threaten the establishment of the Jewish state. The establishment of the Jewish state did not actually depend on the UN resolution of November 29—although that resolution was of great moral and political value—but rather on the possibility of our determining the situation in the country by force."[86] Ben-Gurion's proclamation that force, rather than political processes, would determine the fate of the Jewish state was not a revelation for senior members of the political system, who had long known his views. It was the timing of the American shift that forced him to reveal his position openly and unequivocally to the Yishuv community, as a counterweight to this change in US policy.

The Americans sought to seize the moment. In unrecorded testimony before the Senate Foreign Relations Committee on March 24, 1948, Marshall explained that the reassessment of American support for partition stemmed from the understanding that its implementation would necessitate deploying troops to the region, which in turn would require permitting a significant Soviet military presence in the "Holy Land" and its surroundings. Marshall was quoted as saying that international experience demonstrates that if the Soviets deploy forces to a particular region, they tend to remain there. This would undermine the security interests of Western democracies, according to Marshall, hence the change in the American position. Reporting on

Marshall's testimony, the *New York Times* closed by stating that no domestic political considerations had dictated this shift—thereby exposing Marshall's office as the probable leak for this story.[87]

The myriad forms of pressure applied by the State Department to prevent the establishment of a Jewish state reached an unprecedented level on March 26 when Lovett and Marshall met with Shertok and Epstein in an exchange that bordered on terrifying for the Jewish side. From a historical perspective, Shertok's most significant political act in 1948 might have been his success in preventing a disaster and his skills in thwarting any possibility of a trusteeship approach during this conversation. Marshall initiated the meeting after six months of avoiding any encounter with Shertok. Of all the issues covered during seventy-five minutes of dialogue, it was the topic of Jewish migration that reflected the thrust of the meeting. Marshall repeatedly called for a Jewish-Arab agreement on the scope of immigration, going so far as to ask whether the Jewish Agency would object to the United States receiving large numbers of Holocaust refugees as a way of alleviating the situation. Shertok's formal reply was that the Jewish Agency had no objection to refugees going wherever they wanted and were able to go. Immigration to the United States would resolve the problem for many individuals, he admitted, but it would not resolve the problem facing the Jewish people. "It would not arrest the historical process of the Jewish return to Palestine," he cautiously pointed out. To lessen the tension, he explained, "At the first outbreak of a wave of persecution [of Jews in Arab countries], those of them who will be able to escape will take to the boats and set sail for Palestine. It would never occur to them to go to the US on their own, as they would to Palestine." Marshall had no reply to this.[88] The existential distress of Jews in Arab countries provided tremendous and unmatched leverage domestically and externally. This was evident in the determination demonstrated by Ben-Gurion and Shertok in pursuing a political resolution as soon as possible.

Although Shertok urged the deployment of an international force and admitted that the Arab militaries had numerical superiority, in his conversation with Marshall and Lovett on March 26, he asserted that for invading forces, the confrontation would be "a military adventure," whereas "to us it was the defence of our very lives and of the future of our people. We would never give up the struggle, whereas they might soon get tired of it." Shortly before this meeting, Epstein had met with Henderson, who delivered a number of harsh messages: the United States would never send armed forces to Palestine to implement any policy; "if trusteeship is not accepted by the Yishuv as a basis for a temporary settlement in Palestine, the Jews there will be massacred and face certain annihilation"; it was dangerous to assume that the United States would send armed forces to defend the Jews in Palestine; and if the United States were to lift the arms embargo, the Arabs "might then massacre Christians, particularly Americans, as well as the Jews living in Arab states."[89] It would appear that before that meeting, no US official had ever spoken so harshly to a Zionist representative. The conclusion that both Epstein and Shertok drew from their conversations was clear: on the one hand, "the American administration has no concrete plans for implementing the trusteeship proposal," and on the other hand, "they are confused and do not see any way out."[90]

In an April 4, 1948, meeting with Defense Secretary Forrestal, the Joint Chiefs of Staff reported that they would require an estimated 104,000 troops to implement the trusteeship plan. They were inclined toward the view presented at the meeting by Dean Rusk, director of the US State Department's Office of UN Affairs (and secretary of state in the 1960s), who recommended that half the force be allocated by the United States. Rusk warned that if the United States did nothing, "it was likely that the Russians could, and would take definite steps toward gaining control in Palestine through the infiltration of specially trained [Jewish] immigrants" or by exploiting the civil war that would probably break out. "Moreover, the slaughter of thousands and perhaps hundreds of thousands of Jewish residents would present difficult questions for the United States."[91] His warning echoed the tangible lesson learned by the State Department from the *Pans* affair regarding "communist Jewish infiltration" into Palestine under the guise of immigration as well as the recurring rhetoric about Jewish massacres that had permeated American discourse, as is illustrated in the words of Henderson and the Alsop brothers.

However, Truman's principled opposition to the deployment of American forces to Palestine—independently or as part of an international force—alongside Forrestal's announcement that the military could not allocate the forces needed to implement trusteeship, precluded the pursuit of this proposal. This was compounded by a lack of enthusiasm for the proposal in the British Foreign Office, whose senior officials did not think it had the potential to address the deep, long-term problems of Arab-Jewish relations in Palestine (the Jewish aspiration for partition and independence, a Jewish veto over the political future of a state with an Arab majority, and mass Jewish immigration). By late April, consequently, the option of trusteeship by force was no longer on the table, having been dismissed wholesale. The remaining alternative, therefore, was partition, which the State Department sought to replace over the coming weeks with a proposal for a truce conditional on the Jews not proclaiming statehood and the Arabs refraining from invasion.[92] On April 23, at the initiative of the United States, the Security Council passed a resolution establishing a "truce commission" composed of the consuls of the United States, France, and Belgium in Jerusalem to prevent Soviet intervention and mediating and supervising a truce throughout the country or at least in Jerusalem.[93]

Earlier, on April 9, to ward off American concerns (primarily unfounded) that the Zionists supported a Soviet military presence in Palestine under the guise of a UN trusteeship, Shertok (who shared the Zionist aversion to trusteeship) proposed to Rusk and Lovett that the international force be deployed only to Jerusalem, for the benefit of "the world and civilization." This, he explained, would make it possible to preclude inclusion of the Soviets while at the same time facilitating the Haganah's efforts to gain control over the territories allocated to Jews under the Partition Plan. During the meeting, Shertok categorically rejected American concerns that the Soviets were supplying arms to Etzel and Lehi in order to foment chaos that would necessitate international intervention.[94] On that same day, Etzel and Lehi carried out the Deir Yassin massacre, casting an entirely new light on the inherent threat posed by these two "dissident" organizations.

WEIZMANN AND HIS LOYALISTS COME INTO THEIR OWN

While Shertok was busy with damage control, Weizmann was focusing his attention on a different political track in an effort to reach an agreement with the White House that would benefit the Zionist cause. One of the fruits he hoped to see from this labor was his return to the center of decision-making circles in the future Jewish state. To provide proper context for his efforts, let us take a step back in time to events that preceded April 9. A first indication of the anticipated fruit appeared four and a half months earlier, at a celebratory dinner organized by the American Committee for the Weizmann Institute of Science. The event was held at the Waldorf Astoria in New York on November 25, 1947, four days before the fateful UN General Assembly vote. Each of the approximately two thousand guests paid $250 as a donation to the scientific institute slated to succeed the Daniel Sieff Research Institute in Rehovot. Aside from dinner, the guests enjoyed the sounds of the Boston Symphony Orchestra, which performed gratis. Officially, the event was intended to honor Weizmann and the institute that would bear his name, and unofficially to celebrate the birthdays that month of Weizmann (age seventy-three) and his wife, Vera. In political terms, the event constituted an impressive display of public American Jewish support for Weizmann, a compensation of sorts for the bitter taste left by Neumann's slight in not inviting him to speak at the thirtieth anniversary of the Balfour Declaration a few weeks earlier. Abraham Feinberg chaired the planning committee that organized the event, Rudolf Sonneborn served as its treasurer, and Morgenthau introduced Weizmann. Feinberg delivered the opening address, drawing thunderous applause when he referred to Weizmann, who, "with God's help will be the first president of this new republic, and will guide it through its early years in the family of nations."[95] This was the main political message of the gathering, marking the first time one of Weizmann's prominent allies publicly proclaimed the aspiration to see him become president of the state.

Feinberg's stated desires did not receive much resonance in Palestine, but the *New York Times* coverage, statements by a substantial portion of the American Jewish elite, the presence of Mapai leaders (Shertok, Kaplan, Sprinzak, and Zalman Rubashov) at the event, and the upcoming UN partition resolution guaranteed that the message was received. A few days later, at a large gathering of Jewish organizations in Chicago, longtime Zionist leader Stephen Wise called for Weizmann to be appointed president of the state, as did Isaac Hamlin, general secretary of the National Committee for Labour Palestine, at a subsequent mass gathering in New York, and congressional Representative Emanuel Celler at yet another gathering in New York. In a display of modesty, Weizmann demurely responded that "it is too early to talk about it."[96] This sequence of assertions and their timing constituted both a spontaneous expression of personal admiration for the noted leader and a deliberate, coordinated effort to create expectations that would lead to his appointment when the time came. During the latter half of 1948, as we shall see, cooperative efforts among Sonneborn, Feinberg, and Morgenthau would prove to be exceptionally important in realigning American Zionist power dynamics as they relate to the subject of this study, and in this sense as well, the previously mentioned gathering constituted an important public milestone.

Feinberg had accumulated much of his wealth from the undergarment business during World War II. He met Vice President Truman in 1944 for the first time, and on occasion subsequently. Feinberg presided over the New York section of the American Committee for the Weizmann Institute of Science and would later become president of the institute. He was the founder (on July 2, 1947) and first president of Americans for Haganah, a group that engaged in propaganda for the Zionist cause, including clandestine immigration in particular, fundraising, and arms purchases for the Haganah. Feinberg worked closely with the Sonneborn Institute. Thus it happened that Feinberg, who numbered among the American Jews most deeply engaged in weapons acquisition and therefore greatly valued by Ben-Gurion, was also intimately engaged in efforts to secure Weizmann's appointment as president and in fundraising simultaneously for the Weizmann Institute and the

Haganah.[97] At the same time, Feinberg was also involved in an increasingly fierce dispute with Silver, who was aligned with the Republicans and supported their candidate, New York Governor Thomas Dewey, in the 1948 presidential elections. In the second half of that year, Feinberg would become a key figure in contributing to and fundraising for Truman's presidential campaign during its most sensitive times—but all in due course, although it is worth noting that this is one of the factors obscured by systematic documentation, without which an important key to understanding political developments in 1948 is missing.

Another prominent figure with a comparable network of contacts was Dewey David Stone, founder and chairman of the Board of Directors of the American Committee for the Weizmann Institute, established in 1944. Stone was appointed at Weizmann's direct request and would later serve for more than two decades as chair of the Weizmann Institute's Board of Governors, to be succeeded by Feinberg upon his retirement. A businessman and native of Brockton, Massachusetts, Dewey provided camouflage and contacts for the Sonneborn Institute, playing a key role in covert finances that included funding the purchase of clandestine immigration ships in the United States. On January 31, 1946, Kaplan allocated him an initial $400,000 from the Jewish Agency toward this end, thereby establishing a back-channel link between his business and covert Zionist activities, by means of which the *Pans*, among other acquisitions, were purchased. Based on his long-standing interaction with American Jewry, Abba Eban assessed retrospectively that while many American Jews may have surpassed Stone and his associates in terms of wealth, contacts, and community involvement, what distinguished this group was its total commitment to the Zionist cause and its willingness to shift the focus of its activities from one area to another in the continuous and purposeful pursuit of this commitment.[98]

In the run-up to the 1944 presidential elections, Stone was among the first donors (contributing $25,000) to support a publicity campaign for Missouri senator Harry S. Truman to become a Democratic vice-presidential nominee, alongside the incumbent President Roosevelt. After Stone and Truman's victory and Roosevelt's passing, Truman succeeded Stone in April 1945. About three years later, following a meeting on February 17, 1948, with Weizmann at his hotel in New York, Stone traveled to Boston, where he attended a dinner in honor of himself and B'nai B'rith president Frank Goldman hosted by alumni of the Jewish college fraternity Zeta Beta Tau.[99] During the dinner, Goldman noticed that Stone seemed intensely worried, and inquired why. Stone informed him of his conversation with Weizmann, who was anguished by the president's refusal to meet with him. After all, this was the reason Weizmann had suspended his plans to settle in Palestine, traveling instead to the United States. The two stepped outside of the venue to discuss the matter in the hotel corridor. Goldman related that he had just returned from Kansas City where on behalf of B'nai B'rith he had presented an award to Edward Jacobson. The two decided to call Jacobson immediately but wanted to avoid charging the call to the hotel for fear that this could draw unwanted attention. They therefore decided to collect quarters from the dinner guests to call Jacobson from a pay phone.[100] If we pause for a moment to take a retrospective look, we might somewhat lyrically describe those collected coins as having more weight and value than all the funds raised previously or subsequently by American Jews for the establishment and survival of the State of Israel.

Jacobson was a close friend of Truman's and a business partner in a haberdashery they owned in Kansas City, Missouri. The two had opened it in 1919 after serving together in a field artillery battery stationed in France during World War I (Truman was the commander, and Jacobson was his sergeant). Before their deployment, they had operated a canteen for the regiment. After insolvency led to the closure of their shop in 1922, Truman turned to public life, while Jacobson remained in the clothing business, but their friendship stayed strong. In 1947, Jacobson was operating his own haberdashery in Kansas City. To date, he had demonstrated no interest in Zionism or any form of public activity (his contribution to B'nai B'rith was primarily in the form of membership fees), but in that year, he was enlisted on behalf of the Zionist cause in preparation for the UN vote on partition. His unmediated contacts with Truman on this matter were the reason for his previously mentioned award from B'nai B'rith after he had successfully arranged for Goldman and Maurice Bisgyer, executive vice president of B'nai B'rith, to meet with Truman on January 29, 1948. The fact that this meeting took place only three days after Jacobson approached the president's office attests to the unmediated quality of his personal relations with Truman.[101] There is a direct line between the simple and successful arrangement of this meeting and the trickery by which Jacobson secured Truman's agreement to meet with Weizmann on March 18.[102]

The fact that Stone initiated the renewal of contact with Jacobson as a result of his February 17 conversation with Weizmann underscores the role of Weizmann loyalists in bringing about shifts in the president's position. At that time, Truman was not available, and Jacobson was only able to meet with him on March 13. During that meeting, in an act of despair after Truman repeatedly voiced refusal to meet with Weizmann because he had grown weary of the incessant pressure from Zionists, Jacobson invoked Truman's favorite leader, the seventh president and founder of the Democratic Party Andrew Jackson, whose statue was visible from the White House, comparing Truman's admiration for Jackson to his own admiration for Weizmann. Jacobson had not yet met Weizmann, as Truman, who knew his friend well and knew how much he had helped the Zionist cause a few months earlier, was no doubt well aware. Perhaps because of Jacobson's brazen comparison, or perhaps for another reason that Truman never disclosed, the president, for whom politics was an art, weighed the possibilities once more and, cursing colorfully, agreed to meet discreetly with Weizmann. Goldman was waiting with Bisgyer for news of the meeting at a nearby hotel in Washington. Bisgyer, an acquaintance of Weizmann's, accompanied Jacobson to New York to deliver the news to Weizmann. After receiving a briefing from Stone in the lobby of the Waldorf Astoria, Jacobson went up to Weizmann's room and informed him that the president was willing to meet with him discreetly. That meeting took place on March 18, with Weizmann accompanied by Bisgyer and another Kansas City B'nai B'rith member, Herman Rosenberg, who had also served with Truman during World War I.[103]

Several difficulties overshadowed this meeting: its timing, the day before Austin's announcement at the UN regarding US support for trusteeship; doubts surrounding the president's support for partition; and the latter's annoyance at State Department officials who had allegedly deceived him, although it is not clear whether this was genuine, feigned, or a response to the protests leveled against him by Jewish figures and political rivals.[104] Nevertheless, this was the occasion that gave rise to and consolidated the close, continuous personal connection between Truman and Weizmann, as illustrated by Weizmann's unequivocal reply to Jacobson after the latter called to offer his sympathy following the shift in the US stance: "Don't forget for a single moment that Harry S. Truman is the most powerful man in the world. You have a job to do so keep the White House doors open."[105]

On March 26, 1948, against the background of the unrelenting shock waves sparked by the American policy shift, Weizmann denounced the US position as violating "three established principles" of the Palestine question: First, "to prolong tutelage [i.e., through trusteeship] and delay a final solution based on independence is to increase confusion and bloodshed." Second, "to make Arab consent a condition of settlement is to rule out all chance of a settlement." Third, "to abandon a judgment under pressure of Arab violence is to give an incentive to further violence." He pointed out that any solution would require enforcement, and that there was currently "no other practical solution" aside from partition. The *New York Times* described his statement as an expression of strong support for the Jewish Agency's decision to establish an independent state on May 16 (the forecasted final date of the Mandate).[106] Although Weizmann refrained from attacking Truman, and of course said nothing about their having secretly met, his statement was a public and unequivocal call for an immediate decision in favor of partition and statehood, regardless of the Arab position. As to the trusteeship proposal, Weizmann dismissed it out of hand as a "still-born project" that was "produced on the spur of the moment by some fertile brain in the American State Department." He saw the waning of the British Mandatory government as a process that would naturally and independently of international measures lead to the establishment of a Jewish state, which, he was convinced, other states would recognize.[107] His assessment pointed implicitly to the concrete goal he was pursuing: laying the foundation for American recognition of the emerging state. This, he believed, necessitated another personal meeting with Truman.

In the meantime, Weizmann purchased tickets to sail from New York to London on April 7, 1948, with plans to fly from Paris to Palestine on the twenty-third of the month. He described himself as more or less akin to a displaced person, unable to remain in New York, unenthusiastic about staying in London, and unsure where to go.[108] Supreme Court Justice Felix Frankfurter advised that he postpone his departure by a week, pointing out that "I cannot assure you that staying will not bring frustration and futility any more than I can guarantee that leaving will not result in feelings of might have beens." At the very last minute, on April 6, Weizmann and his wife, Vera, decided to remain in the United States pending the outcome of the UN General Assembly debate on Palestine scheduled for April 16.[109] Weizmann had apparently been only a heartbeat away from missing the opportunity for one of the most significant historical moments and achievements of his life, an event destined to immortalize his memory and inscribe him indelibly in the state's creation story. If he somehow sensed the inner workings of history in the making, he left no record of that miraculous prescience.

In a final political effort, Weizmann wrote a letter to Truman on April 9, seeking to maintain continuity following their March 18 meeting and presenting an unequivocal defense of the Partition Plan as the only political recourse. He pointed out that partition had the support of "two distinguished investigating commissions" (the Peel Commission in 1937 and UNSCOP in 1947) and drew the president's attention "to the psychological effects of promising Jewish independence in November and attempting to cancel it in March." He concluded with the blunt assertion that the choice for Jews "is between Statehood and extermination."[110] David Niles, White House adviser on minority issues, took it upon himself to deliver Weizmann's letter to Truman and promised that he would make sure the president met with him next week, but Truman did not reply to the letter, and no such meeting took place.[111] In late 1941, Frankfurter had written to Ben-Gurion that he knew a modest, unassuming but important man who knew everything that was going on and who was shrewd, intelligent, and well connected. The man was David Niles, from Boston. At that time, Isaiah Berlin had also placed Niles at the top of the list of critical Washington contacts that Ben-Gurion should have in promoting the Zionist cause.[112] But in April 1948, Truman did not instruct Niles or Clifford, his senior advisers and supporters of Zionist interests, on how to respond to the letter. Presumably, the two understood that the president "did not wish to commit himself to any response that could serve as a source for new interpretations of his March 25 announcement," in which he asserted that the trusteeship proposal did not rule out partition at a later stage.[113] However—and this was more important than a response to the letter or a meeting—Weizmann's political objective in writing that letter was confirmed and achieved in full and as formulated.

As is often the case with political processes that lead to the concrete goal, this one took many twists and turns. Another overlooked American Jewish figure who took part in Weizmann's relay race toward statehood was Edmund Kaufmann, president of the Zionist Organization of America in the early 1940s and, from 1944, president of the American Committee for the Weizmann Institute. Kaufmann had also headed the campaign to raise $1 million for the establishment of the Weizmann Institute, and he and Stone were among the first to make personal donations of $100,000 toward this cause. Kaufmann, who made most of his fortune from the diamond business, was among the wealthiest men in Washington, DC. Like Stone and Feinberg, he belonged to the inner circle of Weizmann associates who engaged in a mix of science, business, American politics, and Zionism.[114] On April 10, 1948, Kaufmann wrote to Samuel Rosenman, formerly a close senior adviser to Presidents Roosevelt and Truman, urging him to extract an admission from Truman that he had erred in proclaiming a shift away from the Partition Plan. He argued, "It is my studied belief that the President can be reelected if certain proper things are done and which in justice should be done," because it was not right to promise Holocaust survivors partition and raise their expectations, then suddenly announce a change in policy. Kaufmann argued that the president should follow the model of another admission of error in American history, referring to Abraham Lincoln's letter of July 13, 1863, to General Ulysses S. Grant, admitting that he had erred in asserting that the esteemed Civil War hero was making a military mistake when in fact the latter's move had led to one of the major victories against the Confederate army.[115] Perhaps, as with Jacobson's invocation of President Jackson a few weeks earlier, Weizmann's associates were deliberately drawing on Truman's affinity for and familiarity with the life stories of previous presidents.

Weizmann had already enlisted Rosenman on March 8, 1948, in the effort to persuade Truman to abide by the Partition Plan, as he and Shertok had concluded that "only the president can undo" the US deviation from support for partition. In late February, Rosenman had come to Clifford's aid in formulating American policy on Palestine for the State Department and the Pentagon. Clifford had been appointed to the position of White House counsel thanks to Rosenman's recommendation, replacing the latter in 1946. According to Clifford, Rosenman, a non-Zionist Jew, had taught him how to fill the role of senior adviser to the president and serve him in the best manner possible.[116] Rosenman earned both leaders' trust as a discreet intermediary when he resolved the misunderstanding caused by Austin's statement at the UN on US support for trusteeship, made on the day after Truman and Weizmann's meeting of March 18, 1948.[117] On April 11, Weizmann met with Jacobson. It is highly probable (although there is no verifying documentation) that Niles also participated in this meeting, and that this was the occasion on which Weizmann handed over the letter to Truman that he had drafted two days earlier. On the following day, Jacobson met with Truman, and the president promised him that he intended to recognize the Jewish state once it was established. Jacobson then delivered this news to Weizmann.[118]

On April 14, in an intermezzo of sorts that for historiographical reasons we cannot overlook, Weizmann met in his hotel room with the US ambassador to the UN, Warren Austin, and two of his aides. In his subsequent report to Marshall, Austin related that "Weizmann said he had tried very hard but could not understand the reasons for the 'switch' in the US position. Was it fear of the Arabs? Was it oil? Or was it fear of Russia? . . . Were we afraid that the Jewish state would be dominated by Russia? There was no possible occasion for such fear. Bolshevik agents had tried very hard in the 1920s to get a foothold in Palestine and had failed miserably." Weizmann then repeated the argument he had made in his letter to Truman regarding the "psychological problem" facing Jews: "They were granted independence in November and independence was withdrawn in April." Although Weizmann did not spell it out, it is reasonable to assume that he was referring to the possibility that this problem of false hopes could have political repercussions for the Jewish vote in upcoming US elections and the Jewish view of Western interests in Palestine.[119] In his autobiography, authored just a few months later, Weizmann made the following observation about this meeting: "I must have astonished as well as disappointed them, for I declared bluntly that I put no stock in the legend of Arab military might, and that I consider the intention of Palestine

Jewry to proclaim its independence the day the Mandate ended thoroughly justified and eminently realistic."[120] In contrast, the American record of this meeting, which lasted forty-five minutes, described how the US representatives tried to persuade Weizmann that trusteeship could address the "three essential points" for Jews—immigration, land settlement, and economic development—while also providing an opportunity for the closest possible cooperation between Jews and Arabs, leading to an agreed-upon political settlement. They concluded from his response that "it was clear that his mind is [running] strongly in this direction." Indeed, Lovett specifically drew Truman's attention to this point when he transmitted a copy of the report to him.[121]

Various scholars have queried whether Weizmann's remarks indicated that he was seriously considering setting aside the Partition Plan—a query that seems most astounding on the face of it.[122] After all, throughout his political career, since 1918, Weizmann had categorically doubted the feasibility of reaching an agreement with the Arabs regarding Palestine. The notion that Weizmann might diametrically reverse his position in the course of a forty-five-minute conversation with midlevel officials a month before the end of the British Mandate in exchange for a vague promise of economic development and possible cooperation with Arabs—and only a few days after sending the strongest man in the world a letter stating explicitly that he saw partition as the only solution—is simply and fundamentally baseless.[123] Nor does the press of the time, in its coverage of Weizmann's response to Austin, leave any room for doubt: "The Jewish state will be established on May 15, regardless of what the UN resolves," Weizmann reportedly stated, adding, "The Jews will surely fight and will realize their hopes."[124] This incident, while historically marginal, is instructive for our purposes because it accurately portrays the suspicions toward Weizmann and the lack of appreciation for his influence and the importance of his political engagement, which have become commonplace in historical writings. Weizmann's conclusion regarding the concept of trusteeship was pointed: acceptance by the Jews of trusteeship when "only a few months before we had been adjudged worthy of statehood . . . would have meant to make ourselves ludicrous in the eyes of history."[125]

Directly thereafter, Weizmann met with Rosenman on April 18, 1948. According to Joseph Linton (Weizmann's close adviser and later an Israeli diplomat), who also attended, Rosenman asked Weizmann what proposals he would like to see raised with Truman. At the time, Rosenman was meeting with Truman on a weekly basis in light of his role on the advisory committee that was formulating a strategy for the upcoming Democratic National Convention where Truman hoped to be nominated as the presidential candidate in the November presidential election. Weizmann replied that he wanted the United States to recognize the Jewish state upon its establishment.[126] Presumably, Weizmann hoped, by means of Rosenman's conversation with the president, to give political weight to the personal promise Truman had made Jacobson and to ensure its validity.

Weizmann's belief in the critical importance of securing American recognition of the future state accorded with the views of the two leading Zionist policymakers at the time, Ben-Gurion and Shertok. A month earlier, on March 20, Shertok had attributed decisive importance to recognition of the provisional Jewish government by the UN and the United States, "with emphasis on the United States of America," as a way of blocking continued British control over the country and as a necessary tool not only for the implementation of the Partition Plan but also for the "physical survival of the Yishuv." He was building on Ben-Gurion's demand that "recognition of the government should be expedited. Only if Washington recognizes the Jewish government will it be possible to curb the British military in the country."[127] A few days after Shertok's remarks of March 20, with the United States' public announcement of the trusteeship proposal on the preceding day still echoing in the background, the executives of the Jewish Agency and the National Council announced, as noted, that "no later than May 16 of this year, a provisional Jewish government will be instituted"—a message echoed in *Davar*'s main headline.[128] Thus, for the first time, a target date was set for the establishment of a government. To be precise, the talk surrounded the establishment of a government rather than a state. Notably, however, and in contrast to the Zionist decision-making establishment, whose meticulous distinctions mirrored its ongoing disputes, the prevailing public discourse in the Yishuv regarded state and government as overlapping concepts. The subheadline to *Davar*'s main headline illustrated this starkly: "Opposition to any delay in the establishment of the state."[129]

Two days after his April 18 meeting with Weizmann, Rosenman raised the question of Palestine on his behalf with Truman during the president's weekly meeting with his election advisory committee.[130] Cautious, sober Weizmann, who had had his share of disappointments, did not harbor any grand expectations, and on April 20, he informed Weisgal that he intended to depart the United States nine days later, arriving in London on May 4, then departing to Paris and from there flying to Palestine on May 13 on the eve of the British Mandate's termination. It was incumbent on him to be in Palestine, he pointed out, and after all, he and Vera had already faced greater dangers in the London Blitz during World War II.[131] His close associates in Palestine were as skeptical as he was about his future career in public life.

Weisgal questioned the judgment and wisdom of the Yishuv leadership—namely, Ben-Gurion—and pondered the "reckless abandon" with which local youths were throwing themselves into the fight for survival, though he did add, rephrasing Winston Churchill, that "never did so many (alas, not too many now) owe so much to so few." Despite his criticism, he believed that in light of the fighting underway, near Rehovot as well, it was "unwise and imprudent" for Weizmann to come at that time. Weizmann's scientific protégé at the Sieff Institute, Dr. Ernst David Bergmann, had the opposite advice. In a letter to Vera, he postulated that the Weizmanns would prefer to be in the country as Arab forces invaded, though in his assessment, no one would bother to consult with Weizmann, who would "be forced to confine himself to Rehovot and the Institute." He backed his argument by drawing on another famous World War II quote of Churchill's, promising that "we will know to fight on the beaches and in the hills and in the streets," and he and Vera would "feel the affection surrounding" them. Bergmann further invoked longtime Zionist leader Shmaryahu Levin's acerbic observation about the difference between Warsaw (as a metaphor for London, to which Weizmann intended to travel) and Tel Aviv: "In Warsaw I knew that most of the people on the street were enemies and the few who greeted me were friends; in Tel Aviv most of the people on the street are friends and only the few who greeted me were enemies." He closed on a note of anxiety, as if parting forever, conveying his love to her and the "chief" and pledging to remain loyal as long as he lived.[132]

A letter of April 20, 1948, to Bergmann provides direct evidence of the depths of despair Weizmann had reached as to his personal and professional future at that point, as he awaited an update from Rosenman. He noted that his stay in the United States was coming to an end and appeared to have been a heartbreak and waste of time. Weizmann further added that "nothing has happened and nothing will happen apparently, and when the show is all over, we shall have spent a great deal of money [Weizmann had personally covered the expenses], wasted a great deal of time, made quite a number of speeches, but the result will be very small."[133]

Then everything turned around. At a meeting on April 23, just a few hours before the Passover seder, Rosenman informed Weizmann on behalf of Truman that the president had pledged to recognize the Jewish state as long as the UN did not amend its partition resolution by then. Truman conveyed by way of Rosenman that he wished to have Weizmann be his sole contact on the Zionist side and requested that Weizmann remain in the United States, as he intended to issue an official invitation to the White House after the Jewish state was proclaimed. Weizmann was sworn to secrecy by Rosenman.

According to close associates of Weizmann who recounted the events of the months preceding statehood, only a select group, including Vera, Linton, and Josef Cohn, knew about Truman's promise.[134] In practice, however, Weizmann acted far more responsibly than some of his close associates knew or chose to recall and immortalize with the passage of time. It is known with certainty that, at the time, at least two leading Jewish Agency figures knew of Truman's pledge to Weizmann—Moshe Shertok and Abba Eban.[135] Referring to Weizmann's April 23 meeting with Rosenman and what would happen in the coming months, Eban later observed with wonder that it was hard to believe the words Rosenman had conveyed to Weizmann, as in some sense, they nullified "all the 'hard-headed' theories which deny the personal and human factor in international relations."[136]

On the following day, presumably after receiving an update from Weizmann about Truman's intentions, Kaufmann wrote to Rosenman, presenting a series of requests. In the letter, which reflected Weizmann's political agenda at the time, Kaufman proposed that to counter the lack of clarity surrounding American policy (given its vacillation between truce, trusteeship, partition, and weapons embargo), there was a need for "a simple, dramatic statement," issued by the president, asserting as follows: First, the United States has never wavered in its support for partition. Second, to prevent unnecessary bloodshed, an immediate truce should be called between Jews and Arabs, followed by a provisional trusteeship. This would allow for the implementation of partition without war raging in the background. Because there was no possibility of implementing any other policy, the United States would announce its intention to recognize the Jewish state, which, as proclaimed, would be established on May 16, 1948. Doctor Weizmann would be the first president of Jewish Palestine. He was planning to set sail on the twenty-ninth of the month and would be grateful if the president could meet with him before then.[137] Weizmann's ostensible willingness to accept trusteeship was only a means of relying on declared American policy as a brief, temporary station on the path to partition and statehood immediately upon termination of the Mandate. More important was the fact that this letter effectively grounded the points on which Truman and Weizmann had agreed while also taking into account the message Rosenman had received a day earlier directly linking the establishment of the state to Weizmann's appointment as president as an inseparable part of this agreement.

While Weizmann was working, through indirect dialogue with Truman, to confirm the alliance between the Zionist Movement and the United States as it related to the Partition Plan of November 29, 1947, the State Department was operating along other channels to advance its approach, which diverged from partition. The April 14 meeting between Weizmann and American delegates to the UN marked the only contact between State Department officials and Weizmann during February–May 1948. In retrospect, that may have been one of the key factors in the Department's failure to prevail on the Palestine question. Secretary of State Marshall adamantly refused to meet with Weizmann during this period, and when Frankfurter tried to arrange a meeting in February, he replied that a Supreme Court justice should not be involved in politics.[138] Senior State Department officials such as Lovett and Rusk did not consider Weizmann an essential figure whose views should be taken into account. As a result, they failed to identify the key orchestrator of Zionist policy in the United States, not necessarily at the public or declaratory level but in formulating critical moves behind the scenes.

On April 28, 1948, Lovett met with Nahum Goldmann to assess the possibility of pursuing a truce instead of trusteeship as a way of restoring stability in Palestine, and the issue of the Soviet perspective came up as well. Goldmann, original and sharp-witted as ever, challenged Lovett by asking how the United States would respond if no truce was achieved, the Jewish state was proclaimed, and the Soviet Union immediately recognized it. If the Jewish state finds itself without British or American support, Goldmann noted, it might, in desperation, turn to the Soviet Union, and the Soviets would then have the same right to intervene in the country that the British did in Transjordan. According to Goldmann, Lovett was piqued by this idea and commented that "if the Jewish people wish to commit suicide nobody can prevent them from doing so," stressing that they should not for a moment expect that the Americans would sit quietly and watch the Russians invade Palestine, directly or indirectly, legally or illegally. He added that there were various steps the United States could take, although these fell not within the purview of the State Department but within that of "another" department—clearly implying the Defense Department.[139] Similar warnings about the Soviets intervening in the country by exploiting their recognition of the emerging Jewish state surfaced again in early May among members of the US delegation to the UN.[140]

Concurrently, awareness of the upcoming establishment of the Jewish state steadily permeated the UN arena in New York. American efforts to make the trusteeship proposal a realistic option were repeatedly stymied by a lack of willingness—both disguised and overt—among the British. The British anger over this proposal contributed significantly to its demise. This does not mean, however, that the British hostility to the establishment of a Jewish state had dissipated. On the contrary, at a meeting in London between Lewis

Douglas, US ambassador to Britain, and Bevin and Clement Attlee on April 28, 1948, the British prime minister asserted that the aggression of Arabs from neighboring states seeking to assist their brothers in Palestine was no different from the aggression attributable to the entry of thousands of Jews by sea. In response to the ambassador's reply that the Jews were arriving unarmed, Attlee argued that this had precisely been Hitler's approach: he had sent people masquerading as tourists into Germany's neighboring countries (e.g., Austria) but made sure to arm them soon thereafter. Similarly, Jewish immigrants would soon become soldiers and were already receiving preliminary training in Italy.[141] The British leadership's hostility toward Zionism seemed to grow ever stronger as Britain's withdrawal from Palestine drew nearer. Secretary of State for the Colonies Arthur Creech-Jones, then in New York, reported to Foreign Secretary Bevin on May 2 that in his view the trusteeship proposal was off the table and that the psychological reality and developments in the field since November 1947 had led to the unavoidable conclusion that the Jews were going to establish a state immediately upon termination of the Mandate. Creech-Jones's outlook had changed substantially since his 1935 visit to Palestine, when he had marveled at the achievements of Zionism and, like a disciple of Ahad Ha'am, expressed satisfaction that the Zionists were establishing not a political state but a cultural nation.[142]

Thus the Partition Plan remained the only pragmatic alternative. During the second half of April 1948 and early May, however, State Department officials tried to replace it with a proposal for a truce, which would be conditional on the Jews not proclaiming statehood and the Arabs not invading the country, alongside restrictions on Jewish immigration. Rusk mediated the unofficial back-channel negotiations between the parties, who occupied separate rooms along an entire floor of the Savoy Plaza Hotel. The main stumbling block, he later recounted, was the scope of monthly Jewish immigration. After Rusk had tentatively managed to persuade Shertok to agree to 2,500 Jews per month, Prince Faisal ibn Abd al Aziz (later the Saudi king), the lead Arab negotiator, rejected the possibility, adding that if they agreed to this figure, then the Jews would bring 2,500 pregnant women, and the number would soon double. On the other side of the political divide, Silver described the American proposal as a "trap" intended solely to delay the establishment of the Jewish state.[143]

Far away and unaware of the events behind the scenes, Bergmann continued, keenly but vainly, to await Weizmann's arrival. On May 5, he wrote to the leader's wife, Vera, on the occasion of Weisgal's imminent travel to Britain and the United States. Bergmann told her about the first Hebrew stamps to be issued, one of which included a portrait of the "chief" (Weizmann), but which he had been unable to purchase because the post office sold out one hour after opening, "that shows you" he added, without stating the obvious: the mass affection for Weizmann. Bergmann reiterated his sorrow that she is "not coming now—you would have felt very elated here." As a close associate who knew the sort of information that interested the couple, he shared that "Ben-Gurion is trying to become a dictator, which causes a lot of danger," then relayed a bit of gossip: Mrs. Ben-Gurion (Paula) was reportedly about to leave for Paris "in order to get some suitable stuff from Molyneux!" Of course, he added, "there is nothing more urgent just now." As to the matters of the day, Bergmann recounted that the provisional government was "composed of the old cronies who have learnt nothing and know very little and are not very inspiring." He concluded, "The only comforting feature is that the Jewish people are so much better than their provisional government."[144] Not only did he momentarily forget how old his beloved leader was; more significant was the fact that on the shoulders of these members of the People's Administration rested the outcome of the most fateful issue that Jewish political leaders had faced in the past 1,800 years.

3

THE DECISIVE MOMENTS

The People's Administration evening session of May 12, 1948, opened with a discussion of the effectiveness of efforts to achieve a truce throughout the country or, alternatively, only in Jerusalem. Also discussed at this meeting was the decision to establish a state, which, according to Israeli collective memory and the education system's frequent retellings, passed by "a hair's breadth," with a majority of six in favor and four opposed.[1] In a book he authored a decade or so later, Ze'ev Sharef, People's Administration secretary, observed, "At the end of this joint discussion a decision was reached by a simple show of hands among the ten members of the People's Administration present; the question of whether to accept the truce proposal presented by the US delegation encompassed the decision about establishing the state.... There was a vote, and by a majority of six to four it was decided to postpone the vote on a truce; . . . in any case it was decided that in two days the state would be established."[2]

A footnote in Yehuda Slutsky's *History of the Haganah* and later comments by the editors of David Ben-Gurion's *War Diary* list the names of those who voted for or against statehood.[3] Yet the minutes of the People's Administration meeting contain no record of such a vote, as international relations scholar Uri Bialer discovered while conducting research for his master's thesis at the Hebrew University of Jerusalem in 1971.[4] As far as we know, he was the first member of academia to view these minutes. The absence of a vote (or at least of its documentation) and the multitude of dilemmas resulting therefrom became a matter of public record thanks to a newspaper article authored by historian Yoram Nimrod during the course of his doctoral research at the same university. He concluded his article by appealing to the reader: "As long as you consistently question both old and new conventions, you will not number among those enslaved by myth."[5]

Ten days before the termination of the British Mandate, Clark Clifford made note of the principles that would guide his conduct in the coming days and, as will become apparent by the end of this chapter, the conduct of the United States under Harry S. Truman, despite of opposition by senior State Department officials. First, Clifford noted that "recognition [of a Jewish state] is consistent with US policy from the beginning." Second, "a separate Jewish state is inevitable. It will be set up shortly." Third, "as far as Russia is concerned we would do better to indicate recognition." Fourth, "we must recognize inevitably. Why not now."[6] On the same day, as Clifford was outlining the case for recognition of the imminent Jewish state and linking American conduct in this regard with the interbloc conflict, senior State Department officials led by George Marshall held a meeting with Judah Leib Magnes, president of the Hebrew University of Jerusalem. Among other recommendations, Magnes advised cutting off the cash flow to the Haganah, which cost $4 million a month to run, because "if contributions from the United States were cut off, the Jewish war machine in Palestine would come to a halt for lack of financial fuel." Marshall described Magnes's remarks as "the most straightforward account on Palestine I had heard" and took measures to arrange a meeting between Magnes and Truman.[7]

On May 4, the Jewish Agency Executive section in New York categorically rejected Nahum Goldmann and Moshe Shertok's recommendation to adopt the State Department's truce proposal. The proposal included a commitment by the United States and Britain to prevent an Arab invasion on the condition that the proclamation of state would be postponed by three months. This approach drew the support of Joseph Proskauer, president of the American Jewish Committee, the most prominent non-Zionist organization among American Jewry and whose leaders were known for their close ties with government officials.[8] In a telegram of April 30, 1948, to Ben-Gurion, Proskauer warned him, "Brave words without cold calculated strategy mean merely the death of brave men." On the same day, Shertok advised Ben-Gurion that if the proclamation of statehood were to be postponed beyond May 16 (at the time the Mandate was expected to terminate on May 15), then Ben-Gurion should publish a "modest communiqué" stating that the Jewish government "actually exists."[9] In response to Shertok's willingness to accept postponement of the proclamation of independence, Ben-Gurion refrained from replying to his political messages for several days.

On May 2, Shertok had asked Ben-Gurion to meet him in Athens for an urgent consultation. Descriptions of Shertok in those days, both in Vera Weizmann's diary entries at the time and in the book Eliahu Eilat published several years later, portray him as hesitant and afraid of the anticipated Arab Legion's invasion, which horrified him. According to Vera Weizmann, her husband called on Shertok to stand strong and under no circumstances to capitulate and discuss a truce.[10] In fact, Shertok greatly miscalculated the decision-making locus on the question of Palestine within the American establishment. He overestimated the influence of the State Department, regarding it as the policymaking body, while underestimating the president's authority in political decision-making.[11] A May 7 letter to Mapai leaders from Shertok's close friend David Hacohen, then in New York, starkly illustrates the inclination toward such misjudgment in Shertok's immediate environment. While admitting that he had no expertise or authority to voice an opinion about the mysterious workings of American politics, Hacohen asserted that it seemed to him that for some years, the Zionist leadership in the United States had been relying on the shaky foundation of congressional representatives, senators, the Democratic and Republican parties, and even the president, all of whom put together did not, in his view, carry as much weight as half a dozen State Department bureaucrats working behind the scenes.[12]

These were the historical conditions under which Shertok participated in his memorable May 8 meeting with Marshall and members of his staff, just hours before his scheduled flight to Palestine to participate in the momentous decisions leading up to the proclamation of statehood. The meeting took place against the background of Clifford's May 7 proposal to Truman that he use the routine presidential press conference scheduled for May 13 to announce that the United States intended to recognize the anticipated Jewish state. Truman telephoned Marshall, who strongly objected to US recognition of the Jewish state, and the two agreed to hold a meeting on this matter at the White House on May 12. The president authorized Clifford to present the position in support of recognition at this meeting.[13] At Goldmann and Dean Rusk's suggestion, Marshall decided to meet with Shertok before the latter departed for Palestine. In a discussion with Goldmann on May 6, Rusk had foreseen that without a truce, "the probable course of events will identify Russian and Jewish interests in such a way as to create bitter hostility and anti-Semitism in the Western world."[14] Conversely, Truman began to wonder whether the Zionist Movement would abide by his agreement with Chaim Weizmann. In response to Samuel Rosenman's plea of May 7 that the president announce his intention to recognize the Jewish state on the eve of its establishment (as Clifford also proposed), Truman replied, "Why should I do so, when the Jewish Agency is ready to accept a truce?"[15]

On the day of his scheduled meeting with the secretary of state, moments before the meeting started, Shertok spoke on the phone with David

Niles, who was staying at the White House. During this conversation, and in light of the previously mentioned developments, Shertok felt compelled to deny something Lovett had told Clifford—namely, that three days earlier, Shertok and Abba Hillel Silver told the US State Department delegate to the UN, John Ross, that the Jewish Agency had agreed to postpone proclaiming statehood and to proceed slowly on the matter of recognition.[16] This was the same Ross who had prepared the April 15 document that misrepresented Weizmann's position on trusteeship. Weizmann instructed Shertok and Goldmann, who had secretly orchestrated Marshall's "compelling conversation" with Shertok, to prepare and transmit to Rosenman letters denying that the Jewish Agency was withdrawing its support for the Partition Plan and expressing their own rejection of the truce proposal outlined by Rusk. Rosenman made sure the letters reached Clifford in advance of the fateful May 12, 1948, White House meeting.[17] He also took advantage of the *Yedioth Ahronoth* reporter to convey a message to those in the know in Palestine, who were involved in his networking efforts among US decision-makers: "I have become aware," wrote the reporter, "that Judge Rosenman is firmly opposed to a truce agreement, and he claims that Washington should be called upon to implement the partition and recognize the Jewish state."[18] This item was intended for the eyes of one man only—Ben-Gurion—who as early as 1942 had identified Rosenman's support as essential for the success of the Zionist cause, even outweighing the support of three Jewish organizations thanks to his close association with the president—Roosevelt at the time and then Truman.[19] In my view, it is reasonable to assume that to persuade Shertok to write his letter of clarification to Marshall, Weizmann told him about Truman's pledge to recognize the Jewish state upon its establishment. Yet all that remains of this is Shertok's no-less-than-astonishing confession at the start of the government of Israel's first meeting, on May 16:

> The United States Government's recognition of the Provisional Government as the de facto ruling authority came as a complete surprise to all of us. I want to admit and confess that before leaving for America I heard an assessment that this was possible, but I did not believe it. Perhaps I was among those of little faith in this regard.... It came as a total surprise. The president said that he had been put in a situation whereby he misled Weizmann [with the announcement of the trustee proposal in March]. This made him furious at the State Department, and he tried a few times to reclaim the initiative. Judge Rosenman, who was very close to Roosevelt and in contact with Weizmann, met with the president twice in recent weeks. He inserted in the president's heart the idea [planted the idea with the president] that he had an opportunity to reclaim the initiative by recognizing the Provisional Government if established. Such is his authority. He did not create the fact itself—the Jews created it. Rosenman applied a great

deal of pressure in this regard because he believed that the Jewish government would indeed be established. For this reason, too, Weizmann was of the opinion that the declaration of independence must not be postponed.[20]

In the heat of the moment, Shertok forgot that it was Weizmann who had instilled this "belief" in Rosenman and that Truman had requested that Weizmann be his only contact in the Zionist camp for the purpose of fulfilling his commitment. Nonetheless, his remarks to the ministers are sufficient to attest to the close correlation between the political path adopted, which circumvented potential obstacles to the Zionist Movement's declaring statehood in a manner conducive to the receipt of international legitimacy, on the one hand, and American recognition of Israel and Weizmann's personal contribution in this regard, on the other. These factors corresponded with Weizmann's firm support for the proclamation of statehood at that time and with his appointment as president, as we shall see.

Shertok's May 8 meeting with senior State Department officials ended with Marshall's warning that the Jews, who were feeling encouraged by their military successes, should not expect American military aid if at some point in the future things turned against them on the battlefield. From Marshall's perspective, his warning was ignored. Shertok pointed out that the prevailing feeling among Jews in Palestine and across the world was "now or never." Marshall took this to mean that the Jewish Agency was "prepared to gamble on [a] 'now or never' basis and [on the] possibility of [an] arrangement with Abdullah [the emir of Transjordan] partitioning Palestine between Jews and Abdullah."[21] During this conversation, Robert Lovett put forward the argument that if the Jews proclaimed statehood, the Arabs would proclaim an Arab state throughout all of Palestine, and the two states would end up competing for international recognition. Shertok replied in the spirit of the Zionist Labor Movement, asserting that it was not "a movement given to hunting after formal shibboleths." He continued, "We were usually careful not to put the cart before the horse. Recognition can only apply to something which effectively exists. It would not be our first step to rush headlong into the quest for recognition. We would first have to do some work in building up the State properly." Shertok's downplaying of the critical importance of American recognition from the Zionist point of view was in stark contrast to his earlier remarks, at a March 20 meeting of the Jewish Agency Executive's US section, about the vital importance of American recognition. In my view, his assertion of May 8 in this regard amounted to deliberate manipulation based on his knowledge of Truman's pledge to Weizmann, and it attests to his awareness that the pledge must not become widely known, even if his admission eight days later made clear that he did not believe it would actually be fulfilled.[22] He doubted and was proved wrong. What Shertok truly thought about the importance of American recognition may be gleaned from his remarks at a public assembly in Tel Aviv on the day after Israel's declaration of independence: "One must praise the healthy, realistic political intuition that, after all the doubting and vacillating, subversion and complaining, fear and suspicion, once we took the decisive step, told the lofty leaders of that mighty country [the United States] that they should jump at the opportunity to be the first in the world to recognize the Jewish state."[23]

On May 10, 1948, the day after Shertok departed for Palestine, a fierce confrontation erupted in the US section of the Jewish Agency Executive between Silver and Goldmann as to what needed to be done upon termination of the Mandate. Silver concluded from Shertok's conversation with State Department officials that the US administration was determined not to permit the proclamation of a Jewish government on May 15, and he insisted on declaring immediately that the Jews were establishing their state. Goldmann countered that this would not be the right move and insisted on adhering to the UN plan of establishing a Provisional Council of Government at that time and declaring independence only later, after the withdrawal of British forces on October 1. Isaiah Kenan, who oversaw public relations for the Zionist delegation to the UN (and went on to found the lobbying group AIPAC, the American Israel Public Affairs Committee, in 1951), intervened in their disagreement. He pointed out that the press reporters covering the UN activities in Lake Success were expressing astonishment over what appeared to be reluctance on the part of the Zionist leadership, and he described the political efforts at the UN to thwart a Jewish declaration of independence as attempts to put the chicken back into the egg.[24]

Also on May 10, two days before the stormy White House meeting of May 12 and in preparation for reaching a decision on the Palestine crisis, Lovett held an off-the-record meeting with prominent American journalist Herbert Elliston, editorial page editor for the *Washington Post* (and recipient of the 1949 Pulitzer Prize). He presented the same argument he would pose two days later with Truman: the illegal immigration of Jews to Palestine was composed largely of Soviet agents, who would help actualize Moscow's plans to turn the Jewish state into a base for Soviet activities in the region. Lovett claimed that the prevailing inclinations among large sectors of the Jewish population in Palestine and in particular the workers' parties, to which he attributed substantial public and economic power, would help advance the Russians' plans. In a meeting immediately thereafter with Eliahu Epstein, Elliston stated that he disputed Lovett's theory, arguing that Jewish society was the only democratic one in the Middle East and that the communist threat was several times greater in Egypt. Accordingly, he had recommended to Lovett that the United States recognize the Jewish state immediately upon its establishment.[25]

On the evening of May 10, Clifford spoke with Epstein in preparation for the fateful meeting at the White House and in parallel to Lovett's preparations. The purpose of this conversation was to clarify a number of matters that opponents of recognition were claiming in support of their position that such a move would harm American interests. Their discussion focused on three issues: borders, communism in Palestine, and the anticipated composition of the Jewish state's government. Because Clifford, the most outspoken supporter of Zionism in decision-making circles, was comfortable with the Jewish commitment to partition, he sought to confirm that the claims about Soviet agents infiltrating Palestine via clandestine immigration efforts were unfounded. He also wanted to know whether there was any validity to information received from credible individuals who had recently returned from the Middle East; according to their reports, pro-Soviet inclinations were evident in various circles in Palestine, particularly among the labor camp. He questioned whether such inclinations might not upset the social and political balance of the Jewish state as a democratic state, even more than outside Soviet agents would, and whether a small number of agents sent by Stalin to Palestine might not exploit the situation for its own purposes. Epstein's replies are less germane in this context; the questions themselves attest to Clifford's concerns as the fateful decision on Palestine drew near. As to the third question that preoccupied him—the anticipated composition of the government—Epstein later recounted that Clifford had asked whether Chaim Weizmann would be elected as the state's first president. In reply, Epstein expressed his hope that Dr. Weizmann would indeed become "our first president" and described the composition of the People's Administration.[26] This conversation marked an intersection of two issues that concerned Clifford, who would soon be at the forefront of the struggle for recognition of the anticipated Jewish state—communism and Weizmann.

The American political camp headed by Truman, with Clifford as his emissary, needed unequivocal proof of the Jewish state's affiliation and position in the interbloc struggle, in advance of its establishment and as a necessary condition for supporting it. That proof took the form of Weizmann himself and the role he would assume. Notably, there is no record indicating that, at the time of the May 10 meeting, anyone in the Zionist decision-making establishment had conveyed a promise or commitment of any sort to Weizmann that he would be appointed president. On what basis, therefore, could Epstein have expressed hope, at this fateful political-diplomatic moment on the eve of statehood, that such would be the case? One may reasonably assume that what Epstein described in his memoirs as an "expression of hope" was in fact, in diplomatic terms, an indication that he understood the White House's expectations in this regard. More precisely, he understood the explicit demands of the American political camp led by Truman, which supported the immediate establishment of a Jewish state, and he grasped what this camp required of the Jewish leadership to become fully convinced that the dominant forces in the soon-to-be Israeli political establishment would be aligned with the Western world, in light of the escalating interbloc confrontation. Epstein was considered the appropriate address in this regard not only because of his presence in Washington but also because of his views, given that in the internal dispute among Zionist leaders in the United States, he numbered among those who rejected the possibility of postponing the proclamation of statehood.[27]

On May 11, Arthur Lourie, director of the Jewish Agency Executive in New York, sent a telegram to Shertok stating that Clifford's advice was to "go firmly forward with planned announcement of State" and his impression was that the president was considering recognition.[28] This point is critical to understanding what took place at two decisive meetings, in Tel Aviv and Washington, on the following day. Clifford would not have taken it upon himself to urge the Yishuv leaders to proceed toward proclaiming independence unless he was certain that he had Truman's backing in this regard and that the US decision on the matter was guaranteed (even before the May 12 White House meeting). This conclusion contravenes a prevailing outlook in the historical scholarship, which holds that Truman did not reach a decision until May 14. At the same time, in Nimrod's view, Lourie's telegram decided the internal struggle among Mapai ministers in favor of declaring the establishment of the State of Israel on May 14, 1948.[29]

Lourie's telegram can be used to interpret what happened at the May 12 People's Administration meeting because the content of that telegram implies that in practice, there were two alternatives on the agenda. The first agenda item—discussed at the meeting—was whether to accept the truce "proposed by the American delegation" in the words of People's Administration secretary Sharef in his memoirs.[30] But at least Shertok and Ben-Gurion knew that another American alternative was also on the table, one that originated in the White House—an immediate proclamation of statehood. The misleading description in Sharef's book, implying that the Americans were acting in unison in adopting a position on Jewish statehood, simply does not accord with the historical facts of the time. Moreover, it would have been evident to all that an American alternative originating in the White

House greatly outweighs any alternative that was conveyed by the American consul in Jerusalem and represented views originating in the State Department in Washington. Accordingly, the possibility that a vote on declaring independence took place at the May 12 People's Administration meeting is profoundly unlikely. There was a green light for the establishment of a Jewish state from the strongest man in the world, irrespective of the varied historiographical accounts of the May 12 White House meeting that have emerged. This is the key point.

Furthermore, according to entrenched historiographical folklore, a riotous tumult erupted in the US State Department corridors and amid its delegation to the UN when it became known that Truman decided, on May 14, to recognize the Jewish state.[31] The surprise, however, would have been limited. On May 11, Rusk met with Charles Fahy, a representative of the American Zionist Emergency Council and one of the leading Zionist figures in terms of governmental contacts. Rusk informed Fahy that the US delegation to the UN would not be advocating a truce or any other option because the Americans had come to terms with the fact that the declaration of a Jewish state was inevitable.[32] This information, too, had reached decision-makers in the Yishuv by May 12, when they were supposedly considering the US State Department's truce proposal. In a conversation between Rusk and Clifford on May 8, Rusk presented the official US stance in favor of trusteeship or a truce in place of the Partition Plan and the consequent requirement of establishing a Jewish state within a few months on the grounds that the Jews held only one-third of the territory allocated to them (particularly because they did not control the Negev). Clifford countered by urging "that the United States take no position between now and the 15th which would tie the hands of the United States after May 15th." According to Truman's biographer, Alonzo Hamby, "One did not have to be a cryptographer to discern the word 'recognition' between the lines." Rusk understood the message well, and on May 11, he voiced his opinion that the president would never place himself in a situation in which American action would be the only obstacle to the establishment of a Jewish state.[33]

This was the point at which a central State Department figure's understanding of the political reality finally coincided with the explicit political stance Truman had adopted when he clandestinely promised Weizmann that he intended to recognize the future Jewish state. The underlying premise of most studies of this period is that Truman was inundated with assorted information over several months, during which he examined the question of Palestine, particularly during the month preceding May 14. Yet throughout this time, he did not adopt a clear political stance regarding what he hoped to achieve. That premise appears to be a historiographical impediment to the proper understanding of history.

On May 12, Lourie sent another telegram to Shertok about the announcement of a provisional government scheduled for Saturday, May 15 (it was only on May 12, after the British officially announced that the Mandate would terminate at midnight on the night between May 14 and 15, that the proclamation was rescheduled for Friday, May 14). Lourie proposed that the Yishuv leadership consider the "designation [of] Weizmann [as the] first citizen [of the] new state and President Designate."[34] What may seem at first like a bureaucrat's bizarre intervention in a future state's election and appointment procedures was actually something that Shertok and Ben-Gurion understood perfectly well; that is, it was a clear statement of the expectations among White House decision-makers who supported the immediate establishment of a Jewish state. A few days later, Silver—who headed the Jewish Agency Executive office in New York but had been excluded from Weizmann and Shertok's back-channel contacts with Marshall and the White House in the days leading up to statehood, and who knew nothing of Truman's intention to recognize Israel immediately—voiced his fury over Lourie's May 12 telegram. He described it as one in a series of measures taken behind his back at the time. Lourie "played innocent," claiming that he had sent the telegram at his own initiative.[35]

There was, however, a direct and unequivocal link between Epstein's conversation with Clifford and the two messages Lourie sent from the United States to Shertok and through him to the other senior Mapai decision-makers. That link further extended to another telegram sent on the day after Israel's establishment by Epstein, Robert Nathan, David Ginsburg, and Oscar Gass, four activists from the Jewish Agency office in Washington who had been deeply involved in clandestine contacts in Washington aimed at securing government support for Zionist interests. The four believed it necessary to notify Ben-Gurion urgently (with a copy to Weizmann) that they had a moral obligation to inform him, and through him the members of the Provisional Government, of the major role Weizmann had played in achieving the US government's recognition of the State of Israel. They were certain that if Ben-Gurion knew the details of Weizmann's work, he would join them in admiring Weizmann's great contribution.[36] Was it indeed only considerations of morality and gratitude that prompted this rather peculiar initiative to send a telegram praising Weizmann's efforts at this time, or was it also advice conveyed behind the scenes by a government actor in the White House? Without concrete documentation, one cannot know for certain, but one may wonder.

The fierce argument that broke out at the May 12 White House meeting between Secretary of State Marshall and his undersecretary, Lovett, on the one hand, and Clifford, on the other, has received extensive attention in the historical literature. Of particular note was Marshall's extraordinary statement to Truman, asserting that if the president adopted Clifford's position in support of recognizing the Jewish state immediately upon termination of the Mandate, then Marshall would not vote for him in the upcoming November elections.[37] The import and context of this statement, as well as its aftermath, cannot be understood without examining an event that took place on May 8, the day before Marshall warned Shertok about immediately declaring statehood. That day was Truman's sixty-fourth birthday. In a congratulatory message delivered to the president that morning, Marshall wrote that he was aware of the extraordinary faith Truman placed in him and promised to do his best to grant him the same degree of faith and trust. That evening, contrary to habit, he went to a private party marking the occasion, where he said that while history had yet to discover Truman's true greatness, he had to underscore that all the decisions reached under his administration with an impact on overseas policy were solely in the best interests of the United States. Marshall concluded, "It is not the courage of these decisions that will live, but the integrity of the man." Truman, choking with emotion, could only say to the teary-eyed guests that "he won the war" (World War II).[38]

As a matter of process, it is important to keep in mind that while Marshall and Lovett were certain that the May 12 meeting would determine the US position on recognition or nonrecognition of a future Jewish state and that its outcome might result in a final presidential effort to deter the Jews from taking that step, the conversation in fact took place after the president had already reached his decision.[39] He had even made it known to the appropriate person in his view—Weizmann. The importance of the discussion lies, among other factors, in the question of ascribing a "communist" affiliation to the clandestine immigrants and the consequent fear that the new State of Israel could become a Soviet satellite. The scholarship in this field frequently mentions this as one of the topics raised at the meeting but does not examine its origins or significance because of the natural tendency to focus efforts on uncovering Truman's perspective and deciphering the mix of positions within the US administration.[40] During the meeting, an argument broke out between Clifford and Lovett over the importance of the United States preempting the Soviet Union in recognizing the Jewish state. In the days leading up to the meeting, in fact, the US press had reported a few times on Soviet intentions to recognize the Jewish state soon after its establishment.[41]

From Clifford's perspective, the question of timing related to his aspiration that the United States preempt the USSR in recognizing the Jewish state. In Lovett's view, recognizing the Jewish state before it came into existence would amount to "buying a pig in a poke." He added, "How [do] we know what kind of Jewish state would be set up?" The key word here was "kind"—that is, would it be a Western-style liberal democracy or, heaven forbid, a popular democracy along the lines of Eastern European communist states? To provide a concrete illustration and authoritative backing for his claims, Lovett read excerpts from intelligence sources according to which the Soviets were sending communist Jewish agents, under the guise of clandestine immigrants, from Black Sea areas to Palestine.[42] Behind this information were echoes of the *Pans* affair. Because Truman did not give authorization at the meeting for recognition before the proclamation of statehood, the attendees left with the impression that the position opposing the establishment of a Jewish state and refusing to recognize it immediately had prevailed. Immediately after the meeting, however, Truman instructed Clifford, "I still want to do it [to recognize the Jewish state]. But be careful. I can't afford to lose General Marshall."[43] Given the pending presidential elections and his unstable position in the Democratic Party, which was about to name its candidate, Truman could not allow himself to lose such an esteemed figure in the eyes of the American public.

At a press conference on the following day, when asked how the United States would respond on May 15, Truman replied, "We will cross that bridge when we come to it." In a casual conversation later with Niles, Truman "apologized" for deciding against the pro-Zionists on the previous day. Niles expressed regret that Marshall and Lovett claimed that the Jewish state would be communist, to which Truman replied, "Don't pay any attention to the communism charge, they are always making it. . . . Those two men [Marshall and Lovett] mean well, but they follow their subordinates." In response to Niles's remark that Western recognition should preempt the Soviet bloc's recognition, Truman agreed, adding that they need "to give it the right slant from the beginning."[44] These remarks by Truman on May 13 should be considered in conjunction with an understanding reached on the other side of the governmental divide. On the same day, Lovett proposed, and Clifford agreed, that the United States grant de facto rather than de jure recognition of the Jewish state, and on the following day, Lovett tried to delay the announcement of recognition by a few days. In response, Clifford observed that speed was essential to preempt the Russians and reminded him of Marshall's constant concern that indecisive American conduct only served Russian interests. He cautioned against a postponement of one day turning into two, then three, and so on.[45]

On May 13, Clifford took measures to help the Zionist leadership make appropriate arrangements for US recognition, advising Epstein on the formulation of a letter to the American president on behalf of the Provisional Government. On that day, Weizmann sent a similar letter to Truman, although it adopted an informal tone rather than the necessary legal style. Notably, Weizmann did not hold an official position of any sort in the Zionist Movement, and his letter was therefore without practical significance.[46] At the same time, an incidental remark about Ben-Gurion by Marshall, which accidentally became part of the dramatic White House discussion of May 12, attests tellingly to Weizmann's actual status from the American perspective. During the tense exchange at the White House, the Oval Office received a phone call regarding a United Press news item from Tel Aviv. According to the item, after returning from Washington, Shertok had a personal message from Marshall for Ben-Gurion, the "Premier-designate of the Jewish state." According to Marshall, "In actual fact, no message had been sent to Mr. Ben Gurion, and *I did not even know that such a person existed.*"[47] This is not merely an anecdotal matter, even if it is reasonable to assume that Marshall did know who Ben-Gurion was. His remarks attest indirectly to the status ascribed to Ben-Gurion in the American arena relative to Weizmann. The disparity relates directly to our subject matter because it highlights the American view that the recognized Zionist negotiating partner was Weizmann.

THE DECISION IN TEL AVIV

Ben-Gurion was the axis and anchor of decision-making in the Yishuv. Some months later, *Time* magazine would describe him as "a prophet who carries a gun."[48] His leadership status, which built up gradually over decades and more intensively after the Twenty-Second Zionist Congress in late 1946, became imprinted in the contemporaneous consciousness and historical research primarily because of his conduct throughout 1948 generally, during May specifically, and above all at the People's Administration meeting of May 12 held at the Jewish National Fund Building in Tel Aviv. Ten of its thirteen members were present: Ben-Gurion, Shertok, Mordechai Bentov, Peretz Bernstein, Eliezer Kaplan, David Remez, Pinhas Rosenblit, Moshe Shapira, Bechor Sheetrit, and Aharon Zisling. The absentees were Yitzhak Gruenbaum and Yehuda Leib Fishman, under siege in Jerusalem, and Yitzhak-Meir Levin, who was in New York.[49]

An important speech that Ben-Gurion delivered on May 9 provides a key to understanding historical events and clearing up the historiographical dispute over whether the People's Administration indeed held a vote on May 12. Historian Yoram Nimrod notes that "between the formulation of proposals [in the People's Administration] on May 3 and the proposal for the People's Administration to discuss an immediate declaration [of independence, on May 12], something happened on the street at the newspaper stands. The expectation surrounding a declaration of independence grew stronger from one day to the next, having earlier been a question that did not receive much resonance."[50] Aside from the spontaneous process Nimrod describes, one must also acknowledge Ben-Gurion's decision to shape public opinion in the Yishuv, focusing it on an immediate declaration of independence. Ben-Gurion's speech was part of a celebratory gathering dedicated to opening the first Jewish national fund, with the aim of raising five million Palestine pounds to fund the activities of the future state. Speaking before a resoundingly enthusiastic audience of thousands that filled the national theater, HaBima, including its aisles and exits, Ben-Gurion proclaimed, "In a few days the State of Israel will be established and the first government of Israel in 1900 years will be formed." That statement (in various formulations) was the main headline in most of the daily Hebrew newspapers on the following morning.[51]

The drama of anticipation in the lead-up to independence did not, of course, emerge out of thin air; Ben-Gurion infused it with such great resonance and validity as the main political course of direction in the Yishuv henceforth. His announcement was neither an incidental assertion nor a momentary, emotionally charged rhetorical outburst. Rather, it was a public stance taken in light of the internal political dispute raging behind closed doors, and a determined pledge to pursue independence immediately, without blurring the lines or proceeding only partially toward the desired goal. From Ben-Gurion's perspective as a political leader at a decisive historic moment, there would be no going back. Thus, the assumption that three days later he would oversee a meeting where his position was adopted by only "a hair's breadth" seems utterly unfounded. On the day after Ben-Gurion's speech, *Maariv* pondered, "Those who were touched to their core by Ben-Gurion's enthusiastic speech last night—*a speech unlike any other in the history of Israel*, a prophetic vision about the aspired redemption and salvation of ninety generations, on a precisely exact date, this Saturday night!—asked themselves only one question upon leaving HaBima: And what does Shertok have to offer us? What will he say?"[52]

Before that was to happen, it was necessary to resolve one final, pressing political crisis, given that the matter at hand was the formation of a Jewish state. Specifically, the chief of staff had instructed that defense establishment employees work on Saturday as well. The religious parties then demanded "a complete revocation of this illegal and arbitrary instruction negating the sanctity of the Sabbath as a day of rest." Ben-Gurion responded by ordering that "as long as it is *militarily necessary*—they will work on Saturday."[53] In the interests of providing a full historical context, it should be noted that a month earlier, Golda Myerson had informed the Zionist General Council that when approached by Agudat Israel representatives who were seeking assurance that kosher food would be available to military recruits, "I did not argue with them." She added, "I saw this as one of the happiest moments in my life, . . . that this sector of the Yishuv [the ultra-orthodox] had reached the conclusion that this was the entire nation's battle."[54]

Shertok's participation in the decisive People's Administration meeting and his presence in the country with the onset of the Arab invasion were not self-evident. As reported at the May 3 and 4 meetings of the Jewish Agency Executive's US section, Shertok had been debating whether to fly to Palestine. After losing a vote in the Executive, he changed his mind and decided to remain in the United States. On May 6, Ben-Gurion informed him that he personally disagreed with Shertok's decision to stay in the United States and would prefer that he return to Palestine, as planned, for consultations. A few hours later, Ben-Gurion reinforced this message in a telegram designated, in an unusual move, as "extremely urgent": "I strongly advise that you come immediately. Send us a telegram regarding the arrangements we should make [for your arrival]."[55] Shertok acquiesced. Then, on May 16, only two days after Israel's establishment, when its chances of survival in the face of an Arab invasion were not clear, Shertok suggested that he return to New York to meet with Andrei Gromyko and UN delegates. Although Kaplan and Myerson supported this idea, Ben-Gurion was fiercely opposed: "We are planning a state now, and it is inconceivable that the overseer of foreign affairs be away from the country."[56] Following consultations, it was agreed that it would be Shertok's decision whether to leave, and he decided to remain. Had he chosen to depart, he would have provided fertile ground for his portrayal as someone who, for fear of what was to come, fled the country immediately after its establishment. That would undoubtedly have provided fodder for years to come. Any time he was caught up in a political confrontation within or outside his party, his rivals could indulge in standard political disparagement practices, discrediting him as a leader and public figure at the most critical moment in the history of his generation. Thus it turns out that twice within a span of ten days, Ben-Gurion "saved"—perhaps the quotation marks should be omitted—Shertok's political career. In 1956, when a big fight broke out between the two in advance of the Sinai Campaign, Ben-Gurion had only to mention the virtues of their "1948 coalition."[57] The reference encompassed those two occasions, and the hint at his indebtedness would not have been lost on Shertok.

On May 8, while Shertok was at the airport in New York awaiting his flight to Palestine, Weizmann contacted him to implore that he support statehood during the People's Administration deliberations to which he had been summoned: "Moshe, don't weaken, don't swerve, don't spoil the victory, Jewish state and nothing less."[58] Relying on a secondary source, Abba Eban, who was evidently not with Weizmann at the time of this conversation, offered his own polished phrasing: "It is now or never."[59] On the other hand, Joseph Linton, who was in Weizmann's room at the time of the conversation, attested that Weizmann added on a personal note, "I am an old man, and shall not live to see the state if we do not declare it now." Then, looking at Linton, Weizmann told Shertok, "He is a much younger man. And he will never live to see the state either."[60] Weizmann's entreaty was apt given the outcome of Shertok's meeting earlier that day with Marshall. Rusk's report to his colleagues the following day indicated that "according to Mr. Shertok the Jews are not likely to proclaim their State right away but would start out only by establishing their provisional government."[61] Moreover, according to a May 12 report by Goldmann (who had left New York for London), Shertok did not support the proclamation of an independent state on May 15 (the scheduled date at that time). Goldmann reported that both he and Shertok were of the view that it was necessary at that time to declare the establishment of a provisional government for the sake of managing the Yishuv's internal affairs and to wait until October to seek Security Council recognition of a sovereign state, as stipulated under UN Resolution 181 of November 29, 1947. This was also the position Shertok took at the People's Administration meeting of May 12, 1948.[62]

At the start of the meeting, Myerson described the disappointing outcome of her May 10 meeting with King Abdullah of Transjordan. Although Abdullah did not dispute the mutual understanding they had reached six months earlier, he pointed out that various events had transpired since then, including "the Deir Yassin issue." He added, "At that time I was one and now I am one of five and I cannot. I have no choice and I cannot do otherwise." According to Myerson, she departed from him on friendly terms, saying that "if he wants war, then we will meet after the war." In this context, Kaplan had commented a day earlier, at a Mapai Central Committee meeting, that Abdullah "feels quite trapped, both by Arab public opinion and by the English, and commented on this once publicly, saying that any Arab leader who tries to reach an agreement with the Jews will meet a bitter end. He fears that he might meet a bitter end."[63]

Shertok then reviewed the sequence of events since the partition resolution, as reflected in the positions taken by the US administration. He informed those present that the administration was currently opposed to partition, advocating a truce and trusteeship instead (he omitted the internal conflict in the US administration, to the extent that he was aware of it). Shertok listed four reasons for the US stance: the president's lack of involvement in the matter, the end of the UN General Assembly session, the weakness of Jewish forces on the battlefield, "and the main thing—the greatly escalating tension in relations with Soviet Russia and worsening international crisis as a result. To me it was clear," added Shertok, "that were it not for the fourth thing, which is the main point in my view, the State Department would not have succeeded in turning things upside down.... It is only because of this *overshadowing terror of threat to the United States* that they were able to break through the wall of November 29 [the UN partition resolution] within the American government."[64] In retrospect, this was the most concise explanation as to why the People's Administration needed Weizmann in order to ensure the implementation of the partition resolution in a way that granted Israel the legitimacy and international recognition that would enable it to survive for years to come. Any form of partition that gave the Soviets a presence in the Middle East via the new State of Israel would be counter to US strategic interests. Weizmann's inclusion in the ruling echelon of the emerging state was an explicit indication that the incipient Israeli government had no intention of allowing that to happen and that Israel did not intend to affiliate itself with the Soviet bloc. It also underscored, albeit cautiously, that Israel aligned itself with Western interests in the Middle East. The political pledge between Truman and Weizmann was a concrete manifestation of their commitment to the UN Partition Plan and its implementation, and despite countless crises, it remained in force then and later.

Shertok outlined a narrow set of options for averting the threat of war with Arab countries. He reviewed the US proposal for a three-month truce, which entailed postponing statehood. He also described Marshall's caution at their meeting four days earlier. While commenting that it was not his place to suggest what they should do, Marshall had pointed out that, as a military man himself, "he wanted to warn us against relying on the advice of our military people" because "flushed by victory, their counsel was liable to be misleading" and a prolonged invasion would weaken the Jewish side. The secretary of state had concluded dramatically, as reported by Shertok, that "if we succeed, well and good. He would be quite happy; he wished us well. But what if we failed? He did not want to put any pressure on us. It was our responsibility," and he hoped that we were aware "of the very grave risks involved." Shertok spared his colleagues the harshest point raised by

Marshall—that "if the tide did turn adversely . . . there was no warrant to expect help from the United States."[65]

Contrary to the expert warning issued by Marshall, US Army chief of staff during World War II, the Haganah representatives' assessments were actually free of arrogance. Israel Galili and Yigael Yadin attended the May 12 meeting not at the summons of Ben-Gurion, as one might have expected; rather, it was Shapira and Rosenblit who requested their attendance because they sought authoritative backing for their position, which called for a course of action that would avert an Arab invasion even if this meant postponing statehood. Yadin explained that at that time only about 60 to 70 percent of the enlisted units were armed, and "objectively, undoubtedly" the Arabs had "a major advantage at this time." He cautiously concluded, "The chances are very balanced. To be more honest, I would say that their advantage is great."[66] At this point, Ben-Gurion made his first substantive intervention, informing the others that the Jews had "treasure troves of weapons" due to arrive from abroad as soon as the Mandate ended. "It won't be a 'picnic,'" he added, as the conquest of Haifa and the victories in other battles had made enduringly clear to the Yishuv community. However, the military dynamic created by the Jewish side's enlistment capacity and armament would tip the balance, he firmly asserted. His conclusion was that "we have all the chances, with losses and severe blows, to achieve victory."[67] Remez, who was far more pessimistic, warned against relying on miracles. He admitted: "I fear the past will not extend to the future," adding, "I do not want to be defeated by the Arabs now. It would not be sweet."[68]

As the People's Administration meeting continued, nearing its end, and the above-mentioned meeting of Truman, Marshall, and their assistants began, two additional meetings were also convening to discuss the situation and what should be done. A subset of the National Council Executive (five members headed by Yitzhak Ben-Zvi) gathered in Jerusalem to formulate a position that would be conveyed to Remez, who was concurrently participating in the People's Administration's meeting. While Zorach Warhaftig supported an immediate proclamation of statehood, the other participants backed Mapai delegate Avraham Katznelson's position, which, subject to learning Shertok's stance, tended toward accepting the truce proposal and postponing the declaration of statehood by three months. In practice, their position did not have any impact on the decision-making process, and their deliberations amounted to the final death throes of this body as it approached dissolution.[69] Such was also the case with a telegram that Fishman sent from a besieged Jerusalem to Ben-Gurion at 6:00 p.m., requesting that it be "recorded" that he, Gruenbaum, Kolodny (Moshe Kol of the Aliya

Hadasha party), and Eliyahu Dobkin support "the declaration of the Jewish state and the establishment of a provisional government immediately upon termination of the Mandate." The telegram, dispatched while the People's Administration deliberations were in full swing, provides further evidence that the final decision did not depend on a "hair's breadth" of 6–4 votes, as two People's Administration members who were not present—Fishman and Gruenbaum—voiced had their positions explicitly and in real time.[70]

Meanwhile, in Tel Aviv, the Mapai Central Committee convened on May 11 for a meeting that continued, with breaks, until May 12. All were in suspense to hear what Shertok had to report from New York. The key statement in his speech was: "The risk of postponing the announcement of a Jewish state or a government—I'm not dwelling on the minutiae of wording—outweighs the risk of taking this step."[71] What Shertok described as "the minutiae of wording" was in fact the heart of the dispute: not whether to declare but what to declare—a government or a state? Shertok's downplaying of this dispute before the Mapai Central Committee and the fact that he did not put it to an official vote before members of the People's Administration (even though Rosenblit noted during the debate on statehood that "Shertok said: perhaps declare a government but not a sovereign state") indicate that Shertok had accepted Weizmann and Ben-Gurion's verdict, in the same order, even if only in the chronological sense.[72] Publicly, it was announced that the Mapai Central Committee unanimously decided to propose that, upon termination of the British Mandate, the People's Administration immediately declare the establishment of the Jewish state and its provisional government.[73] At a May 13 press conference, Shertok embraced Weizmann's position, declaring that the Jewish state would be established "now—or never!"[74]

Shertok apparently refrained from insisting on his approach or trying to enlist a majority in its favor, and not only in acquiescence to Ben-Gurion's demands the moment he returned to Palestine, on May 11, as Ben-Gurion's biographer, Michael Bar-Zohar, asserts.[75] No less important was Shertok's consideration of Weizmann's position (even though he doubted the latter's guarantee of impending US recognition). Although eight days earlier, at a meeting of the Jewish Agency Executive US section in New York, Shertok had supported the truce arrangement that involved postponing statehood, he did not advocate a truce at the May 12 People's Administration meeting. Perhaps he concluded that an invasion was inevitable, and he was primarily concerned with ensuring international support for Jewish statehood in light of the new reality. Given the circumstances, he concluded that "the issue could not be forced." The question, as he saw it, was what political facts they should establish on the ground given the legal vacuum that would result in Palestine, as far as the UN was concerned, once the Mandate ended. He answered that it was preferable "to declare a provisional government of the Jewish state, so as to make it clear . . . that there is an independent state in Eretz Israel [Palestine], without explicitly stating that a sovereign and independent state exists as of today." His proposal was at the heart of the dispute that erupted when the People's Administration turned to the next agenda item—"the declaration of a state." Ben-Gurion opened the discussion: "First we need to reach a political decision on whether we are declaring a state or not declaring one, declaring a government or not declaring." From this, we may surmise that Sharef's version—in which the discussion of a truce "encompassed the decision about establishing the state"—was unfounded, at least as far as Ben-Gurion was concerned at the moment of truth. Furthermore, notably, in none of his public or archival writings, to the best of our knowledge as of this writing, did Ben-Gurion ever claim that a 6–4 vote had taken place. On the matter of proclaiming a government rather than a state, Shertok had the support of Rosenblit, Bernstein, and Remez. There was no vote on this matter either, at least according to the minutes. It would appear that the matter was decided following the steadfast position voiced by Myerson, who participated in the meeting as a member of equal standing even though her rank was only that of Jewish Agency Political Department manager: "That [declaring a government] won't help us. We need to go all the way. . . . We make the declaration and must ourselves [rather than the UN] declare the establishment of the state. And if we do it—then it should be down to the last detail. . . . That's what the world is waiting for. And if there is a declaration—then we must do it fully!"[76] Perhaps this was why Ben-Gurion had insisted so stubbornly on including Myerson as a member of the People's Administration on behalf of Mapai at Remez's expense—insisted and failed. He preferred her, not as the "flag for the [Middle] East" that he had previously raised so boldly but as a proactive stateswoman who could skillfully instill a genuine sense of "now or never."

The issue of borders surfaced during the debate on establishing the state. Ben-Gurion set the tone in this matter, expressing opposition to the delineation of borders because it remained unclear whether the UN would prevent a war with the Arab states, whether a war would break out, and whether the UN would intervene with force to impose borders. In the event of a war without UN intervention, he foresaw the following outcome: "We will capture the Western Galilee and both sides of the road to Jerusalem, and all this will be part of the state if our strength lasts. Why commit?" On this matter, at least, Sharef was right in observing that "he suddenly saw." In the vote on specifying borders as part of the proclamation of statehood,

opponents prevailed by 5–4. The minutes did not indicate how each participant voted (or who did not participate). From the statements they made, it
appears that Zisling, Shapira, Bernstein, Ben-Gurion, and evidently Kaplan
opposed mentioning borders, while Rosenblit and Sheetrit favored doing so.
My assessment, based on the rather vague statements of the remaining participants, is that the two additional proponents of a reference to borders were
Remez and Bentov, and it was Shertok who did not vote. After yet another
round of discussion surrounding Ben-Gurion's conditions for the security
portfolio appointee, which once again ended inconclusively, the participants
decided by a 7-vote majority to name the state Israel. The meeting was then
brought to a close.[77]

The dispute over the formulation of Israel's declaration of independence
is beyond the scope of our discussion. Nonetheless, it is important from a historical perspective as well to consider how Ben-Gurion, who polished the final version, viewed it. We should also make note of Shertok's complaint to his
collaborator regarding the final version—"he spiritually slaughtered us."[78]
When the People's Council convened on May 14, just hours before the declaration of independence, to discuss and approve its final version, Ben-Gurion
responded to the various comments raised: "The purpose of the declaration is
not to engage in political inquiries (and we have many political matters to settle); rather, its purpose is to lay the ground for proclaiming independence. . . .
None of the drafters of this document has any pretense that it is absolutely
perfect. The purpose was only to present those matters that, in our opinion,
lay the foundation, for us, for the Jewish people, for world opinion, and for
the United Nations, of this thing we intend to do today, why we are declaring independence."[79] That it was not "absolutely perfect" means that this was
not a quintessential canonical document, even though over time every mark
and every comma it contains or omits has effectively gained such status. Because we cannot avoid some mention of the actual declaration of the State
of Israel's establishment at 4:00 p.m. on Friday, May 14, let us consider the
following description from a pamphlet intended for Mapai delegates in the
Diaspora. For our purposes, it offers a compellingly authentic account of
the event in terms of the political and leadership contexts we are examining:

> Those of us here, in this hall, do not, of course, grasp the significance of the
> event. We cannot grasp it. We have sat through so many meetings here—with
> the very same people—that it is hard for us to sense, with every fiber of our be-
> ing, that there has never been such a meeting, neither here nor anywhere else,
> not in our time and not in thousands of years, and there will never again be
> one. And it is hard for us to sense that the people who are so familiar to us have
> become different, at this moment.[80]

Concurrent with this event, ten members of the People's Council convened in the courtyard of the National Institutions compound in Jerusalem to mark the historic occasion, which they could not attend because of the siege on Jerusalem. They found the entrances to the courtyard crowded with widows from Kfar Etzion and their fatherless children, who, while waiting for the Red Cross in order to claim their husbands' bodies, gazed with haunted looks at the council members. The meeting concluded without festivities.[81]

The Arab forces' invasion began on Saturday. Unlike the events of Saturday, October 6, 1973, the invasion of 1948 did not come as a surprise. In fact, the press reported on it in advance. An editorial in *Haaretz* on the following day stated, "The state's glorious and exalted Sabbath [day of rest] is behind us. Now comes the grueling mundaneness [absence of sanctity] in which we must *conquer* the state we proclaimed during the sanctity of Sabbath."[82] The word "conquer" was emphasized. The United States recognized the State of Israel de facto on May 14, eleven minutes after the termination of the British Mandate. The time in Israel was 12:11 a.m. on May 15. The decision to grant de facto recognition resulted from a hard-struck bargain between Clifford and Lovett on behalf of Truman and Marshall on May 13–14. Their disagreement ended with Marshall conceding, although he did so without any loss to his prestige or status. A contemporaneous account of the deal reflects the undisguised bitterness of Marshall's undersecretary, who knew how to appeal to historians who craved tasteless anecdotes that invariably come at the expense of methodical historical research: "The President's political advisers, having failed last Wednesday afternoon to make the President a father of the new state [Israel], have determined at least to make him the midwife."[83] Those documenters of history also blatantly overlooked the sting of this sexist, suggestive anecdote: a father "does the deed" (grants recognition) before the birth (of the state). At an event in honor of Truman a few years later, Abba Eban, adopting a style of speech favored by Israeli leaders across the generations in referring to their wives, would remark that Israel will always recall those "who went with us in the wilderness, in the land that was not sown."[84] In less romantic terms, *Haaretz* admitted that the full story eluded it: "Over the past two months all signs have indicated that the US government was interested in postponing Jewish independence and would not look kindly on our establishing a state. But it turns out that alongside this visible policy, there was another policy, hidden from sight, which allowed America to accept the existence of the Jewish state if declared."[85]

It was not the case, however, that the United States was compelled to accept the situation. Rather, there was a deep division of interests within the American administration, and the recognition of Israel was indicative of the power of Truman's pledge to Weizmann in shaping US action at the decisive moment. About twenty minutes after the United States recognized Israel, Lovett reported the fact to James Forrestal. The defense secretary noted in his diary that Lovett had informed him that the decision was reached sometime in the previous twenty-four to forty-eight hours and conveyed to him and Marshall at a meeting in the White House. Contrary to Marshall's strong warnings to Shertok just a week earlier, Lovett noted that the Jewish forces were better trained and equipped than the Arabs and could almost certainly handle themselves.[86] According to a widespread anecdote recorded later by Rusk, some of Marshall's friends told him that he should resign because of the incident. Perhaps recalling his remarks of May 8, on the occasion of Truman's birthday, Marshall reportedly replied, "You do not accept a post of this sort and then resign when the man who has the Constitutional authority to make a decision makes one."[87]

The Appointment: Weizmann Returns to Center Stage

Let us backtrack a bit: Shertok was about to fly from New York, via Geneva, to Palestine on May 8, but his flight was delayed because the Air France aircraft was experiencing engine trouble. Instead, he flew on May 9, by way of Paris and Athens, reaching Palestine on May 11.[88] The delay in Shertok's arrival prompted Ben-Gurion to allow Meyer Weisgal to leave for Europe, and from there to clarify Weizmann's position on declaring statehood. Before Weisgal even departed, however, Shertok arrived in the country and reported on Weizmann's position. As a result, Weisgal left for Europe on May 12, at Ben-Gurion's request, for a different purpose altogether. At 7 a.m. that morning, he sent a telegram to New York saying that he would be arriving in London and "will phone chief [Weizmann] same day."[89] Thus his flight coincided with the decisive People's Administration meeting that discussed declaring statehood. In his autobiography, Weisgal stated that the purpose of this trip was to clarify Weizmann's position. This may indeed have been the original purpose when he began to make his travel arrangements, but once Shertok arrived in the country, there was no urgency for Weisgal to leave for Europe. Shertok could definitively report on Weizmann's position. At the May 12 People's Administration meeting, Shertok reported that Weizmann unequivocally supported the immediate declaration of statehood: "Dr. Weizmann is opposed to any postponement on our part."[90]

In my view, the purpose of Weisgal's travel was to consult clandestinely with Weizmann regarding the political position Ben-Gurion wanted to assign him once the state was established, and this of course necessitated his prior consent. This presumes that Ben-Gurion had the exclusive authority to select

Weizmann for the position of Provisional State Council president. Although there is no documentation to this effect, it is reasonable to assume that the choice of Weizmann as president was also the outcome of Ben-Gurion conceding to pressure from his colleagues, Remez and Kaplan—two Weizmann loyalists within the Mapai leadership and two of its four delegates to the People's Administration, who, in the spirit of Meir Grabovsky and Dobkin's stance of March 6, demanded that the position go to Weizmann. On May 14, after the State of Israel was proclaimed, Kaplan made a public statement referring directly to the People's Administration's discussion: "With much joy and trepidation, we unanimously decided to establish the state."[91]

After speaking with Weizmann, Weisgal telephoned Ben-Gurion's office, either on the night of May 12 or the morning of May 13, and left the agreed-upon message—"Yes"—although no record of it could be found. At 11 a.m. on May 13, Ben-Gurion's security adviser Reuven Zaslani (Shiloah) sent a telegram to the Dorchester Hotel in London, where Weisgal was scheduled to stay, confirming receipt of the information: "ANSWER IS YES HOORAY."[92] It is safe to assume that Zaslani, who was staid by nature, would not have cheered Weizmann's agreement to a process that was already underway. Cheering the president is another matter. Weisgal's reply, dispatched from London on May 13 and arriving in Palestine on the following day, stated, "SPOKE TO ZAKEN [old man, i.e., Weizmann] NEW YORK YESTERDAY WILL COOPERATE FULLY stop Deem it most important your chief [Ben-Gurion] send him appropriate message Waldorf Astoria on the fifteenth STOP Awaiting word from you Dorchester regards. Meyer."[93] This was a dramatic telegram, the importance of which, in terms of shaping the final chapter of relations between Zionism's two leading figures, cannot be overstated. With what exactly was the "zaken" expected to "cooperate fully"—the declaration of independence or the position he was to be offered? The words are seemingly open to both interpretations, but the final clause of the telegram—"appropriate message"—points unequivocally to the position Weizmann was to be offered. This is confirmed by a telegram that the five senior Mapai leaders—Ben-Gurion, Kaplan, Myerson, Remez, and Shertok—sent to Weizmann immediately following the declaration of independence, which stated, "We congratulate you on the establishment of the Jewish state, to whose creation, of all the people living among us, no one has contributed more than you. Your position and help at this stage of our struggle fortified all of us. We look forward to the day when we see you as the *head of the state* under conditions of peace. Strength and fortitude."[94]

The telegram, with its carefully chosen wording, was intended not as a casual, obligatory compliment but as a response to a request or, more precisely, a demand, conveyed by Weisgal's telegram, that Ben-Gurion and his associates in the Mapai leadership abide by their part of the agreement reached by the two leaders. Hence the telegram contained a concrete political commitment: Weizmann's placement at the "head of the state"—that is, a commitment to elect him as president of the state.[95] For the benefit of readers not familiar with the nuances of Jewish politics in Palestine, the *Washington Post* explained that the post of president of the Provisional State Council was "tantamount to provisional president of the new Jewish state." An editorial in the leading weekly of Britain's Jewish community, *The Jewish Chronicle*, informed its readers that the most prominent member of their community had returned to center stage.[96] A week earlier, on May 13, Weisgal, evidently fully committed to his mission, had managed to "plant" the information about Weizmann's anticipated appointment in the London Jewish weekly's editorial.[97] Thus, to put it lyrically, Weizmann and Ben-Gurion arrived hand in hand at the finish line of the Zionist race.

Accordingly, it was neither for reasons of modesty nor as a perfunctory show of respect but to prepare Israeli public opinion for the upcoming presidential appointment that Ben-Gurion included the following statement in his speech "to the Yishuv and the people" broadcast on the *Voice of Israel* on May 15: "Of those still living among us, this evening I will mention only one great man who, whether holding an official position or not, whether one agrees with his opinions or not, has always remained the people's choice, and no one living among us has contributed as much as he did to all the Yishuv-related and diplomatic conquests of the Zionist enterprise—Dr. Chaim Weizmann."[98] On the following day, as the Provisional State Council was discussing the selection of council president, Ben-Gurion once again hinted at Weizmann's position during the leadership's internal dispute. He noted that he disagreed with Weizmann on one occasion but "fortunately, not recently"—a clear testament that during the stormy debate among Yishuv decision-makers in the lead-up to independence, Weizmann had been among the proponents of statehood here and now. To remove the least shred of doubt, Ben-Gurion asserted that Weizmann "also sees the need for us to fight, and also insisted on declaring statehood."[99]

On Sunday, May 16, 1948, at the Provisional Government's first meeting following the declaration of independence, it decided to submit a proposal to the Provisional State Council nominating Weizmann as its president. The government voted in favor of this proposal by 9–2, with Mapam ministers Zisling and Bentov opposing. Zisling justified his stance by asserting that the president should only be elected once a Constituent Assembly was established.[100] The Provisional State Council affirmed Weizmann's appointment that day by a majority of 13–2, with the Revisionists opposing and the Mapam members and Communists abstaining after a few failed attempts to thwart the nomination. In presenting Weizmann's candidacy, Ben-Gurion completely ignored the political context of his appointment, focusing only on the biographical and symbolic aspects, as noted: "It is inconceivable that Chaim Weizmann not serve as head of our state. It may not be necessary for Weizmann, but it seems to me that it's a moral imperative for the Yishuv and the people."[101] The moderate Mapai members rejoiced. Yosef Sprinzak informed Weisgal on May 18, "I have already congratulated Weizmann as the first president of the State of Israel." Weisgal, who arrived in New York after the telegram, promised—in contrast to his threat a year and a half earlier when Sprinzak was slow in delivering the Histadrut's grant for the Weizmann Institute of Science—that "a hundred cigars" were on their way to him.[102]

A *Washington Post* article published the day after Israel's establishment stated, "The President . . . had made up his mind almost two weeks ago to recognize quickly if the floundering U. N. failed to reach a decision, and if the Zionists proclaimed their nation. He confirmed his plans to Judge Samuel I. Rosenman of New York, who visited him ten days ago."[103] Rosenman had apparently leaked the story to immortalize his part in the historical chapter of Israel's declaration and establishment, and in the process, to the consternation of Truman's advisers, disclosed a fact they would have preferred to keep confidential. Lovett, furious, telephoned Clifford and charged that the article "stultified the President, that he would then have been playing a double game, trying to get trusteeship at UN while having made up his mind to recognize." Clifford, seeking to calm Lovett down, replied that the president had decided to announce the recognition of Israel on Friday (May 14). In subsequent internal consultations, Clifford and his colleagues decided that, if asked at the daily press conference, White House Press Secretary Charlie Ross would refrain from answering the question directly.[104] Accordingly, when asked by one of the reporters, Ross indeed replied that he could not say exactly but that the president had been thinking about it for some time.[105]

As Truman had promised Weizmann, by way of Rosenman, in April, the two met ceremoniously in Washington on May 25. Weizmann's entourage was headed by Abraham Feinberg, with Maurice Bisgyer overseeing technical matters. Two days later, still exhilarated by the event, Feinberg described it to members of the New York delegation of the Weizmann Institute of Science at the Waldorf Astoria Hotel: the teary-eyed gathering of "literally hundreds" of reporters and photographers at the entrance to Union Station in Washington, assembled to witness one president arriving to visit another as the flag of Israel flew over the site of their meeting at the Blair House (the presidential guesthouse, where Truman was staying while the White House was undergoing extensive renovations). On the eve of the meeting, Lovett and Marshall were summoned to the site to neutralize any official symbols that could have transformed de facto into de jure recognition (thereby granting greater prestige, legitimacy, and standing in the international arena) and to ensure American adherence to the embargo as a means of moderating the hostilities in Palestine and constraining Jewish territorial expansion.[106] In this context, we should also note that Weizmann's influence had its limitations: until January 1949, his efforts to achieve de jure recognition and have the embargo lifted met with failure. The lack of understanding surrounding Weizmann's actual status in Israel's decision-making process is evident in Ernest Bevin's demand that Truman, at his meeting with Weizmann that day, insist that Israel immediately announce its acceptance of a truce (to include Etzel and Lehi), during which it would agree that Jewish immigration be limited to women and children.[107] Weizmann had indeed returned to the center of the political stage, but he continued to lack influence in matters of security, which were the core issue in 1948.

Years later, Abba Eban described Weizmann during the weeks preceding statehood as engaged in cultivating the dream of US recognition of Israel.[108] Yet the struggle had not been over recognition but rather Israel's establishment and declaration and the political identity of the Jewish state. This was the dream in which Weizmann was engaged and to which he and Ben-Gurion, each in his own capacity, contributed at the decisive moment in May 1948. When a May 17 editorial in *Davar* stated that "with the selection of Dr. Chaim Weizmann as president of the Provisional State Council, it is as if the image of an independent Israel in our generation has been completed," the author of the editorial was unaware of just how historically accurate those words would turn out to be.[109] In retrospect, it would appear that the choice of Weizmann did indeed establish a very specific image for the newly formed state as Western in inception and essence. That was the intention of the senior participants in this political move on both sides of the Atlantic—Ben-Gurion and Truman. The message conveyed by the close contacts that led to the immediate recognition of Israel and the appointment of Weizmann—the person Truman marked as his confidant on the Zionist side—as president of the Provisional State Council was not intended to be shouted from the rooftops or have immediate international implications. Yet its significance was well understood in the international arena. In a May 21 telegram to Shertok, Eban (Israel's envoy to the UN) noted increasing reports in the American press regarding State Department concerns about a rift between Britain and the United States over Palestine, which, according to the *New York Times,* could facilitate Soviet involvement in the Middle East. He then added a post-script, stating that "Weizmann appointment has made a profound impression in U.N. circles. During the final days before the 15th of May, his opposition to the U.S. truce proposal had become generally known and had psychological effects."[110] It was neither symbolism nor recognition for past deeds that informed the selection of Weizmann as president of the Provisional State Council in conjunction with the decision to establish the State of Israel. His appointment reflected an interest in publicly proclaiming that the new Jewish state was directly and unequivocally affiliated with the Western world.

PROVISIONAL STATE COUNCIL PRESIDENT: ABROAD

Just before the Provisional State Council voted to elect Weizmann as president, Ben-Gurion made a point of explaining that if elected, this would by no means make him a member of the Provisional Government.[111] In so doing, he established a clear delineation between the executive of the state and the yet-to-be-defined powers of the Provisional State Council president. Ben-Gurion sought to prevent Weizmann's involvement in concrete security matters. Weizmann was evidently aware of the expectation that he would fill the role of the emerging state's moral anchor, as indicated by the closing words of the message of thanks he sent his associates in Israel, by way of Ben-Gurion: "Zion will be redeemed by justice." These were precisely the words with which he had closed his somber speech shortly before being ousted from the role of Zionist Organization president at the Twenty-Second Zionist Congress in December 1946, at which time he also added the words "and not by any other means."[112] This time, under the circumstances of existential war, as opposed to the violent struggle against the British, he omitted those words. The Waldorf Astoria Hotel was a day late in raising Israel's flag (in line with the custom when hosting a head of state) because it did not have the proper flag. Weizmann's view, informed by the spirit of morality, was that the new state's flag should feature the lion of Judah holding the tablets of the Ten Commandments, but his approach did not prevail.[113]

Weizmann's appointment as president altered his plans only slightly. Having heeded the advice of his senior adviser, Weisgal, back in April, when he decided to remain in the United States rather than travel to Palestine (given the difficulty of protecting him at his home in Rehovot), he now had to abandon his plans to travel to England (which had become hostile) immediately after his scheduled meeting with Truman on May 25. That meeting marked the fruition of Truman's promise to Weizmann, via his close associate Samuel Rosenman, on April 23: to recognize the Jewish state upon its establishment and to do so officially and ceremonially by inviting Weizmann to the

White House. Most of the discussion between the two dignitaries focused on Israel's formal request for a $100 million loan from the United States.[114] At a press conference following the meeting, Weizmann's indiscreet remarks attested incidentally to the degree of his disconnection from the battlefield and the Israeli reality. His promise that if a truce were achieved, Israel would agree to withdraw from Jaffa and Acre because "they do not belong to us" (under the November 1947 Partition Plan) provoked discomfort in Israel, to put it mildly. Foreign Minister Shertok, opting for diplomatic language, responded by describing this statement as "unjustified" because it was currently not possible to foresee how the war would develop, and it was better to refrain from such commitments.[115] An editorial in *Maariv* was less circumspect, noting that hundreds and thousands of young people were "putting their lives at risk at this moment," and the hundreds of bereaved families "did not authorize the president of Israel to relinquish, in one breath, what they had conquered with their hearts' blood."[116]

On the day after his meeting with Truman, Weizmann sailed for Paris, where he spent June in a futile attempt to persuade French government officials to recognize Israel. From there, he continued to Switzerland with the intention of returning to Paris for the start of the UN General Assembly session in mid-September and traveling to Israel at the end of the month. His travel plans, finalized on May 21, indicate that Weizmann believed he should stay away from the hostilities in Israel and devote most of his time to rest and recovery. He preferred to arrive in Israel after the hot summer months, which were hard on his health, and this meant late September. During his free time, he planned to complete the epilogue for his autobiography, *Trial and Error*, which would cover the period since the UN General Assembly resolution of November 29, 1947.[117]

From the public and diplomatic perspective, it seemed curious that Weizmann remained in Europe, which naturally led to speculation. In early August, George Jones, an adviser to the US ambassador in London who was considered an expert on the Middle East, informed James McDonald, the designated US envoy to Israel, that if Weizmann were to settle in Israel at that time, four hundred to eight hundred soldiers would have to be deployed to protect his home in Rehovot. While McDonald surmised that the troops were necessary to protect Weizmann from Arabs, Jones claimed that they were necessary to defend Weizmann from Israeli extremists who would try to kill him. McDonald regarded this contention as indicative of British efforts to cast doubt, in every conceivable way, on the legitimacy of Israel's government so as to justify not recognizing it. When McDonald arrived in Israel, Myerson resolved the "riddle" of Weizmann's delay, explaining that everyone knew Weizmann could not handle the summer heat in the country and therefore was not due until late September.[118]

Another factor was the unresolved dispute over the president's powers. Two and a half months after his appointment, with the scope of his powers still undefined, Weizmann intended to instruct Weisgal to inform Shertok of his resignation. He could, of course, have done so directly, but he was averse to exacerbating tensions. Weisgal, however, kept Weizmann's complaint to himself. The rationale Weizmann gave for threatening to resign was that he was not receiving updates about political moves and his impression was that "the course of militarism" had taken over the Israeli reality: "I am not in a position to cover with my name all that is going on at present in Palestine and to accept everything which the Government does without being able in any way either to influence it or to prevent it." Yet it appears that what troubled him most in those days were rumors that reached him in Vevey, Switzerland, about happenings at the Sieff Institute (the current Weizmann Institute of Science). He learned, without receiving advance notice, that the "course of militarism" had taken over the institute, headed by a scientist loyal to him, Dr. Ernst David Bergmann. The operations of the institute were being redefined to meet wartime needs, and the scientific basis on which Weizmann had founded the institute in 1934 was being redirected. Weizmann had never been a pacifist and was actually well versed in the technological and financial link between science and the military in developed countries, as he had personally excelled at this interface in times of war. However, as historian Benny Morris points out, he was also upset by the disconnection and estrangement that emerged between him and his right-hand man, Bergmann, who was enlisted by Ben-Gurion. The wholesale transition from independent theoretical and applied academic research for strictly civilian purposes to applied military research under government auspices was, according to Bergmann, a valuable contribution to the establishment and security of the State of Israel. Weizmann opted to convey his grievance to Weisgal, who was on a fundraising campaign in Mexico—mainly for the purposes of documentation "for the sake of history," as he tended to do from time to time. In practice, he was content with blaming Shertok for what he considered the unnecessarily quick adoption of irresponsible Balkan-style conduct.[119]

Following this rebuke, Shertok hurriedly wrote to Israel's UN envoy, Eban, who was aware of Weizmann's displeasure. According to Shertok, Weizmann was "wrongly" assuming that he had been elected as president of the state, whereas he was only president of the Provisional State Council, and despite having had the difference explained to him, Weizmann continued to cultivate this illusion. Eban replied that "unfortunately [this] misunderstanding [is] shared by the US president and almost entire diplomatic world. [The] chief's [Weizmann's] impression" was that the council president provisionally held the position of head of state until elections to the presidency took place. Eban added that this impression originated with a telegram sent to him by his friends in Mapai—that same telegram sent on the day of the state's establishment stating, "We look forward to the day when we see you at the *head of the state*."[120] However, Ben-Gurion's standing as the foremost national figure leading the Israel Defense Forces' (IDF) campaign of military conquests, alongside Israel's battlefield victories, prevented the emergence of a competing focal point of power at the head of the state.

BEN-GURION'S STANDING IN SECURITY MATTERS

Shertok, who had been away from the country for nine months (from August 1947 to May 1948, except for a few days around the start of 1948) related retrospectively that "the main and most stunning revolution" he discovered upon returning home was the formation of an army in the Yishuv. He had no doubt as to who had instigated this "revolution"—Ben-Gurion.[121] In line with this observation, and in what might come as a surprise to those who only remember their deteriorating relations over the next decade, it was Shertok who dubbed Ben-Gurion the "founding father" of the State of Israel. In a speech before the Mapai Council on June 18, 1948, and in light of criticism voiced by Mapam leaders and senior officers in the Palmach (the Haganah's strike force) regarding Ben-Gurion as defense minister and his management of the war, Shertok stated that there were many things the Jews' adversaries were not taking into account. He listed the strong Jewish spirit and the courage of Jewish youth, the measures taken to acquire armaments and the Jews' determination to establish a state, "and another thing they have not taken into account . . . David Ben-Gurion, David Ben-Gurion the man, the visionary, the aspirer, the darer, the operator. And David Ben-Gurion the symbol, whose personality, whose life story, encapsulate the heroism of the country's pioneering and fighting generation."[122] His remarks drew thunderous applause, according to the minutes, but even more significant was the fact that this style of speaking, which has since become routine in Israeli politics, had been utterly absent in Mapai's customary public discourse and within the Labor Movement from its inception until that formative moment. Ben-Gurion did not need confirmation of his status from Shertok of all people, but the historical fact is that the latter took it upon himself to crown Ben-Gurion—"the man and the symbol"—as someone who, with body and soul, personified the generation that realized Zionism and founded the state.

Two days after Shertok's "coronation" speech, the *Altalena*, a weapons-laden ship arranged by Etzel, reached Israel's shores. Its arrival blatantly violated the terms of the first UN-mediated truce between Israel and Arab states. On June 22, after a stormy debate about whether to turn the weapons over to the new state's authorities, the IDF shelled and sank the ship *Altalena* off the shores of Tel Aviv. On the following day, prompted by Etzel's central command, hundreds of participants in the funeral procession for casualties of the incident, while en route to the cemetery, burst into the courtyard of the Histadrut building on Tel Aviv's Allenby Street. They brought the work underway to a halt and interrupted an Executive Committee meeting. Simultaneously, at a meeting of the Provisional State Council in the Prime Minister's Office a few streets away, Ben-Gurion was delivering a fiery speech. As he wound down, he declared, "Blessed is the cannon that shelled this ship. That cannon should stand by the Temple, if it is built. Of course, it would have been better if there had been no need to use it and if they [Etzel] had turned the ship over. But since they did not, the best thing was to sink it." The imagery he invoked should be viewed in the concrete political and ideological context of his target audience: Ben-Gurion was reacting to remarks by the president of the global Mizrachi Movement, Meir Berlin (Bar-Ilan), and the resignation of religious ministers Fishman and Shapira from the government in protest over its refusal to authorize the release of five Etzel leaders arrested for their part in the incident.[123] After all, Ben-Gurion specifically and the Labor Movement more generally would never entertain the idea of rebuilding the Jewish Temple, at least not before the Messiah's arrival, a cynic might add. Reciprocally, Etzel fighters who had joined the ranks of the IDF boycotted the latter's swearing-in ceremony on June 28 in protest over the *Altalena* affair. A poster issued by the Herut Movement, headed by Menachem Begin, declared, "One day—maybe soon—you will liberate our country from the whip held in the shaky hands of a small Jewish tyrant, just as you were able to liberate the land from the whip held by Hitler's disciple—Bevin."[124]

The significance of the *Altalena* affair for our purposes is captured by the remarks of Yohanan Bader, a leader of Herut, ten days after its founding on June 15, 1948, as the successor to the Revisionist Movement: "Is it not true that the government of Israel is an incidental assortment of individuals not elected by the people, whose status and influence and the keys they hold are a product of the previous period, a product of Mandate stipulations regarding 'cooperation' between the British and the [Jewish] Agency, and a product of this cooperation, which in fact continued almost until the very end?"[125] In terms of the Provisional Government's legitimacy, this outlook did not differ from that of senior officials in the US State Department and the British Foreign Office. At a gathering of workers' associations in Tel Aviv, concurrent with the Provisional State Council discussion, Pinhas Lubianker (Lavon), one of Mapai's most brilliant young leaders, sharply observed, "Today the State of Israel is more a desire than a reality, and we must make the Yishuv desire to become the bearers of the reality of our state."[126] This was a credible and accurate description of the State of Israel five weeks after its birth.

The fate of the Palestinian refugees was one of the main topics of discussion when the Mapai Central Committee convened for the first time after May 12. The meeting took place on July 24, 1948, shortly after the start of the war's second truce, which followed the "Ten-Day Battles" (July 9–18). During those battles, the IDF captured Lod and Ramle, among other areas, and at Ben-Gurion's orders expelled tens of thousands of Palestinian residents from the two cities. At the meeting, a few of Mapai's prominent political figures who had joined the growing circle of bereaved families voiced their opinion on the matter of Palestinian refugees and forced transfer. Shlomo Lavi and Shmuel Dayan spoke in favor of transfer and barring refugees from returning to their homes, while Sprinzak insisted on knowing who was entitled to establish "facts of dispossession and the forcible removal of Arabs from the country" and by what authority. The question in the air was whether, by virtue of the heavy human toll they had paid, bereaved fathers were more entitled than others to issue political rulings surrounding the cost entailed in losing their son. Ben-Gurion, in characteristic fashion, distinguished between the start of the war, when Arabs "who harmed us" were differentiated from those who did not, and the present circumstances of all-out war involving "solidarity, whether we want it or not," whereby belonging to a particular population group automatically triggered a collective verdict. He illustrated his point: "What sin did a million Jewish babies commit? They were Jews and had to be slaughtered because Jews had to be slaughtered." He then returned to his premise of the previous year and the looming threat of extinction: "The Arab people has never in its history produced a Beethoven or a Goethe. They wanted to destroy Tel Aviv and we had to destroy them. Had they succeeded in their plot, there would have been no outcry around the world, just as there was no outcry when six million Jews were slaughtered. The world did not come to our aid when Jerusalem was shelled. The intention was to destroy Jerusalem. Tragically, we stand only by our own power and this is our final fortress. And when force is needed—it is needed. Otherwise we will be destroyed."[127] In contrast with the May 12 Mapai Central Committee meeting, this time, "the Central Committee meeting found it appropriate not to conclude its deliberations with written resolutions."[128] In effect, Mapai had adopted a stance opposing the return of Palestinian refugees in principle, which by implication unofficially authorized their expulsion from newly conquered areas if the hostilities resumed. At the same time, the responsibility and obligation to formulate a political position on the issue were, in practical terms, transferred from Mapai bodies to senior party members entrusted with handling the state's affairs in this area—namely, Ben-Gurion and Shertok.[129] This was a testament to the degree of faith and appreciation that leading Mapai members generally felt for the two, and to the confidence that their actions would be informed and purposeful under the complex circumstances of the time. In other words, it reflected recognition of their achievements over the past year since the publication of the United Nations Special Committee on Palestine (UNSCOP) report.

In the military sphere, however, Ben-Gurion's powers were still constrained, notwithstanding his success in navigating a series of severe crises within the General Staff and thwarting a decision to establish a ministerial committee on security matters.[130] On September 26, 1948, the government considered Ben-Gurion's proposal to conquer parts of the West Bank (including Latrun, the Old City of Jerusalem, and Mount Hebron). Three Mapai ministers—Shertok, Remez, and Kaplan—were most vocal in opposing renewed hostilities on the Jerusalem front. Ben-Gurion lost the vote, which in later days he dubbed a "lasting tragedy." A few days later, he sought to re-raise the issue of an attack on the West Bank for government discussion, but the General Staff commanders persuaded him to refrain from doing so because such action would necessitate attacking on other fronts as well. Ben-Gurion had to make do with an angry diary entry: "Happily for us, these [people] did not have to vote on most of the actions taken this year."[131] Although his approach remained belligerent, he was also closely attuned to the political context of military actions. On the day following the "lasting tragedy" meeting, the prime minister stated at a meeting of the Provisional State Council that "if only local military considerations had been allowed to determine matters, we would not only have implemented the November 29 UN resolution [i.e., secured the Partition Plan borders] but, in my view, would also have been able to implement the Biltmore Program"—that is, conquered the West Bank as well. Ben-Gurion did not for a moment doubt the ability of the United States and the USSR to ensure that their decisions were implemented in Palestine, but he pointed to the difference between "what a government says and what it is prepared to do." The mistake of those who had advised against establishing the state on May 14, he said (hinting with veiled anger at Shertok and Remez), stemmed from their "not knowing how to differentiate between what *an American representative* [Marshall] *says and what the American military does.*"[132]

On the evening of September 29, Ben-Gurion instructed Chief of Staff Yaakov Dostrovsky (Dori) to dismantle the Palmach headquarters. That morning, Ben Dunkelman, commander of the 7th Brigade, had insisted that Ben-Gurion concentrate forces against Egypt in order to liberate the Negev; otherwise, it would be lost. In his diary, Ben-Gurion noted, "He's right, but it's necessary that most of the government understand this." Later that day, Ben-Gurion informed the General Staff of "the political problems that are now intertwined with the military situation—an attack on Latrun and a general attack, why in my view [option] A is possible, [and option] B—not now."[133] That is, despite the government's decision, Ben-Gurion had not changed his stance and was still arguing that under the present political circumstances, it was possible and necessary to attack Latrun. Zaslani reported to Shertok, who had left to participate in the UN General Assembly session in Paris, that Ben-Gurion had stated at a General Staff meeting that as long as the question of Palestine was being debated there, Israel would refrain from action that could be interpreted as aggression, conditional on the degree of US preparedness to deploy troops (on behalf of the UN) against Israel. In light of past experience, Shertok could certainly have taken this to mean that military action was pending and all that was needed was an appropriate reason to attack.[134] In preparation for the next government discussion on breaking the military standstill, Ben-Gurion took measures to ensure a different voting outcome. To this end, taking into account the General Staff position, he shifted the focus from central Israel to the south. During the months of the truce, Yadin and Yigal Allon (Palmach's commander-in-chief) urged him to do this.[135]

Until the government vote of September 26, 1948, Ben-Gurion had, according to his records, raised military issues only with the General Staff and the government. After finding himself in the minority thanks to three Mapai ministers, he changed this practice and took steps to initiate a "friendly persuasive meeting" with Remez and a number of second-tier Mapai leaders (including Grabovsky, Shaul Avigur, Levi Shkolnik, and Beba Idelson). At an October 5, 1948, meeting, he stated that "there is now no reason to fear sanctions, particularly in the south, and the British on their own will not provide open support [to Egypt]." Once again, Remez was strongly opposed.[136] On the following day, the political figures whose vote—"happily for us"—had not been needed in the past convened and adopted "the most serious decision since we decided to establish the state," in the prime minister's words. The ministers approved an attack in the south by a majority of 8–3, with one abstention. Surprisingly, the supporters included Remez, who explained that he was convinced by the certainty with which Ben-Gurion described the "high likelihood of victory."[137]

On the morning of October 6, Ben-Gurion heard from Bisgyer of B'nai B'rith, who was visiting Israel, that the United States had changed its position.

Bisgyer informed him that as a result of Edward Jacobson's discussions with Truman, the president instructed Marshall not to pursue the Bernadotte Plan "in its entirety" (as the secretary of state had announced on September 21 on the advice of Lewis Douglas, US ambassador to Britain). Under the Bernadotte Plan, the Jewish state would have encompassed the Galilee and a narrow strip along the shore stopping north of Ashkelon. Instead, Truman instructed Marshall to adhere to the November 29 Partition Plan to which he himself had publicly committed. Jacobson had approached Truman at the request of Weizmann, who urged him to meet with the president immediately because the Negev was designated to receive hundreds of thousands of Jewish refugees (we will return to the circumstances of this request). Following Marshall's sweeping September 21 declaration, delivered without the president's prior knowledge, American Jews began exerting pressure on Truman, which now bore some form of fruit in the public arena. Although Truman did not issue any statement, developments behind the scenes were sufficient to prepare the ground for the coming military action.[138] Truman's position, that the Negev belonged to Israel, played a decisive role (in light of Zaslani's telegram to Shertok) in the decision to launch Operation Yoav on October 15. The thrust of the matter was clear to Ben-Gurion: the Americans would not deploy troops or proactively seek sanctions against Israel in the Security Council.[139] The political tumult in Israel, which lasted about two weeks, took place and reached resolution without any conscious involvement by Weizmann, who arrived in Israel on September 30, 1948. Indirectly, however, in ensuring Israel's control over the Negev, his involvement contributed substantially to creating the conditions for Operation Yoav. Following the conquest of Beer Sheva on October 20—the main strategic and symbolic achievement of Operation Yoav—David Lazar wrote in *Maariv*:

> Our opposition leaders are not in an enviable position right now—neither on the left nor on the right. Last night the prime minister spoke in Tel Aviv, and who among our greatest "maximalists" would not sign their name, with both hands, to the text of his *proud* speech, full of self-confidence and dignity? "In order to reach the Negev"—said Ben-Gurion—"we no longer need the help of the United Nations or the mercy of the Egyptians. . . . Now the Egyptians need our mercy." Indeed, it is very hard to criticize or have a dispute along party lines with the minister of defense and the coalition government—against the background of *such* a formulation of our political and military situation, when in their heart of hearts the opposition members are also full of gratitude toward the government for bringing us *such* glorious achievements. The Israeli army has cleared the path to the Negev for us. The government of Israel has cleared the path to elections for itself.[140]

4

THE POLITICAL FOG IN THE LEAD-UP TO ELECTIONS

The year 1948 was marked not only by proclamations and battles but also by elections. The Jewish state's elections were expected to take place in October, while November 2 was the scheduled date of elections in the United States, with the presidential race at the forefront. Ultimately, Israel's elections were postponed until January 25, 1949, while the United States, as usual, held its elections on the scheduled date. The elections and their outcomes—unexpected in the United States and as expected in Israel— had an impact on historical developments during the Jewish state's first year. They took place against the backdrop of the Cold War as it began to escalate and the war over Palestine as it approached a decisive stage on the battlefield. From the Israeli perspective, there were three main items on the US-Israel agenda: de jure recognition, a $100 million loan for preliminary economic stabilization, and recognition of Israel's battlefield territorial gains as legitimate. Other weighty issues—such as the exhaustively discussed fate of Jerusalem, the Palestinian refugees, the possibility of an imposed arrangement, whether to engage in direct or indirect talks with Arab states, and Israel's admission to the UN—were considered less acute at that stage.[1] For our purposes, the key players in these political developments were the American envoy to Israel, James McDonald, and the American Jews loyal to Chaim Weizmann. The latter's input became evident during the second half of 1948 and early 1949 in two spheres: financial backing for Harry Truman's election and a series of power struggles in the Zionist Organization aimed at undermining Abba Hillel Silver's political standing in the American Zionist Movement. These spheres are related in various ways to the main issue before us now; namely, the consolidation of Israel's political establishment.

A few days after the UN partition resolution of November 29, 1947, Clark Clifford informed Truman of a conversation he had held with Edmund Kaufmann, the Washington-based millionaire who numbered among Weizmann's closest loyalists. In that conversation, Kaufmann voiced appreciation for the president's efforts; praised him for living up to his promises, unlike Roosevelt; and expressed hope that he would keep his promises to the Jews. Truman replied that he had not promised anything to the Jews; he had simply been implementing the Democratic Party platform. Clifford also conveyed Kaufmann's certainty that once the presidential election campaign was underway, many Jews would be prepared to contribute to Truman. This drew the president's attention, yet he still doubted the effectiveness of the promise and "commented that when election comes around they [Jews] would say that we've [the Democrats have] done nothing for them recently. Clifford added that they would be off and on sixteen times by then."[2] These vacillations would come to an end in June 1948 and would be repeatedly put to the test subsequently.

On June 22, 1948, Truman appointed James Grover McDonald as the special representative of the United States to Israel. Internal State Department correspondence described McDonald as a "professional Zionist." He had previously served for many years as chairman of the President's Advisory Committee on Political Refugees and as a member of the Anglo-American Committee of Inquiry established in 1946 to examine conditions in Mandatory Palestine. Concurrently, Eliahu Epstein was appointed Israel's official envoy to Washington, backed by the tremendous trust in him that Weizmann expressed in a letter to Truman following their May 25, 1948, meeting and a request issued by Moshe Shertok in his official capacity. From Israel's perspective, the exchange of diplomatic representatives signaled to the international community that the United States regarded its recognition of Israel as official rather than transient. On the day of McDonald's appointment, Jacobson visited Truman, and on the following day, Kaufmann, jubilant over the appointment, sent a telegram to David Niles praising the "excellent" choice and expressing his view that the best possible candidate had been chosen for this position. Clifford informed McDonald that his appointment was intended to ensure a credible line of communication with the president regarding developments independently of the State Department.[3] From Weizmann's perspective, this appointment ensured a foundation on which he could continue to cultivate close relations with Truman even at a great distance.

In July, as the first truce approached its expiration and the second phase of fighting (the "Ten-Day Battles") was about to erupt, Robert Lovett briefed Epstein on the State Department's current thinking regarding US recognition of Israel: recognition of the state was unconditional and unreserved; the only limitation was that the recognition of Israel's government was still provisional, as elections had not yet taken place; when elections took place, de jure recognition would follow. In a telegram to Shertok, Epstein described this as a substantive policy shift for the State Department, given how grudgingly it had accepted Truman's de facto recognition of Israel.[4] The shift was attributable to a change in James Forrestal's military assessment. In light of the battlefield victories achieved by the Haganah (and later the Israel Defense Forces [IDF], established on May 31, 1948), the US secretary of defense had concluded that "the most useful bulwark against Soviet infiltration in the Middle East is a strong, democratic Jewish state." The State Department adopted this approach, subject to the condition that Israel remain a "compact state" within the territory of Mandatory Palestine.[5] From time to time during this period, the United States unofficially readjusted its reasons for withholding de jure recognition, depending on developments on the battlefield. After the first truce expired, State Department officials insisted on clarifying the borders of the Jewish state for the purposes of granting de jure recognition, given that "tomorrow you might reach the gates of Amman" (after its shelling by the air force). From the American perspective, its withholding of de jure recognition served as a warning and means of curtailing unrestrained Jewish military expansion. The United States was concerned that if Israel delivered too fatal a blow against the Arabs, pro-Western Arab regimes could collapse, paving the way for Bolshevism to invade the corridors of power in the Arab world.[6]

These political circumstances presented Israel's decision-makers with a twofold dilemma: first, how to ward off efforts by the State Department, with British backing and under the auspices of UN mediator Count Folke Bernadotte, whose plan was to limit the territorial contours of the Jewish state; and second, how to extract as many concessions as possible from Truman at that time (in particular, de jure recognition and a substantial bank loan), given the prevailing assessment in US political discourse that he had little chance of overcoming the Republican presidential candidate, Thomas Dewey.[7] It is difficult to determine whether or to what extent Truman was aware that the Zionists were pressing for de jure recognition at the earliest possible date not only because they considered it vital but also because they doubted his chances of being reelected in November and did not want to miss this window of opportunity. In retrospect, it would become evident that their intensive campaign of persuasion helped somewhat in moderating State Department initiatives that undercut Israeli interests, even if it did not achieve the intended objectives.

In short-term retrospect, the failure of Zionist efforts during June–October attested to the relative powerlessness of pro-Israel White House officials, and of Clifford and Niles specifically, in addition to Weizmann and his loyalists, in the face of a president who, for his own reasons, was not interested in adopting their political approach. This was especially evident in the repeated rejections of Israel's request for a $100 million loan from the US government–controlled Export-Import Bank. Israel claimed that the loan was necessary to absorb Holocaust refugees. The prevailing view in the State Department, however, was that a premature loan could bolster Israel's war effort and prolong the fighting. Oscar Gass, the economic consultant who had helped promote Israeli interests in Washington, believed that the American lack of enthusiasm rested on the "vulgar conviction" among most of those involved that Jews had "plenty of money" to manage on their own. The State Department's excuse for dragging its feet was that it did not want to give Israel an incentive to wriggle out of discussing the Bernadotte Plan. For appearance's sake, this provided a seemingly professional, principled explanation—that is, the bank refused to assist a state that was engaged in war and had not yet obtained political stability (as if most of its loans just a few years earlier, to European and other countries at the height of World War II, had not been of this nature). Weizmann, backed by Jacobson, framed Israel's needs as commensurate with Truman's "historic assistance" on November 29, 1947, and May 14, 1948, but even the US president viewed Israel's conduct at that time as indicative of imperialist aspirations and a lust for conquest, which would only be stated if restrained.[8]

The situation in Israel gave American diplomats who arrived in the country during this period a different perspective. The first to arrive, on July 7, 1948, was Charles F. Knox, counselor of the US mission to Israel, who experienced the routine shelling of Tel Aviv by Egyptian planes during the "Ten-Day Battles." He participated in the popular practice of guessing which nearby street would be shelled and whether the next bomb would land on them. At the end of this round of fighting, Knox began to document daily experiences of this purportedly "imperialistic" country, including the ludicrous clothing of soldiers, whose uniforms spanned the gamut of possibilities, and who had to report for duty with sheets, shoes, and kitchenware from home. In letters devoid of any formality, he focused on day-to-day life, documenting his impressions as an astute and experienced observer of social phenomenon in a foreign land, having come to Israel from Caracas, Venezuela. His conceptual world, like that of his addressees, was not local. In a conscious effort to adapt, he described the besieged settlements of the Negev: "It's very much like our southwest settlements in the days of the Indian wars." Knox was encouraged by his observation that Israel's Jews differed from US Jews in conduct and appearance. "Here they have lost their inferiority complex to a large degree and consequently are not aggressive in manner." He was less accurate in describing their physical appearance, claiming that they were tall, tanned, and often blond. "I have never, anywhere, seen such healthy, handsome children," he asserted effusively, and "everything possible here is done for the little ones," he added without hyperbole. There was a stated and almost excessive effort to protect their physical and mental health, he explained, but this was understandable in light of the tremendous, widespread suffering the young generation experienced. Little children, he observed, were considered "the only certain future seed left to Israel." Knox also noted that there was less consumption of alcohol than in any other city he had known during his nineteen years of diplomatic service, whether because of its quality or its price. As to his travels across the country, he described how soon after venturing outside of Tel Aviv, be it to the south, north, or east, one encounters signs warning against crossing the border. He marveled at the local concept of distance and relayed to his sister that after touring the seaside city of Netanya, he learned that the border was a good distance away—six miles, he marveled—"far away, thank God."[9]

McDonald landed on August 12, 1948, and met with Shertok on the following day. In the spirit of the time, Shertok generously suggested that the government lend McDonald a vehicle (no longer customary practice). He also reported on preparations for a census and elections. Apparently, the facts changed when they were discussed with Americans: from August through October, Israel's political and institutional establishment operated on the presumption (indeed, decision) that elections would take place in November or December, but Shertok told McDonald that elections would take place "sometime in January 1949." In a letter to George Marshall, McDonald wrote that he was convinced that the provisional government was determined to hold elections "at the earliest possible moment."[10] Despite this report, in late August, Marshall prepared a memorandum to Truman stating that the United States should grant Israel de jure recognition only after its elections, scheduled for October 1, and the subsequent establishment of a permanent government. At that point, Marshall explained, there would be enough evidence that the government of Israel rested on the will of the people, exercised control over its territory, and was prepared to abide by its international commitments. In conjunction, the United States would grant de jure recognition to Transjordan (in response to the British interest) in expectation of Britain's concurrent recognition of Israel. In subsequent days, Marshall continued to adhere to this assessment of the scheduled date of elections, out of an interest in preventing Israel from relaunching military efforts.[11] Yet this assessment presented an obstacle for Truman, who believed that de jure recognition was essential for improving his chances of securing the "Jewish vote" at a time when all the surveys and most of the commentators predicted that Thomas Dewey would win.

Within two weeks of his arrival, McDonald invoked the privilege, granted by Truman, of approaching Truman directly. On August 24, 1948, he informed the president that if the United States took action in the Security Council to promote UN sanctions against Israel, in the spirit of the recurring threats to Israel conveyed by the State Department, then, according to what he had learned from conversations with David Ben-Gurion and Shertok, "they would fight both the US and the UN" because "what we have won on the battlefield we will not sacrifice at the council table." No doubt McDonald also recalled Weizmann's vehement statement to him in early August—that if the Security Council decides to take the Negev from the Jews, "every Jew would have to be carried out bodily." These belligerent statements on the part of Israeli leaders were undoubtedly part of McDonald's indoctrination into the ways of Zionist politics, but in retrospect, they also attest to the concrete importance Israel ascribed to conquering the Negev. Marshall refused to concede, and in consultation with Truman maintained the position that it was essential to thwart Israel's aggressive intentions of fully exploiting its military advantage to seize the Western Galilee and parts of Jerusalem beyond what the Partition Plan allocated it.[12]

A month after his arrival, McDonald advised Truman that now was not the appropriate time to grant de jure recognition, regardless of the date of Israel's elections. He believed that such a move would reinforce the moderate members of the provisional government, who were interested in preventing renewed hostilities to the extent possible. His position was apparently based on conversations with Eliezer Kaplan on September 9 and 10. He was further bolstered by Bartley Crum, his colleague on the Anglo-American Committee of Inquiry and editor of the liberal newspaper the *New York Star,* who had arrived in Israel for a visit. Crum reported his findings to Clifford, with whom he had a long-standing relationship.[13] Marshall angrily rejected the recommendation on September 17. Presumably, the secretary of state would have been even angrier had he known that McDonald's report on his September 8 meeting with Ben-Gurion and Shertok omitted the prime minister's explicit and pointed assertion—which the US envoy chose to record only in his diary and without embellishment—that there are "only two alternatives: US mediation directly between parties or war."[14] Marshall, who was not kept fully abreast of all the local developments and learned from his ambassador to Britain that Israel had postponed elections to November 15, reached an agreement with Truman that de jure recognition would apply to the government, not to the State of Israel (in line with Lovett's assertion in his July 8 conversation with Epstein). He held that de jure recognition need not be granted before the moderates' efforts proved to be successful. Marshall preferred to "stimulate and aid" the provisional government's moderates "in retaining effective control of a permanent government" once elected. He buttressed his position by referring to the interbloc crisis resulting from the Soviet blockade of Berlin, arguing that "premature recognition . . . would aggravate unrest throughout [the] Moslem world at this critical juncture."[15] The gap between the global leader's perspective and the battlefield reality as perceived by Israel's decision-makers left a window of one month (which might have been less were it not for the "lasting tragedy" decision) before full-scale hostilities were renewed on the southern front.

Marshall further informed McDonald of the State Department's belief that "we now have a most favorable opportunity to persuade both parties in Palestine situation to cooperate with Mediator in his truce and mediation efforts." On September 17, 1948, the very day Marshall dispatched this telegram to McDonald, Lehi assassinated Bernadotte in Jerusalem.[16] In a letter to his sister, Knox wrote, "We knew through our information service that the Underground were going to kill somebody—we just hoped it wasn't us." The following day saw the publication of Bernadotte's political plan, which Ralph Bunche, his deputy and successor, had actually drafted. Security surrounding the US delegation was tightened for fear that as a "last gesture" before exiting the historical arena, one of the undergrounds would try to assassinate a member of the American diplomatic delegation to Israel. Ernest Bevin's efforts to present the Bernadotte Plan as a sacred "political last will" to resolve the question of Palestine were fueled by his view of Britain's geopolitical needs in light of the steadily escalating Cold War. In this context, British military commanders sought to preserve corridors for military movement throughout the Middle East by maintaining indirect control in the Negev, which in turn, in their view, required curtailing and delineating the territorial reach of the Jewish state.[17] In early October 1948, Truman thwarted this process because, among other reasons, of the potential electoral damage it could cause him in the last month of the presidential race. To understand the circumstances of Truman's move, it is necessary to look at the role money played in the political arena.

"Money Time": Friends, Confidants, and Clandestine Contacts

The president knew the value of genuine, timely support and knew how to express appreciation retroactively, personally as well as politically, when such support yielded dividends. Quite possibly, proximity to the president and active engagement on the part of Zionist advocates loyal to both Truman and Weizmann also contributed to Israel's campaign to thwart the Bernadotte Plan. Importantly, it was only the reciprocity of their loyalty to both Truman and Weizmann that made their engagement at this time truly significant. While it is difficult to gauge the value of their involvement retrospectively, we can still identify some of its effects. The main impact of their contributions is discernible from historical records available to us. Perhaps these bread-crumbs were intentionally left for future documenters; perhaps they result from a less-than-meticulous weeding of material designated for posterity or from the natural inclination of retirees to relate some of their "past glory" when contemplating their life's work. In any event, we must approach the is-sue with a clear understanding that we have only a partial picture of the con-tribution these loyalists made to the new state. The common thread running through the mix of issues we will address was the matter of political financing that by its nature remained hidden from view.

Alongside the achievements, fears, and failures that characterized 1948, there were also occasional moments of amusement. One day, for example, David Horowitz received a letter in Yiddish from an elderly American Jewish woman who also enclosed a one-dollar bill. The letter stated, "I'm sending you this dollar, so that you have something to start with."[18] To alleviate the continuous financial hardship Israel had known since its founding, Henry Montor, the leading figure in the United Jewish Appeal (UJA) during the 1940s, met with several prominent Jewish Wall Street personalities on June 17. The participants, whose companies managed tens of billions of dollars, in-cluded Maurice Wertheim, father of renowned historian Barbara Tuchman and founder of the investment firm Wertheim & Co.; Benjamin L. Buttenwi-eser, a partner (like Felix Warburg, who died in 1937) in the investment bank Kuhn, Loeb & Co.; André Meyer, chairman of Lazard Frères & Co.; and Wertheim's partner, Frederick G. Steiner, father of renowned literary critic George Steiner. Montor sought their assistance in raising funds for a $500 million loan for Israel. Wertheim's position was that such a loan should only be granted two years later, after Israel had achieved military and political sta-bility, and that investors would only be willing to participate in such a loan if a body such as the Export-Import Bank or the World Bank first granted a loan of its own. Wertheim—a non-Zionist and former president of the lead-ing Jewish organization in the United States, the American Jewish Com-mittee, and whom Ben-Gurion had described as "my loyal friend"—noted that the UJA had other issues on its agenda, including raising $45 million for the Jewish community of New York. Meyer described a loan of half a billion dollars as "utterly unrealistic. In fact, he thought that the whole program in

Palestine [Israel] was unrealistic." He was sentimentally sympathetic, he admitted, but he did not see how the State of Israel could become a "going concern" anytime in the future. Buttenwieser voiced support for what the Yishuv had achieved and compared its pioneers to the revolutionaries who founded the United States, but he added that American Jews should remember that they are Americans first and must not be seen to demonstrate more interest in the fate of Palestine's Jews than that of their next-door neighbor. As such, a loan in the amount of half a billion dollars "was utterly out of the question." Buttenwieser warned that if it turned out that Jews were making very substantial donations to the UJA, "it must ultimately cause great concern to the Christians of America" because this would mean that they were not allocating similar funds to their own community.[19]

Montor summarized the speakers' collective position: a $500 million loan was out of the question, a loan in any amount at that time would dissuade government bodies from lending money to Israel, and there was no basis on which a business loan could be considered economically viable from Wall Street's perspective. Employing the style of a classical Zionist "sermon," Montor tried to shift the debate's center of gravity: First, many American Jews were rapidly accumulating wealth to the extent that some of those whose entire capital had once amounted to $50,000 were now donating that amount annually to the UJA. Second, because these Jews identified with Israel's struggle for independence, they were prepared to join the cause. That is, there might have been no basis for a regular business loan, but there was certainly a basis for what may be described as a "sentimental loan" of something like $250 million for twenty years at an interest rate of 2.5 percent. Montor added that while he did not wish to be melodramatic in a conversation with bankers, it was essential to bear in mind that if the settlement of Palestine had been guided by logical, economic considerations, then "the whole venture by Jews in Palestine was fantastic, and despite the advice of all the experts, Jews had gone forward." This was not a matter of granting economic aid for Israel's Jews, he pointed out, but of creating the capacity to absorb half a million Holocaust survivors from Europe and Jews from Muslim countries. Wertheim, Meyer, and Buttenwieser insisted that the UJA could not be transformed into a general lender, be it based on sentiment or business. Buttenwieser insisted that the UJA should focus on investing in US-based institutions. The meeting concluded without establishing a channel for the immediate flow of cash, and the participants agreed to meet again in a few months. Their position drew support from Harry Dexter White, Henry Morgenthau's senior adviser in the treasury and author of the memorandum that served as a basis for establishing Israel's new currency (the Eretz Israel lira) on August 17, 1948. In effect, the Jews of Wall Street had been given an opportunity to change the fate of Israel and its population and perhaps also to ease the suffering caused by war and reduce bloodshed. Yet they opted to send Israel back empty-handed at the most difficult and decisive moment in its history, at the height of its war of independence and amid its preparations to receive Jews from Europe and Islamic countries.[20]

In the final analysis, we should also note that White, who turned out to be a Soviet spy, died two months later, and Wertheim passed away in May 1950, three weeks before the expiration of the two-year period he had designated for reconsidering a loan to Israel. A year earlier, Wertheim and Buttenwieser had heeded Golda Myerson's and Montor's repeated pleas to establish a framework for a "popular" rather than "sentimental" loan.[21] This led to the preliminary groundwork that eventually enabled the formation of the Development Corporation for Israel (Israel Bonds), providing a basis for worldwide fundraising for Israel once it was able to stand, following the war and the elections. Ezriel Carlebach, who at one point derided Montor—charging that "of the doctrine of Zionism he knows nothing; of the doctrine of tumult and propaganda and the 'campaign' and banquets he knows full well"—actually had no idea about Montor's efforts.[22]

Two weeks after Montor's unfruitful June 1948 meeting, Teddy Kollek, head of the Defense Ministry delegation to the United States, called on Morgenthau to help fulfill an "extremely urgent" order he had received from Ben-Gurion: to arrange an airlift of one hundred tons of powdered milk and fifty tons of powdered eggs to the besieged city of Jerusalem within ten days before the first truce expired. In this context, Dov Yosef, who handled the city's affairs on behalf of the Jewish Agency Executive, had proposed that the cities of Tel Aviv and Haifa refrain from consuming hard cheese and eggs for a while and that the dairy cooperative Tnuva deliver all its products to Jerusalem. Kollek, fully committed to the cause, approached Morgenthau with the request that he "immediately" telephone Forrestal and ask that the US Armed Forces allocate the necessary supplies from their warehouses in Greece, Italy, and Germany. Thus the drama of the siege on Jerusalem, although it digresses from our discussion, illustrates Kollek's characteristic chutzpah, which would continue to evolve in the years after he became Jerusalem's mayor. At that moment, it was apparently the urgency of the hour that led him to think that he could enlist Morgenthau (perhaps because of the latter's affection for Dov Yosef, the man who had introduced him to Zionism in the early 1940s) in summoning Forrestal, by phone, to take up the Zionist cause. We do not know the outcome of this telephone call—if it indeed happened—but a partial solution was provided by Hadassah, which arranged the urgent transport by ship of about seventeen tons of powdered eggs.[23]

Dov Yosef's daughter Leila, who served in the Palmach, was killed in October 1948 near Kibbutz Dorot in Sha'ar HaNegev. Two months before her death, she described the mood of the time: "They used to say disparagingly that a young woman's role was to amuse the army. This is a vulgar statement, but essentially it's true." Leila refused to accept the rank of an officer even though she had held positions of command during the war and even though a family friend, Ben-Gurion, expressed his confidence during her youth that she would become "one of the prominent [women] leaders in the country." Of her experience in the Palmach she stated, "In reality our lives sometimes seemed bleak, but neither praise nor chic photos in the newspapers were what determined our value." Rather, the day-to-day life, "in which young women willingly bore every heavy burden—this is what inscribed them in the pages of history."[24] The aspiration to be included in the "pages of history" stemmed from self-awareness and identification with the needs of the hour in realizing the Zionist vision, and in this context, Hadassah and the young women of the Yishuv made a unique contribution to achieving the political goal.

The lack of money and the severe shortage of eggs, which Israel was desperate to remedy, reflected one aspect of the Jews' powerlessness in 1948. The record of the closed-door meeting Montor convened would have been lost to history had the customary banking practices surrounding Zionist matters prevailed. Instead, the meeting's minutes provide a peek into behind-the-scenes political workings. Only by bringing them into the picture, even momentarily, can we understand Montor's importance and weight in the financial apparatus, without which it is doubtful whether Zionism and the Yishuv would have achieved sovereignty and overcome the initial obstacles of maintaining it. Appreciating this fact is essential to understanding the nearly existential need for the role Montor played. Otherwise, it would be difficult to grasp certain aspects of the fierce struggle that took place in the inner circles of the American Zionist Movement in 1947 and the first half of 1948, and that erupted into the public consciousness of US Jewry with ever-growing intensity during the second half of 1948 and early 1949.[25] In Israel, immersed as it was in its war of independence, the power struggles within the American Zionist Movement, relations between the state and the Zionist Organization (particularly with respect to US Jewry), and Silver's status all seemed like undecipherable and sometimes random background noise. It turns out, however, that there was a close correlation between certain aspects of these issues and some of the themes addressed in this study, a correlation that some of those who were most involved sought to obscure. Here, we shed light on just a few of its manifestations, which survived the barriers of documentation and the passage of time.

In late June 1945, at Ben-Gurion's request, Montor began enlisting the seventeen millionaires who participated in the conference that led to the founding of the Sonneborn Institute. From that point forward, as far as Ben-Gurion and Kaplan were concerned, he was a supremely reliable confidant for the financial arrangements and weapons provisions required by the Jewish state, in addition to his role in the UJA. In July 1947, another organization that took part in these activities was established in New York—Americans for Haganah. Its primary purpose was to wage a propaganda war for the hearts and minds of US Jewry to secure their sympathy for and identification with the Haganah's objectives and activities in the areas of illegal immigration, settlement, and security while incidentally cultivating their aversion to Etzel and Lehi and the public activities of these groups' supporters in North America. The US section of the Jewish Agency Executive provided half-hearted patronage for the organization by virtue of the Haganah's role as the Yishuv's recognized military body, given that Silver and Emanuel Neumann would have preferred not to reinforce the "leftist" element of Yishuv society, which, as we know, controlled the Haganah. The main instrument employed by Americans for Haganah was its bimonthly magazine, *Haganah Speaks*. The news items and many photographs that appeared in this magazine made it, in retrospect, an unmatched source of information (even in Israel) on the 1948 war and its fighters. The organization's founder and president, Abraham Feinberg, had announced Weizmann's candidacy for president of the state on November 25, 1947, in the context of his extensive involvement in establishing the Weizmann Institute of Science. On December 1, David R. Wahl was appointed executive director of the organization.[26] In early 1948, Rudolf Sonneborn decided to close his clandestine organization and, in its place, establish a legitimate entity named Material for Palestine, Inc., whose mandate was to purchase military supplies not designated as arms (such as uniforms, tents, and ambulances) for the Haganah and to provide official coverage for occasional clandestine activities.[27]

Sonneborn and Feinberg were part of the "progressive" front that fiercely opposed Silver and Neumann at the annual Zionist Organization of America (ZOA) conventions in July 1947 and July 1948. During the first half of 1948, Silver and Neumann made a concerted effort to at least weaken, if not shut down, the two organizations headed by Sonneborn and Feinberg. They were politically astute enough to recognize these groups as potential bases of power for individuals who identified mainly with Weizmann, and to some extent with Ben-Gurion, in the Zionist Movement's internal struggle. There was no shortage of formal reasons: beginning with the aspiration to put an end to separate fundraising among US Jews because it ostensibly undermined UJA activities (even though the two organizations cumulatively raised the equivalent of 0.5 percent of what the UJA raised); continuing with the covert and legally questionable, or illegal, activities of Sonneborn's and Feinberg's organizations, which could tar official Zionist bodies; and concluding with an aspiration to grant the Zionist Organization of America with an educational and culturally current image, free from the taint of military matters or daily politics in light of the founding of the state. The IDF's establishment on May 31, 1948, and the announcement that Etzel and Lehi would be merged into it—so that presumably all would be working together—provided a rationale for Silver to demand the closure of Americans for Haganah. The US section of the Jewish Agency Executive adopted a decision in this spirit on June 10, and Silver notified Feinberg about it on that very day.[28]

In a scathing letter, Feinberg responded that until the state had come into being, his organization had operated under the guidelines of the Jewish Agency as the representative of the Jewish interest. Now, however, only the provisional government had the authority to direct Americans for Haganah. Feinberg somewhat disingenuously invoked the patriotic military allure that infused his magazine, asserting that the public relations aspect of Israel's security measures justified keeping his organization operational since it could reach broader Jewish and non-Jewish audiences than Zionist organizations could. Naturally, this allure earned him an entry ticket and standing to engage in the internal Zionist political discourse in the United States, and it was one of his main sources of power. In closing, Feinberg asserted that Israel's government representatives—that is, members of the security delegation headed by Kollek—were aware of his decision and sympathetic toward it. Kollek, furious, reported to Shertok that "Abe [Feinberg]" was "acting like a child" and that his "rude" letter to Silver had almost destroyed his organization's last chance, although in light of the *Altalena* affair, *Haganah Speaks* was able, at least for the time being, to justify its continued existence.[29] While this confrontation, which might in the larger context seem like a relatively minor personal and organizational power struggle, was apparently coming to a close, the political battle remained far from resolution.

Another matter occupied some of Feinberg's time in those days, as Samuel Rosenman related years later. On a number of occasions during May and June, he and Feinberg held evening meetings on the rear balcony of the White House along with Clifford; Matthew Connelly, Truman's appointments secretary; Frank Walker, chairman of the Democratic National Committee (DNC) during 1943–1944; and Robert Hannegan, Walker's successor, who chaired the DNC from 1944 to 1947 and, as Truman's longtime friend and fellow Missourian, had orchestrated his appointment as Roosevelt's vice president. One of the aims of these gatherings, which Truman occasionally attended, was to coordinate fundraising for his nomination as Democratic presidential candidate.[30] Truman's foremost biographer, David McCullough, whose work earned him a Pulitzer Prize, observed that the first half of 1948 was politically one of the most difficult and humiliating periods that any American president had known. During these months, the Republican-dominated Congress impeded the implementation of Truman's policy, undermining the Marshall Plan for Europe's rehabilitation, and in the latter half of June, the Soviets blockaded Berlin to take over the city. Concurrently, the Democratic Party was eroding from within and, weary and desperate, was also subject to a battering from without. Democratic congressmen from a number of southern states announced that they were withdrawing their support for Truman given what they considered his overly liberal approach to civil rights, and instead, they formed the Dixiecrats Party, headed by South Carolina governor Strom Thurmond. On the other side of the Democratic divide, former vice president Henry Wallace enlisted supporters to back his independent bid for president as head of the newly formed Progressive Party, whose platform included transferring control over nuclear weapons to the UN. Along with seasoned New Deal policymakers, Franklin Roosevelt Jr., President Roosevelt's son, led an initiative to replace Truman as the party's presidential candidate with the esteemed US military commander who had defeated Germany, Dwight Eisenhower. With Truman plummeting in the polls, the media portrayed him as clumsy and pathetic. It was at this point in his biography that McCullough chose to insert the president's favorite political saying: "If you can't stand the heat, you better get out of the kitchen."[31] As it happens, the "balcony meeting" participants were able to stand and overcome the heat of the kitchen.

On July 15, 1948, the Democratic National Convention, opening on a note that resembled the start of a political funeral procession, elected Truman as presidential candidate, thus launching the race between him and Republican candidate Dewey. For our purposes, it was at this nadir in the US president's public career, which coincided with Silver and Neumann's efforts to disband Americans for Haganah, that Feinberg began to fortify his position as the foremost "mover and shaker" by establishing himself as a discreet intermediary between Democratic Party presidents (Truman, John Kennedy, and Lyndon Johnson) and the Israeli leadership, a role he maintained over the following two decades. It was during the latter half of 1948 that his contribution gradually became clear. His behind-the-scenes influence was due mainly to what ultimately emerged as the most surprising US election outcome of the twentieth century, which forms a backdrop for our discussion.

The Zionist Organization of America held its annual convention on July 3–5, 1948. At this gathering, Silver and Neumann managed to score a victory over the opposition faction, of which Feinberg was a leading member. During one of the sessions, the opposition faction, led by Louis Lipsky and Montor, asserted that senior ZOA members bore a grudge toward the Israeli leadership under Weizmann and Ben-Gurion. Lipsky underscored his support for Mapai and the cooperative aspects of Israel's economy. Likewise, the opposition openly declared its personal, party, and economic support for Mapai's approach. Nonetheless, the opposition's defeat tied Ben-Gurion's hands, and on July 13, he instructed Feinberg to implement the decision taken by the Jewish Agency's US section and dismantle Americans for Haganah, even though he was actually furious about Neumann and Silver's extremely weak statement of support surrounding the *Altalena* incident. The reason he gave was "the need to preserve unity" in the Zionist Movement. Officially, Ben-Gurion was acting in accordance with an earlier understanding—that in matters relating to American Jewry, the local section has the authority—as reflected in his instructions to Kollek in December 1947: "Under no circumstances are [you] to agree to the dissolution of our friends' group [Americans for Haganah] or the special fund [Sonneborn Institute], or to cave into any pressure in this regard—unless the full assembly of the Executive decides to do so."[32]

Wasting no time, Silver published a statement on July 13, 1948, on behalf of the US section, stipulating that Americans for Haganah immediately cease operations—as the formation of the IDF rendered it unnecessary—and that henceforth information about IDF operations would be disseminated through the Israeli diplomatic delegation's information office and various Zionist bodies. Feinberg and Sonneborn responded that after fulfilling preexisting commitments, they would dismantle their organizations by October 1. However, they had no intention of heeding Silver and Neumann's order. Instead, Feinberg and Sonneborn coordinated their next move with Meyer Weisgal, Weizmann's top associate: on July 16 *Haganah Speaks* announced the formation of a new entity, Americans United for Israel, which would be neither subordinate to nor dependent on the Jewish Agency. In a letter to Sonneborn, Feinberg stated that in addition to continuing to disseminate current information about Israeli military activities and enlisting support for the transport of remaining refugees to Israel, the new body had the following objective: "diminishing and if need be eliminating the power of the very dangerous group of men now running the Zionist Organization of America, and who might eventually run the State of Israel if their plans mature." This group, he asserted, strives to achieve "political control of another country through control of its economy."[33]

On August 22, about a month later and amid the second truce, the Zionist General Council convened in Jerusalem for its first meeting since independence. Ben-Gurion began his opening speech by stating, "We are now in the midst of a profound revolution, the revolution of Jewish independence that has yet to conclude, and not all of its outcomes are given or known in advance." He warned against drawing a clear divide between the Zionist Organization and the state "out of a premature assumption that the state already exists and lies packaged [ready and complete]." Silver and Neumann, in contrast, insisted on a clear division between the two entities, arguing that otherwise, Jews would be faced with the question of a "dual loyalty" to Israel and their country of citizenship. The two sought to shift the main base of the Zionist Movement to New York and position some of its key departments there, including a political information department (to replace the political department), the economic department, and the organization department. In this context, it is noteworthy that Ben-Gurion's first political act after being elected to the Jewish Agency Executive in 1933 was to have this body adopt a decision to transfer the organization department from London to Jerusalem. Thus he would naturally have seen the proposed relocation as a matter of great sensitivity and potential damage. The concern in Mapai was that implementing what the ZOA leaders proposed would legitimize the nomination of Silver as sole chairman of the Zionist Organization.

The Zionist General Council (ZGC) deliberations concluded on September 4, 1948, with the selection of Kaplan as the only government minister to remain on the Jewish Agency Executive (without a portfolio). In his place, the ZGC appointed Israel Goldstein, the General Zionists representative and president of the United Palestine Appeal (UPA, the financial branch of UJA in charge of fundraising for Palestine) as director of the finance department, subject to the condition that he move to Israel. Neumann, after proclaiming to Mapai delegates that the organization department's work was not "Torah from Zion" and would be better handled by experts in America, had to retreat and concede the function to Zion. Given the circumstances of 1948, when Ben-Gurion challenged the American Zionist leadership—charging that "for us Zionism was not only the redemption of the Jewish people, but unconditional personal identification, as a matter of life and death, with the realization of this aspiration"—they had no reply. Berl Locker, a second-tier Mapai leader, succeeded Ben-Gurion as chairman of the Jewish Agency Executive, and Silver was reelected as chairman of its US section. During their two-week stay in Israel, Silver and Neumann expressed complete identification with the General Zionists' platform for the Constituent Assembly elections. Neumann even asserted that he saw himself as a "compatriot" and pledged that before long, he would return to live in Israel, although he did so only in 1979, a year before his passing. Silver remained a rabbi in Cleveland, even though immediately after the Partition Plan resolution was adopted, he had informed his congregation at Tifereth Israel (The Temple) in Cleveland that he was considering the possibility of making aliyah and building his home in Eretz Israel, in the new Jewish state—if it needed him. Whether he was needed or not, the conjectures about his immigrating to Israel to provide a focal point for leadership and political power and uniting the right in the struggle against the left's dominance in Israel remained in the realm of mere expectations.[34] Ben-Gurion summed this up in his characteristically merciless style: "Singing 'The Tikva' in Cleveland is a Zionist act, fighting and building the Negev is a Zionist act, but is there no difference between them?"[35]

After the ZGC meeting, *Haaretz* issued the first interim report card for the new political system, thereby launching its own campaign to be crowned the intellectual vanguard of Israeli public discourse. "There has emerged among us a community of professional politicos whose capacity for concern and understanding centers on representing the limited interests of their parties while entirely overlooking the common good," decreed the editorial. "The people have turned its affairs over to politicos of limited mindset," and "does not remove them from political life." Therefore, "it pays a heavy price for its neglect and it will continue to pay an inestimable price," the newspaper charged, disparaging those leaders who only three and a half months earlier had enabled the formation of a sovereign Jewish state after more than 1,800 without political independence.[36]

From a slightly more pragmatic perspective, one might conclude that Mapai, whose organizational capacity was a pillar of its power, had not yet had the opportunity to undertake a thorough overhaul of the visible institutional structures that would shape relations between Israel and the diaspora. Beyond the matters of principle arising from this reality, which necessitated systematic thinking that the circumstances did not allow, there was also the mundane personal dimension of politics. Golda Myerson was posted as a delegate to Moscow and therefore could no longer serve on the Jewish Agency Executive; Shertok's position as head of the Executive's political department became redundant with the establishment of the Foreign Ministry; and Ben-Gurion, who as part of the Jewish Agency had focused all his efforts on security following the Twenty-Second Zionist Congress, was now doing the same for the provisional government. The lack of attentiveness demonstrated by Mapai, preoccupied as it was with the war and the consolidation of state institutions, gave General Zionist delegates from the United States an opportunity to maneuver it into a position of weakness. The long deliberations at the ZGC meeting, which according to *Haaretz* reflected the whims of politicos, in fact stemmed from Mapai's need to extract itself from a bind. Ultimately, the party managed to preserve Jerusalem's seniority over New York as both the beating heart—in terms of consciousness, organization, finances, politics, and culture—of Zionist life and the seat of leadership for the Zionist Organization.[37] We will consider the concrete conclusions that Mapai drew from its momentary indecisiveness later.

The fact that Ben-Gurion was forced to step down officially and against his will as chairman of the Jewish Agency Executive, and that management of the agency's finances was reassigned to a figure identified with the General Zionists, was seen in the American Jewish public discourse—with Silver and Neumann's prompting—as a clear victory for them, even if many of their wishes remained unmet. Feinberg, who had arrived in Israel with members of the American delegation to the ZGC meeting, urged Ben-Gurion to establish an organizational financial apparatus that would allow UPA funds to be channeled directly to Israel. Otherwise, he warned, Morgenthau would resign as head of the UJA because the ZOA was seeking to exert political control over the monies funneled to Israel. Ben-Gurion took his words to heart but preferred to postpone the confrontation to a later date, after the war. In Jewish Agency meetings before the ZGC gathering, Neumann had made no effort to conceal the fact that the aim of relocating the economic department (which in practice oversaw trade and industry) to New York was to use it as a tool to channel private capital to enterprises in Israel.[38] That is, on the one hand, he and Silver sought to draw a clear division between the Israeli government and the World Zionist Organization, making the division publicly evident by removing government ministers from the Jewish Agency Executive and by not allocating UPA funds for Israel's security needs, thereby avoiding charges of "dual loyalty." On the other hand, while ignoring the political power relations in Israel, they sought to regulate and, from their position outside the country, set the state's economic and development priorities by controlling the flow of UPA funds designated for investment, job creation, and immigrant absorption.[39]

It was under these circumstances that, on September 10, Montor announced his resignation as vice president of the UPA and, in practice, as the person in charge of overseeing the diverse day-to-day activities of the UJA under Morgenthau's leadership. Without directly naming the two, he attributed his resignation to Neumann and Silver's efforts to undermine progressive forces in Israel and sabotage their economic freedom. Drawing on the jargon of US discourse, Montor disputed the right of General Zionist supporters to undermine Mapai's economic leadership of the State of Israel. As a result of these developments, the Zionist political movement in the United States entered a period of chaos that would last about six months. Although Goldstein had "promised" Kaplan, and in effect teased him, saying that he had no doubt Montor would lose, the confrontation eventually ended with the decisive defeat of Silver and Neumann and their dismissal from the Jewish Agency Executive in February 1949.[40] First, however, it was necessary that Truman and Mapai win the elections in their respective countries, and at this stage, everything was still shrouded in fog, particularly in the United States. Moreover, just as Montor was making his move, Feinberg's moment arrived.

Unlike the Republicans, for whom campaign financing never posed a problem, Democrats faced a challenge in this regard. Their sources of funding depended less on wealthy individuals or entities and more on small donations from a broad base of supporters with less financial power. One study on this issue described Feinberg, with an undertone of antisemitism, as the archetype of a Democratic fundraiser.[41] In fact, Democratic fundraising efforts required a good deal of coordination and collective strategizing, alongside discreet personal relations. On September 9, 1948, at 4:45 p.m., Kaufmann, along with DNC chairman Senator Howard McGrath, met with Truman at the White House. One of the outcomes of this meeting was a September 16 letter from Truman to Kaufmann. The letter, unusually warm even for the genre of presidential letters of appreciation, conveyed Truman's apology that his commitments prevented him from participating in a ceremony marking Kaufmann's appointment as president of the Leo N. Levi Hospital Association in Hot Springs, Arkansas, a B'nai B'rith initiative. Truman promised Kaufmann that, as he had told him when they last met, "I feel strongly that it is in the interests of the United States to assist the State of Israel in all ways that are reasonably possible." This statement echoed Kaufmann's earlier pledge to Clifford following the adoption of the Partition Plan. At 5:00 p.m., following the previously mentioned meeting, President and Mrs. Truman met for tea with members of the DNC Finance Committee.[42]

Among the twenty participants at this gathering were Kaufmann and Feinberg. Truman admitted to his guests that he was aware that most people expected him to lose the election. He believed, however, that if he had enough funding, he could reach the masses of voters with his message and win the election. When the gathering concluded, most of the attendees, including Feinberg but not Kaufmann, continued to the DNC headquarters, where McGrath, who moderated the discussion, stated, "Well, boys, we have a problem." Silence descended, according to Feinberg's description. There was a need for money to fund Truman's plans for a whistle-stop campaign throughout the southern and midwestern states, including Iowa, Texas, Oklahoma, Missouri, and Illinois. Moreover, a suitable candidate was needed to chair the fundraising committee for Truman's election campaign. Bernard Baruch, a wealthy anti-Zionist Jew whose aversion to Zionism softened in the aftermath of World War II, agreed to provide $2,500 for Truman's campaign headquarters to purchase balloons and noisemakers during the Democratic National Convention. But he declined the president's request to chair his fundraising committee, as did other potential candidates in light of the lack of funding and low probability of victory.[43] The youngest member of this group, Feinberg, had to leave to catch the train to New York, but before leaving, he declared that considering the president's support for Israel, it was essential that he receive a fair chance. Feinberg therefore pledged on behalf of himself and Kaufmann to raise $100,000 toward this goal within two weeks. Feinberg later recalled, with no small measure of satisfaction, that instead of two weeks, only two days passed before he informed Connelly (Truman's close adviser), as the latter was about to set out for Truman's regular weekend sailing trip on the presidential yacht, that he had secured the total sum pledged.[44]

Evidently, however, Feinberg's recollection was inaccurate. It actually took him less than twenty-four hours, as the yacht, with Connelly on board, set sail at 4:00 p.m. on the day following the gathering at DNC headquarters. A week later, on September 15, 1948, Feinberg was granted a personal visit with the president at the White House, alongside McGrath and William Boyle Jr., a close political associate of Truman's from Kansas who would chair the DNC during 1949–1951.[45] On the following day, Truman sent his warm letter to Kaufmann, and on the day following that, he set out for his whistle-stop tour of the southern and midwestern states. This date, September 17, also marked the assassination in Jerusalem of Count Bernadotte, whose plan for Palestine was published the next day. The struggle over Palestine and the struggle for the presidency were merged, as far as Ben-Gurion, Weizmann, and their US Jewish supporters, as well as detractors (principally Silver), were concerned.

On September 21, as noted earlier, Marshall announced the adoption of the Bernadotte Plan "in its entirety." A week later, Epstein, having seemingly lost touch with reality, identified "two fronts" at a meeting of the Jewish Agency Executive's US section: public opinion and Truman. He urged that "every possible man and group of people" be called into action to put pressure on Truman to uphold his pledge. As if the entire fate of Israel rested on his shoulders personally, Epstein declared, "I believe this is the best way to break Bernadotte's Plan, if Truman gives us de jure recognition or a loan, or even if he says something." His objective of applying constant pressure on Truman in the coming weeks, which were also the final stretch leading up to the presidential election, corresponded well with Silver's agenda. The "dual loyalty" that so preoccupied Silver and Neumann a month earlier had apparently dissipated without a trace. Silver now informed his colleagues that he had already been in contact with the Republican candidate, Dewey, regarding the Bernadotte Plan (Dewey had yet to review it) and that on the following day (two days later, in fact) a full-page ad was due to appear in the press, signed by the American Zionist Emergency Council, which he headed. The statement appeared on September 30, 1948, in the *New York Times* and *Washington Post* under the heading "Another Reversal—Another Betrayal," echoing the trusteeship proposal from March. It accused the administration of formulating the Bernadotte Plan in cooperation with Bevin and charged that "the American people have a right to know" how President Truman planned to reconcile the Democratic Party platform, which supported the Partition Plan borders and held that any change depended on Israel's agreement, with Marshall's position, which unequivocally endorsed the Bernadotte Plan.[46]

At this meeting, the US section addressed other matters as well. It first considered a report by a committee established to examine the dissolution of Sonneborn's organization, Material for Palestine, Inc. During the ensuing discussion, it came up that two days earlier, Americans for Haganah had announced that, contrary to its commitment to cease all activities by October 1, it actually intended to continue publishing *Haganah Speaks*. Silver was furious: "These people have since come to think of themselves as superior to any Zionist authority on the American scene and accordingly acted as such. The same people are behind Material for Palestine, Friends of Israel, the Zionist opposition, and now the attempt to break up the United Palestine Appeal." Jewish Agency funds "were used to build up a political machine. Now we have the task of dealing with this Frankenstein," Neumann charged. Toward the end of the meeting, the discussion focused on an announcement by the Committee of Contributors and Workers, a group headed by Feinberg with Sonneborn and Lipsky, among others, in leadership roles and a membership of about one hundred UJA donors and fundraisers. The committee called for the reprioritization of UJA activities in light of Montor's resignation. Its members strongly backed Montor's insistence that funds collected for Israel be channeled directly to the state, with no mediation or intervention by anyone in the American Jewish community.[47] It was clear that they were referring to Silver and Neumann. This was a direct, explicit, and unequivocal threat to their leadership of the American Zionist Movement. Feinberg was preoccupied that day, September 28, with an admittedly local but no less acute and dramatic problem, to put it mildly.

On that day, President Truman was speaking in Oklahoma City, delivering his only speech on communism during the course of the campaign. The speech was a planned response to Dewey's attack against him a few days earlier, in which the latter charged that the administration was not dealing firmly enough with suspected communists in its ranks. That argument turned out to be one of the most successful in the Republican Party's arsenal during the campaign, and Dewey's supporters tended to invoke it mercilessly against the president. The midwestern states were particularly receptive to this claim, which is why Oklahoma City was the chosen setting for the president's response. A crowd of about twenty thousand gathered to hear Truman. More significantly, because the approach to communism was such a sensitive and explosive topic in American discourse at the time, Truman's address was also broadcast live by radio for the first time during the campaign. At a time when television was still in its infancy and radio was considered the fastest and most popular way to transmit news, this was no trivial matter.[48] Among the audience was Jacobson, who had come to visit his friend on the road and lent Truman his hat, promising that it would bring him good luck. To broadcast the president's speech, his staff needed one more thing—money. Specifically, they needed an immediate $40,000 because without payment in advance, the radio staff refused to broadcast the speech. The campaign's dire financial condition was an open secret, the cash available to the president's entourage had all been spent, and a sense of despair and inertia was creeping up on his close associates. Were the broadcast to be canceled, it would have provided fuel for propagandizing the president's overall shortcomings. At the last minute, Truman telephoned Feinberg to say that if he could not make this sum available, the campaign would be in an extremely awkward situation because the speech and its broadcast had already been announced. Feinberg accepted the challenge and ensured the urgent allocation of the necessary funds.[49]

Sometime later, in a report summarizing the activities of Americans for Haganah between July 1947 and December 1948, Executive Director Wahl wrote as follows under the somewhat obscure heading "Project B":

> Prior to the Presidential election last fall, the Democratic Party was experiencing difficulty in raising the necessary campaign funds. To those concerned with the welfare of Israel it is no secret that many commitments and many concessions have been wrested from President Truman in the face of strong

opposing pressure from his own State Department and from many of his military experts. When it was made known that funds were needed if there were to be any hope of Presidents Truman's reelection, it was decided to use this opportunity to make a sizable contribution. Americans for Haganah advanced $40,000 toward the gift which was presented directly to a Presidential aide specifically for the campaign of the President. There is little doubt that the contribution has already paid dividends.[50]

The funds donated to the organization clearly went to a purpose other than their designated aim. Did they serve the political and security objectives for which they were donated? From an informed contemporaneous as well as retrospective view, the answer is definitely affirmative. It would be easy to present this redirection of funds as political corruption. Yet practices and arrangements that are customary at a certain time and place as a regular and legitimate part of the familiar rules of conduct can, at other times, in other settings, and from a different perspective, seem morally and legally questionable at the very least. One can, of course, delve into the issue more deeply, but for our purposes, it is enough to include this incident in the mix of murky events that characterized 1948. In later years, it would turn out that Wahl, who immigrated to Israel in the 1950s and worked as a librarian at the Weizmann Institute of Science (where Feinberg's standing would obviously not have been an impediment), was an active agent for the Soviet KGB at the time of the previously mentioned incident.[51] That is probably enough reason to return to our narrative and examine the main points of Truman's speech against communism in Oklahoma City.

In his address, the president attacked the Republican Party for trying to paint a distorted picture of communism as a powerful force in American life. In the context of our discussion, this mirrored the reality in Israel relative to the picture that British Foreign Office and US State Department officials were trying to paint. In the spirit of Weizmann's letter to him in advance of the UN Partition Plan resolution, on this matter precisely, Truman asserted that the Democratic Party's economic program had brought prosperity, security, and confidence to the American people, "and confident people do not become Communists." He continued, "People who are well-fed, well-clothed, well-housed, and whose basic rights are protected [at least white men, it should be added] do not become victims of communism." By invoking the horror of communism, Republican leaders were trying to make voters believe that they had "a monopoly on patriotism," Truman proclaimed, calling out to the audience in Oklahoma City and listeners on the radio, "Don't let them fool you!"[52]

Nevertheless, surveys as well as the forecasts of the major newspapers across the United States pointed to a decisive victory for Dewey at that time and throughout October. Three weeks before the election, *Newsweek* polled fifty leading political commentators, every one of whom predicted a defeat for the president. On the eve of the election, 771 daily newspapers (65.17 percent), accounting for 78.55 percent of the readership across the United States, supported Dewey, whereas only 182 newspapers, accounting for 10.03 percent of the readership, supported Truman. Two weeks before the vote, Dewey had a 6 percent lead over Truman in a Gallup poll, and professional gamblers were placing bets at odds of 15–1 against Truman. In any event, the president departed Oklahoma to continue his whistle-stop campaign with help from the state's governor, who, immediately after Truman's speech against communism, raised funds from local donors that enabled the campaign tour to continue.[53]

During this period, Truman also had to respond to growing Zionist pressure against the adoption of the Bernadotte Plan by the UN General Assembly. Shortly before departing for Israel, Weizmann managed to dispatch a telegram to Jacobson imploring him to appeal immediately to the president to prevent the plan's authorization, but Jacobson received the message only after returning from Oklahoma to Kansas City. In the end, Weizmann's fervent telegram had no impact whatsoever. Truman learned about it only after he had already conveyed to Lovett, via Clifford, his concerns about the overemphasis on the Bernadotte Plan. Clifford came away from a conversation with Lovett on September 29 convinced that the president had not completely rejected Marshall's position when presented with it back in early September, nor had the president's staff responded to the secretary of state's announcement that he intended to issue a statement of support for the plan once it was published. Presumably, Clifford assumed that under the circumstances, there had been no need for a public response by the president. During the September 29 conversation, Clifford conveyed Truman's strong reservations about promoting the Bernadotte Plan at the UN General Assembly to the State Department, which was enough to undermine its legitimacy. Marshall, in response to Lovett's report on the previously mentioned conversion, asked him to inform the president that this was a balanced plan, as evidenced by the strong yet equal pressures he was receiving from both the Jewish and Arab sides, which "may cancel each other." Nevertheless, the secretary of state now had no choice but to temper his efforts. In the background of this tense exchange were concerns on Truman's side about the possibility of a strong public reaction by Marshall, which could hurt the president's chances in the elections, and about Marshall's upcoming hospitalization and subsequent resignation.[54]

Had it been concern about Jewish electoral pressure that motivated Truman and his staff to take such a firm stance against the State Department a month before elections, they would no doubt have drawn attention to this fact to extract commensurate dividends. That they did not do so points to two complementary and mutually reinforcing possibilities: First, Truman's substantive position on the best approach to the Middle East from an American perspective had, appropriately, informed his governance in this regard. Second, the Truman administration genuinely appreciated the financial support that came from Weizmann loyalists, as well as their political support in the domestic Jewish electoral arena in the face of Silver's agenda, and it expressed this appreciation politically in a manner that was discreet yet also remarkably advantageous in practical terms.

A Final Political Effort: The Lead-Up to US Elections

During the month preceding the presidential elections, Shertok, in Paris for the UN General Assembly, and Epstein, in Washington, had to tiptoe diplomatically between what appeared to be an outgoing Democratic administration and an incoming Republican one, according to the prevailing consensus on the election outcome in the United States. Silver was the Zionist Movement's reliable link with Dewey and with John Foster Dulles, the Republicans' designated choice for secretary of state. Whether or not Silver actually supported the Democratic Party, as did the vast majority of US Jews, what we do know is that in four consecutive presidential elections, from 1940 to 1952, he took a public stance in support of the Republican candidate. Efforts to bridge Truman's aversion to Silver were unsuccessful, and in fact the president's antipathy only increased after the September 30 publication in leading newspapers of the provocative full-page ad initiated by Silver. Conversely, employing questionable diplomatic judgment, Epstein systematically briefed Silver on the substance of his discreet conversations with Truman's close advisers Niles and Clifford regarding the president's intentions surrounding the Bernadotte Plan.[55] Epstein appeared to be categorically ignoring the fact that Silver was increasingly aligning with Dewey and that his clash with Feinberg was not unrelated to the latter's standing as the Zionist Jew closest to Truman at that time. Naturally, this confrontation also had a personal dimension, but that was of secondary importance relative to the mix of issues described previously, which placed Silver and Feinberg on opposing sides of the US policymaking process generally and American Jewish policy toward Israel specifically. Their diametrically opposed attitudes toward Weizmann were perhaps the most overt indicator of their different outlooks within this mix of issues.

The closer the elections of November 2 drew, the more acutely Israeli leaders felt the disappointment of not being able to extract any sort of public political gain from Truman. In a "last chance" effort, Shertok urged Epstein to try to expedite Israel's admission to the UN through associates of Truman who were sympathetic to Zionism. Shertok suggested that to keep his own hands clean, Epstein could argue that if Israel's admission were delayed, Israeli public opinion would blame the United States, which would have negative repercussions in Israel's upcoming elections.[56] Epstein took this as authorization to present what was good for Israel as equivalent with Mapai's aspirations.[57] Ten days before the US elections, Shertok despaired of trying to extract a political gain from Truman and urged Epstein to have Zionist sympathizers apply pressure on Dewey to issue a public commitment that would bind him after the elections, thereby compelling Truman to regard such a preelection commitment as part of the future victor's agenda.[58] As they drew closer to the finish line, the two candidates issued nearly simultaneous declarations, even without Shertok's advice from afar. First Dewey and then Truman made pro-Israel statements, but in contrast to Shertok and Epstein's aspirations, the promises they made had no immediate effect.[59]

Another promise, of a much more local nature but important in itself, came from Morgenthau, who was visiting Israel at Ben-Gurion's invitation. On October 22, he toured Kibbutz Negba, which, having been devastated by Egyptian shelling, had just gained a margin of security with the conclusion of Operation Yoav. The day after he observed the brave men and women defending Negba, Morgenthau sent an impassioned telegram to Montor imploring him to raise $450,000 urgently for the reconstruction of the residential and agricultural infrastructures of this kibbutz that symbolized Jewish pioneering and liberty in the Negev. Specifically, the funds were to be raised at an upcoming conference of Jewish community leaders scheduled for two days hence in Pittsburgh, Pennsylvania, where participants planned to coordinate efforts opposing Silver and Neumann. Only a few days later, Morgenthau was able to report at a press conference that the city of Philadelphia had allocated the requested amount, following his plea to Montor. On this occasion, Morgenthau declared that "in Israel there is a hard core of democracy and a bulwark against the spread of communism." He added that "a dollar invested in Israel" by the American government "would be much better than the hundreds of millions of dollars being spent in a not far distant country [Greece] which as far as I can see is going down a rat hole."[60] Such is the power of the dollar that even devoted socialists such as Negba's HaShomer HaTza'ir members needed this money, despite its branding as a tool in the struggle against Soviet communism. Even for Ben-Gurion, the occasion justified a defense of Mapam's legitimacy, as he told Morgenthau that, despite its differences of opinion with Mapai, Mapam "would never take orders from Moscow that contravene the Jewish interest."[61]

Ben-Gurion would certainly have drawn comfort from Morgenthau's demonstrated willingness to confront Silver and his cohorts over the management of UJA and from his pledge that if Montor left, he, too, would step down as chairman. Conversely, Ben-Gurion would have been less pleased with Weizmann's remarks of October 27 at the inauguration of a new settlement along the Tel Aviv-Jerusalem road—Tal Shachar (Morning Dew), in honor of Morgenthau—where Weizmann voiced discomfort over "the spirit of militarism that may be permeating our people."[62] The main conclusion Mapai's leaders drew from Morgenthau's visit is perhaps reflected most clearly in a statement by Yosef Sprinzak in January 1949 at the crucial moment in the struggle for control over the UJA: "There is no personality who can replace Morgenthau at this moment. We do not have the authority to release him from the millions needed for our children here."[63]

On October 28, as Morgenthau was speaking at the press conference and winding up his visit, Truman's campaign tour arrived for two days in New York, home to millions of Jews. Speaking before a crowd of 16,000 supporters gathered, thanks to a concerted effort, in Madison Square Garden, Truman praised the people of Israel, who "created out of the barren desert a modern and efficient state, with the highest standards of Western civilization."[64] These were not mere words but rather a deliberate indication of precisely the type of Israel he supported and an explicit delineation of his expectations from the state in the interbloc confrontation. It was at this moment that Silver chose to publicize a telegram he had sent Dewey thanking him for ratifying the Republican presidential platform position on Israel. A day earlier, influential Republican senator Robert Taft of Ohio, for whom Silver was a political confidant, had issued a statement in a similar spirit. Silver's telegram delivered its sting in its closing sentence. He praised Dewey for supporting the position that Israel's borders not be changed without its consent, a cause for which "you spoke up at a time when others"—namely, Truman—"were silent," which "is a tribute to your sincerity and forthrightness."[65] Beyond the personal insult, this was an explicit call to US Jews who held Zionism and Israel dear to their heart, from the foremost Zionist leader in America, to vote for Dewey rather than Truman. The timing was carefully chosen as a slap in the face to the president and a means of sabotaging his campaign in New York. Had Dewey won the elections, Silver would undoubtedly have framed his move as evidence of his deep political insight and a valuable contribution to Dewey's victory. The reward would likely have been Silver's selection as Israel's and the Zionist Movement's inside man with the Dewey administration. Would his political career then have skyrocketed, reaching its zenith in the Israeli public arena? We cannot know, for history chose a different course, one that led to his downfall and to the omission from collective memory of the major role he played in the struggle for Israel's statehood.

From an Israeli perspective that is slightly less sympathetic than customary to New York Jews and their political judgment, it appears that at the most decisive moment in Israel's seventy years, a significant portion of New York Jewry cast their votes for president based on various factors other than the welfare and existence of an independent Jewish state in the Middle East. In his October 28 Madison Square Garden speech, Truman verged on declaring an open rift with Marshall regarding Israel's borders. He asserted that the state "must be large enough, free enough and strong enough to make its people self-supporting and secure" and made no mention of the Bernadotte Plan, as the *New York Times* observed in the opening paragraph of its main headline story, which covered the presidential visit, and as *Haaretz* echoed for its Hebrew reader.[66]

Governor Dewey defeated Truman by a majority of 61,000 votes out of nearly six million, while Wallace received more than half a million votes in New York State (accounting for nearly half of all the votes he received at the national level, suggesting that a vote for him was a progressive-radical protest vote without concrete political impact). Many of Wallace's supporters in New York were Jews, most of whom were potential Truman voters whose choice of Wallace could have cost Truman the presidency. In Ohio, Taft and Silver's state, Truman won by a hair's breadth of 7,107 votes out of 2.9 million, and Wallace drew 37,000 votes. Likewise in California, Truman defeated Dewey by a majority of slightly under 18,000 votes out of a total of four million, while Wallace received 190,000 votes. In Illinois, too, the results were close, with Truman winning by a majority of thirty thousand votes out of nearly four million. Only 29,194 additional Jewish votes in favor of Dewey, as Silver hoped—for example, 3,554, 8,933, and 16,807, respectively from Ohio (Cleveland), California (Los Angeles), and Illinois (Chicago)—would have been sufficient for Truman's defeat. In a tone of genuine concern mixed with customary Jewish self-consolation, *Haaretz* editorialized that at least "the election outcome proved that Truman's policy towards our problems did not sabotage his victory."[67]

There was someone who took pains to ensure this. Silver's declaration of support for Dewey was somewhat moderated within the American Zionist arena by the funds Feinberg raised so that the president's last election speech, in St. Louis, could be broadcast by radio and a large announcement Jacobson published in the *Kansas City Jewish Chronicle* on October 29. In this announcement, alongside photographs of Truman and Weizmann to-gether and a series of pro-Truman statements, Jacobson vehemently pointed out to Silver that, as he knew, Truman was "not given to empty words and vague promises."[68] Truman's victory on November 2 demonstrated that this was also how most American voters viewed his leadership. An editorial in *Al Hamishmar* summarized the election results using the jargon popular with its readers: "Reactionism won. This time too it stole the opinion of the masses."[69] At least Negba (and other HaShomer HaTza'ir kibbutzim such as Yad Mordechai and Nirim) benefited from this "theft" to the extent that there was one.

In the months leading up to the presidential elections, Truman actu-ally made no concessions to Israel or Israel's and Zionism's supporters in the United States: neither UN membership nor wholesale dismissal of the Ber-nadotte Plan with its proposal for a territorial exchange between the Western Galilee and the Negev; no loan, no de jure recognition, and no removal of the arms embargo. Even his affirmation of his commitment to the November 29 borders could be interpreted as potentially casting doubt on the validity of Israel's battlefield gains. Nevertheless, during the months leading up to the US elections—through commission as well as omission—Truman granted Israel something more important at that moment than all of the above combined: the leeway and time to implement Operations Yoav and Hiram without any real international intervention before, during, or after their ex-ecution. In a letter to Weizmann on the one-year anniversary of the UN Par-tition Plan, Truman reiterated his public preelection pledge, affirming that the United States would grant Israel de jure recognition immediately after its Constituent Assembly elections on January 25, 1949.[70]

A FINAL POLITICAL EFFORT: THE
LEAD-UP TO ISRAELI ELECTIONS

With the US elections decided, the military and political reality in Israel as it approached its Constituent Assembly elections still remained an open ques-tion. The dilemma of whether and how to try to shape the outcome in terms of American interests surfaced increasingly in closed-door discussions and public discourse. On November 13, during the annual UN General Assembly session in Paris, Marshall held a side meeting with Shertok. A week and a half earlier, the Security Council had called on Israel to withdraw to its pre–Operation Yoav boundaries, although a preelection intervention by Tru-man had weakened the force of this resolution.[71] Shertok made it clear that his government (and he) would refuse to abide by the toothless resolution, which lacked any threat of sanctions or immediate military intervention. In response, and this time from a different perspective, as he marveled at Israel's military gains, Marshall reiterated his May 8 warning not to "overplay your hand" militarily. The secretary of state conveyed that "we were not necessarily concerned as to what [a territorial] agreement [contained] as long as it did not involve conquest by war." Marshall cautioned that if Israel flouted or defied the UN or the Security Council—that is, refused to withdraw or renewed its military attacks—"it seemed clear it would be unable to gain admission to the United Nations, and that such other matters as loans and de jure recognition would, of course, be affected." Shertok explained that Israel had to maintain a policy of neutrality between East and West for a number of reasons: the political assistance it was receiving from the Soviet Union in UN deliberations, the many Jews living in Soviet territories and the fear of being disconnected from them, and the arms it was receiving from Czechoslovakia. On the final point, Shertok underscored that Israel had first approached the United States, and the United States had been the first to refuse. He pledged that Israel would not allow Eastern bloc military bases on its territory, but by the same token, it could not allow the Western bloc to establish bases therein because that would result in the Soviet Union severing relations.[72] In many respects, their conversation had the tone of a concluding summary, marking the end of Marshall's tenure as overseer of US policy in the Middle East. Presumably, this was not the type of encounter Marshall had intended.

Two weeks earlier, with only a few days to go before the presidential elections, Lovett had informed Marshall that expert forecasts were predicting a 5 percent lead for Dewey. Therefore, Lovett continued, and given the rumors about Israel's elections being postponed to December, as well as Arab and British concerns, it was vital to consider "the immediate next step in light of [a] possible change of Administration." As a seasoned civil servant who appreciated that his position derived solely from belonging to the leadership charged with conducting American policy, Lovett pointed out that the national election, "regardless of its outcome" (ostensibly, one must add) "gives us a new chance to review our Palestine policy." Lovett suggested that Marshall inform Dulles, who was on the US delegation to the General Assembly, about the immediate and long-term security concerns stemming from "Russian infiltration" in the region "through well-known methods."[73] He was almost certainly hinting at the various observations related by the vice chief of the Imperial General Staff for the British Army, Lieutenant General Gerald Templer, regarding Soviet interests and activities in the Middle East, as conveyed by British ambassador Lewis Douglas a day earlier. For our purposes, the most instructive point concerned the possible consequences of migration prompted by the Jewish-Arab conflict. First, in obligatory British fashion,

Templer's October 28 briefing reiterated the argument that, with Soviet help, thousands of Jews from Soviet satellite countries had managed to reach Palestine, which complicated matters for Britain and was the primary cause of its withdrawal. Second, the economic waste resulting from the departure of 350,000 Palestinians "set back by years plans for ME [Middle East] economic and social development which might go far to immunize ME against communism." Third, the Soviet interest in disrupting stability in the Arab world "is fostered by increasing difficulties of Jewish communities in ME, particularly in Egypt and Iraq." In the short range, this would upset the public order, and in the longer range, the disappearance of Jewish merchants—"economic mainsprings in many Arab states"—would "cripple national economies."[74]

Throughout the war of independence that followed Israel's establishment, the British Foreign Office and US State Department continued to nurture the claim, both in conjunction with and independently of the elections in Israel and the United States, that Israel was on the verge of falling into communist hands. The realist strategic concern that preoccupied them did stem in part from developments in Israel, but at its core, it probably derived from the potential for an ever-strong Soviet foothold in Arab countries through the exploitation of the Arab-Israeli conflict. We cannot know whether, in the absence of this conflict, such a development would have been prevented. What we do know is that ten days after Israel's establishment, Bevin postulated that the Soviets were hoping to increase their influence in the Middle East through the Jewish state, and in December 1948, he predicted that within five years, Israel would become a communist state. The British foreign secretary based his assessment on the fact that most of the new Jewish immigrants came from beyond the Iron Curtain where they had been exposed to a communist worldview, whereas there was no comparable influx of Jews from the United States and Britain, where they would have acquired a democratic worldview. Considering the decades-long democratic practices of the Yishuv and the Zionist Movement, which Bevin had encountered on more than one occasion, that argument appears hollow. Around this time, British Defense Minister Albert Alexander rendered his opinion that Israel was more likely than any Islamic country to become a communist state.[75] It is notable that seventy years later, neither alternative has materialized, but both featured persistently in the British American discourse of 1948, accompanied by an ongoing effort to publicize information in support of these claims.

A stark example of this systematic effort was the concern voiced by "Americans and British in London" (on the occasion of Ambassador Douglas's visit to Washington) over the extent of arms, aircraft, ammunition, and maintenance crews being flown to Israel on a nightly basis along the Prague-Tel Aviv route, as reported by *Newsweek* on December 6, 1948. Thanks to this support and these supplies, the weekly knowingly concluded, Israel had managed to build the largest aircraft fleet in the Middle East. And if this were not enough, the article continued in polished diplomatic style, indications were that Israel had been infiltrated by Soviet political agents, some of whom were reportedly already staffing government positions. McDonald strongly denied this assertion, adding that there was no evidence of any noteworthy communist infiltration, nor were there any identifiable communists or communist agents in the Israeli government bureaucracy.[76] British and US officials even described Etzel's and Lehi's activities throughout 1948 as guided by motives that served Moscow. These claims were backed by intelligence suggesting that agents from countries across the Iron Curtain were infiltrating their ranks.[77] At an October 10 meeting of the Joint Chiefs of Staff with Forrestal, George Kennan, director of the State Department's Political Planning Staff, reported that thirty-three members of the "Stern Gang" (Lehi) who had a direct part in Bernadotte's assassination had returned from Israel to Czechoslovakia, having left it in order to carry out the operation.[78] While these claims have no basis in reality, they did reflect a prevailing mindset among senior US officials.

The new state's international orientation—between East and West—was an important issue at the time. Mapam's identification with the Soviet "World of Tomorrow" clashed with Mapai's inclination to regard the United States as the decisive power to ensure the young state's survival.[79] A particularly harsh assessment of the international threats posed by the Jewish state was that of Harold Beeley, who had served as secretary of the Anglo-American Committee in 1946. Of the British Foreign Office staff, Beeley evidently had the most influence on Bevin's position on Palestine in those days. On December 23, 1948, at a meeting with the US deputy ambassador to London that addressed the likelihood of Israel becoming a communist state, Beeley stated that the Jews currently in Palestine and those destined to arrive were not, as a group, communists and did not want Israel to become a communist state. On the whole, he added, they tended toward the West, and the experience of those arriving from beyond the Iron Curtain only detracted from any aspiration to adopt a similar regime in Israel. Up to this point, he was correct, from a retrospective outlook, and even at the time, it was hard for him to deny the manifest reality. Nonetheless, Beeley was convinced that Israel would become the "communist capital" of the Middle East because the presence of a communist party, even if small, provided an ideal locus for a Soviet base of operations in neighboring countries. Whether the government of Israel was aware of it or not, according to him, this hinged on the

Soviet Union. After the immigration of Holocaust survivors was completed, Beeley continued, immigrants from the Soviet Union and its satellite countries would have their turn. He assessed that the Soviet Union would seize control over this wave of immigrants, as it was doing at the time in Romania, where Zionist activity had been suspended and the Romanian Communist Party was overseeing Jewish emigration. Beatty predicted that at some stage, Israel would realize that to cope with the immigrants who had already arrived, it would be necessary to suspend immigration. The Soviets could then torpedo that policy, he postulated, by deploying ships full of immigrants whose arrival in Israel would negatively impact its economic planning.[80] As it turned out, if even the smallest fraction of Beeley's forecast about communist activities being exported to Israel proved to be true, it still left no imprint whatsoever on Israel or the Middle East in either the near or long term. As to the wondrous vision of Soviet-deployed ships laden with Jews bound for Israel against the wishes of the Jewish state, it existed only in Beeley's biased intellectual imagination. Nonetheless, his remarks are of value in exposing the type of information, analysis, and professional interpretation regularly channeled to Bevin and others responsible for shaping Britain's Middle East policy at the time.

The Americans had their own "professionals." In mid-November 1948, Samuel Klaus, special assistant to the Department of State legal adviser, arrived in Israel for a visit. Klaus, who was Jewish and possibly a CIA agent, had been sent at McDonald's initiative in response to Bernadotte's assassination. In certain American bureaucratic circles, the assassination had succeeded the *Pans* affair as an amplifier of rumors about communism in Israel. McDonald sought to refute these by having Klaus conduct a thorough, authoritative investigation. The adviser remained in Israel for about two months. Ben-Gurion, who met with him a few days after his arrival, noted in his diary that Klaus had come "to check whether this is a red country."[81] Five weeks later, McDonald could report to Niles that "his friend" Klaus "is proving a Godsend to us," as he had managed to investigate the ideological identity of the Labor Movement in depth. McDonald urged Niles to convey that the president should at least make a "clear promise" before the elections in Israel, stating that he would grant de jure recognition and a loan. According to McDonald, this would have a tremendous impact on the outcome. He also took the opportunity to convey how delighted Weizmann was that he had correctly predicted Truman's election victory.[82]

Notably, Weizmann, like the other government ministers and senior officials, also met with Klaus, but he had "difficulty" finding time for a second meeting. He explained to his close associates that "I do not like spies." Klaus's

(250-page) report remains classified. However, a summary by Foreign Ministry official David Meron, who accompanied Klaus, and the main findings Klaus shared with McDonald present a credible if incomplete picture of his observations. First, the state's close ties with the Jewish Agency, including its financial dependence on the agency for immigration purposes, gave the United States significant collateral to prevent undesirable developments in Israel—namely, alignment with the Soviet bloc. Second, the present administrative arrangements allowed for the infiltration of many agents from the Soviet Union, and the State Department's information about the presence of communist agents in Israel was correct. In such a small country, even a small network of disciplined agents could take over the government, but their being small in number also made it easier for domestic intelligence services to identify threats to the regime. Third, the state's economic development and capacity to absorb hundreds of thousands of immigrants in a brief period depended on its cultivation of private entrepreneurship and the import of capital from the United States, and this capital must flow not out of Zionist sentiment but on a solid business basis. This finding was reminiscent of Montor's closed-door talks with leading Jewish Wall Street figures. Fourth, the hopes aroused by prominent American personalities who predicted that the Jewish state would foster economic development in the Middle East and spread a pro-Western outlook throughout the region were unfounded. Fifth, the senior command of the General Staff and brigades was in the hands of Jews who had long been in the country or had an Anglo-Saxon background. Some served in the British or American armed forces during World War II and were inclined toward the style of training and discipline customary in the US military. There was widespread hatred toward the British and appreciation for the Soviet Union for allowing arms purchases from Czechoslovakia, but the Soviets did not provide direct military aid, nor did they have military experts stationed in Israel. The IDF did have among its ranks communist agents who arrived with the waves of immigrants from Eastern countries and who took instruction from Moscow. Sixth, politically, the real communist threat in Israel came from Mapam, not from the Israel Communist Party, whose power was limited. Mapam protected its standing by propagandizing its friendship with the Soviet Union, but conversely, its realistic approach to domestic issues and immigrant absorption weakened its pro-Soviet outlook at the practical level. Even individuals who might have served as a communist vanguard were reluctant to do so because the Soviets were unwilling to permit Jewish emigration. Klaus postulated that American assistance in developing large-scale irrigation projects, which would also benefit Mapam kibbutzim, would be likely to undermine the party's pro-Soviet inclination. The fact that the

Mapam-affiliated kibbutz movement, HaKibbutz HaArtzi, was willing to re-construct Kibbutz Negba with funds obtained by Morgenthau—a prominent American capitalist—seemed to validate this observation. Indeed, Negba was the kibbutz that most symbolized the contribution and sacrifice made by Mapam's predecessor, HaShomer HaTza'ir, during the war of independence. Seventh, the affinity felt by a significant portion of the Jewish population for Soviet-bloc countries derived from a sentimental longing for their homeland, which they nonetheless left because they were oppressed there. Eighth, the legal system, judicial practices, and juridical training in Israel was based on the British system and devoid of any Soviet influence. Ninth, there was very little unemployment. In the absence of industrial enterprises with a large workforce, there was no basis for activities by organizations that controlled masses of workers, and in any event, there was no basis for class warfare in the spirit of communist doctrine. Tenth, the international media operated unre-strictedly, presented opinions freely, and was highly regarded, while military censorship was limited.[83]

McDonald summarized the main points of Klaus's investigation: There was no substantive Soviet activity or influence in Israel. The findings actu-ally indicated the reverse, and to strengthen ties, officers from Israel should be invited to American military academies and government officials should be invited for practical and substantive training. In the second week of Janu-ary 1949, Ben-Gurion held a meeting with Klaus (which he did not record in his diary) to review the latter's visit. The prime minister told him that the government to be formed after the elections would not include parties that, while in the coalition, would attack its foreign policy. This was a reference to Mapam, McDonald explained in his report to the State Department.[84] Ben-Gurion did not make any explicit promise in this regard, as the elec-tion results were still unknown, but this was certainly a message to decision-makers in Washington, signaling that he was attuned to US sensitivities and prepared to take them into account in forming a coalition. This aspect is im-portant to understanding why Mapam found itself excluded from the first coalition Ben-Gurion formed after the elections.

As elections to the Constituent Assembly drew closer and campaigns became more heated, US and Israeli diplomatic delegates, in Tel Aviv and Washington, respectively, sought to shape their outcome, including by mak-ing use of Israel's previous requests in various areas. While presumably self-initiated, these envoys' efforts were fully aligned with their instructions. At a meeting Epstein held with Lovett and State Department officials on De-cember 21, 1948, the Americans pointed out that Israeli willingness to take "constructive steps" by withdrawing troops from Lebanon and lifting the blockade on Egyptian troops in Al Faluja (near present-day Kiryat Gat), in the spirit of the November 16 Security Council resolution, might place the United States in "a much stronger position to support Israeli admission" to the UN in advance of elections. In a letter summarizing the meeting, Epstein told Lovett that the upcoming weeks would be decisive, and he requested that the Security Council approve Israel's admission before January 25, 1949 (the date of Israel's elections), as he believed this would have a determinative and dramatic impact on Israeli public opinion. Epstein reiterated the importance of de jure recognition and a loan, emphasizing that anything that happened in the coming weeks would have repercussions beyond the issue itself and could shape the course of long-term relations between the two governments.[85]

Almost concurrently, McDonald was relaying his forecast to the State Department, predicting that Mapai would receive 30–35 percent of the votes and Mapam 18–20 percent. He postulated that Mapai would form a coalition with the center and liberal right. Accordingly, he recommended strengthening those elements that clearly supported Western "political freedom and socio-economic justice" by issuing an immediate announcement of de jure recognition, or at least of a loan, which Mapai could use as clear evidence of US reliability.[86] Two days later, McDonald wrote to Clifford (with a copy to the State Department), asking whether he had received these recommendations. "The struggle for the soul of Israel will be decided in and by Labor movement," he asserted. Timely action by the president on a loan and de jure recognition "could checkmate Russian attempts [to] weaken predominant moderate pro-western forces during [the] present electoral campaign."[87]

Israel, however, opted to play chess using the strategy it had been employing since Operation Nachshon in April. On the afternoon of December 22, 1948, it launched Operation Horev southwest of Beer Sheva. A week earlier, the Security Council had turned down Israel's request for UN admission. Those accustomed to viewing the events of the past year as "miracles," lamented a Davar editorial, "cannot explain why the miracle that was supposed to occur this month is lagging behind."[88] Would a different Security Council decision have prevented this operation? The government deliberations leading up to the operation indicate that it was not a significant consideration. This time Shertok, in Paris, was not asked his opinion, and Rosenblit's request to hold a government meeting before launching the operation only came to fruition, as Ben-Gurion made clear, thanks to divine intervention: rain delayed the launch by a few days. Only Remez and Bernstein voiced opposition to the operation. This time, even Rosenblit and Kaplan supported military action in the south, which obviated the need for a vote.

The aim, according to Ben-Gurion, was to eliminate "our conflict with Egypt by expelling them [Egyptian troops] from the Negev" in order to bring the entire war to an end.[89] As far as the United States was concerned, Israel's action took McDonald's recommendations off the agenda for the time being.

The IDF's battlefield success, as it crossed the international border with Egypt on its way to conquering El-Arish on December 28, prompted US demands, accompanied by British threats, that Israel withdraw its forces. Under presidential orders, McDonald delivered an explicit warning to Shertok, Ben-Gurion, and Weizmann on December 31, although the seriousness of the US warning was most evident in a message delivered via Clifford to Feinberg and from him to Shertok a day earlier.[90] On January 2, 1949, Israel completed its withdrawal from Egyptian territory, and three days later, McDonald reiterated his recommendation that the United States immediately grant Israel de jure recognition or at least approve a loan, as a means of counterbalancing Israel's forced withdrawal. He pointed out that the military and public opinion view the withdrawal as a substantial loss that would cause Israel to "bleed to death" and provide extremists (in American eyes) on the right and the left (namely, Herut and Mapam) with election campaign propaganda.[91]

On January 10, Weizmann informed McDonald that in a few days, five teams of Weizmann Institute scientists would be setting out to conduct a survey of the Negev. Perhaps he was sharing this information as a way of discreetly conveying the Israeli leadership's trust in the Truman administration, or perhaps in gratitude that the president had consistently supported Israel's territorial inclusion of the Negev, even at the cost of a temporary and unintentional military confrontation with Britain. Israel, he pledged, would welcome American cooperation in exploring the region's minerals, including "iron ore, possibly two million tons, chrome, potash, oil in unknown quantities and possibly uranium." With the nuclear age just dawning, this last item was of course at the top of the list. About a week and a half later, Weizmann informed McDonald "in strictest confidence and not to be transmitted" that early findings revealed radioactive rock formations, although it remained unclear whether they contained uranium or thorium. The researchers believed that the material flowed downward from a more elevated source, Weizmann explained, promising that the search would continue. McDonald consulted Knox in deliberating whether to pass the information along and concluded that a head of state would not provide information to another head of state's representative unless he wanted the information to be reported, even if he claimed otherwise.[92]

In the absence of Israeli records, we cannot know whether Weizmann had consulted with Ben-Gurion before disclosing this. The fact that no noteworthy sources of uranium in the Negev have come to light does not detract from

Weizmann's display of trust in his contacts with Truman, perhaps bolstered by an assumption that this information would reach the Americans anyway. In any event, this was an unmediated testament, following immediately after the conclusion of hostilities, to Israel's alignment with the potential interests of the Western world in the Negev. McDonald was hardly apathetic to this dimension. Far from the decision-making center and swept away by the importance of his mandate, he adopted a fleeting idea proposed by his staff and wrote to the State Department on January 18, 1949, stating that with Israel's elections approaching, nothing could more effectively buttress the political forces supporting it in the United States than a commitment made during the presidential inaugural speech (two days hence) to grant de jure recognition and a loan to Israel.[93] As one might expect, Truman's inaugural speech made no mention of Israel. Ten days before the Constituent Assembly elections, Knox voiced concern that if Mapai did not win, a confrontation was likely to erupt between the right and the left, resulting in a military coup.[94] Apparently, the pattern of regime change Knox had encountered in South America during his previous diplomatic assignment did not necessarily apply to Israel.

Ultimately, the United States granted Israel de jure recognition six days after its elections. In contrast, the US government–owned Export-Import Bank announced on January 19 that it would grant Israel a $100 million loan for economic and public development. A day earlier, Foreign Secretary Bevin had informed the Parliament of Britain's intention to release the last of the detainees held in Cyprus.[95] Was the US decision to take a monetary approach, of all the potential means of influencing the elections, informed by a measure of antisemitism—in the sense that Jews understand the "language of money"? We can say with certainty that the answer is no. *Davar* described the loan and the release of detainees as evidence that the "final doubts about the political and economic stability of the Jewish state" had dissipated, although it was clear that the timing was meant to benefit Mapai in the final days before the vote. The public, however, was not troubled by this, McDonald reported to his superiors, though Herut and Mapam were accusing the provisional government of having sold out to the West. An editorial in *Al Hamishmar* described the US and British measures as "an attack of friendliness" and a sign of Israel's possible submission to imperialist forces. Herut vowed that "the plot for foreign intervention will be unraveled!" And *Maariv*'s Carlebach rushed to issue his verdict: "This money is given to sovereign states as a bribe," and regardless of how it is used, "a bribe remains a bribe."[96] There were times in the past when this was the only form of a "bribe" received by politicians in the Jewish state, whether during elections, as discussed next, or at other times.

5

THE PARLIAMENT AND THE PRESIDENCY

ELECTIONS TO THE CONSTITUENT ASSEMBLY: BETWEEN WAR AND PEACE

The political process that produced the electoral system for Israel's Constituent Assembly and the developments during the preelection period effectively demonstrate the political and institutional strength of the young State of Israel. The fact that Israel arranged and held systematic elections as soon as the administrative, technical, security, and political conditions allowed was not a natural or historical inevitability. The initial preparations, which included formulating rules for the electoral system and voting process, took place amid a war, with alternatingly intensifying and waning hostilities, and in an atmosphere of severe uncertainty fueled by fierce internal debates on a variety of issues.

The success of these preparations and subsequent elections was due to the steadily honed capabilities of the Zionist Movement and the Yishuv, which had cultivated and maintained an efficient democratic system, capable of fostering mutual trust, restraint, and cohesion, and of curbing specific parties' desires for power and domination.

Historical records and secondary sources regarding the elections to various institutions of a parliamentary nature that served the Zionist Movement, the Yishuv, and the State of Israel over a number of decades—namely, the Zionist Congress, Assembly of Representatives, Constituent Assembly, and Knesset—are quite scanty and incomplete. Despite the historical significance of those election results and the scholarly attention devoted to concurrent events, it is hard to find systematic, academic, historical studies on the electoral systems of, and elections held during, the Yishuv era and early statehood.

The same holds with regard to elections to the Constituent Assembly, except for Zeev Tzahor's overview and Yehiam Weitz's discussion of the Herut Movement.[1] In Tzahor's view, one could not have extrapolated the

Constituent Assembly election results from the Yishuv-era election results, as the number of qualified voters increased by about 40 percent (from 303,000 to 506,000) between November 29, 1947, and January 25, 1949, when the Constituent Assembly was elected. And this demographic shift would have been compounded by radical political changes attributable to the establishment of the state and the war of independence.[2] This chapter will discuss some of the notable milestones on the road to these elections, which marked "the first time the people of Israel elects its government," as David Ben-Gurion observed in a speech before the Mapai Council shortly before election day.[3]

The Provisional State Council approved the Order of the Elections on November 18, 1948, but did not specify a date.[4] At its next meeting, a week later, Interior Minister Yitzhak Gruenbaum suggested holding the elections for the Constituent Assembly on January 25, 1949. The proposal was approved unanimously. Quite strangely, this event—certainly a historic decision in the annals of the new state—was completely omitted from the minutes of the State Council meeting.[5] An editorial published in *Davar* on the following day stated that "setting the date for the elections removed the last sign of 'temporariness' from the institutions of our state. . . . Even the most sober among us would feel and admit the historic weight of the event we are facing."[6] This was also a sign of sovereignty. Yosef Sprinzak, chairman of the Provisional State Council, concluded, "Now, let us wish all of us elections that will honor the State of Israel."[7]

A foreign policy crisis erupted following the downing of five British planes by the Israeli Air Force at the end of Operation Horev in the Negev, on January 7, 1949, and it had a direct bearing on the domestic Israeli mood. With the Constituent Assembly elections drawing near, the prevailing feeling was that the submission of the lists of voters a day before actually launched the electoral process.[8] *Haaretz*, which had initially bemoaned the lack of "a central issue" in the elections, changed its mind two days later, underscoring the political rifts between Mapai, Mapam, and Herut.[9] At a speech in Petah Tikva, Menachem Begin, leader of the right-wing Herut party argued that "the choice is either Abdullah and Bevin near Petah Tikva, or us on the Jordan River." In a radio campaign speech, Moshe Sneh, then a Mapam leader, declared that Mapam's goal was to drive the invaders completely out of the country, across the Jordan, and establish "an independent, democratic Arab state" next to Israel, with an economic union, in the spirit of the UN General Assembly Partition Plan resolution and as if nothing had changed in Palestine during 1948.

Speaking before the Mapai Central Committee on November 30, 1948, the party's secretary-general, Zalman Aharonovich (Aran), had argued that as an election strategy, "the party should move to an offensive" in the sphere of foreign policy.[10] The conditions that prevailed during the second week of January 1949, with the end of the fighting in the south and the shooting down of the British planes, allowed Israel to demonstrate firmness in the international arena that served Mapai's interests as the elections approached. The calm on the battlefield was further reinforced by the launch of armistice talks between Israel and Egypt on January 13, an event whose historical significance is reflected in *Davar*'s headline: "The First Direct Israeli-Arab Negotiations Has Begun."[11]

The combination of these political, military, and diplomatic circumstances, which were unrelated to the upcoming election and which Moshe Shertok described as a godsend, laid the foundation for his decisive statement. In one of his most brilliant political speeches, delivered before the Mapai convention on January 12, he said: "It is not the question of what the gentiles will say that should guide our political considerations, but rather the simple question of what we will say." Shertok asserted that the choice before the voters was whether Israel was heading toward war or toward peace—not in the sense of peace as a desirable vision, or war for lack of any alternative, but whether "the political initiative should aim at renewing the fighting and continuing the conquest, or whether it should be directed toward achieving peace."[12]

Haaretz hastened to question Shertok's candor and his choice of "peace or war" as the main election issue, as it was hard to know whether this step would increase or reduce the number of votes for his party: "To the extent that the public mood is, for example, against leaving the 'Triangle' [an area near Kfar Saba] and the Old City of Jerusalem in the hands of Abdullah, many of those who were inclined to vote for Mapai may vote for the opposition parties, only because of Mapai's compromising position on this question." The newspaper reported that "interestingly, the top echelon of Mapai was sure that the public wanted peace immediately."[13]

Herut and Mapam, whose political views clashed with Mapai's and with one another's, each passionately defended its position. Begin compared the dialogue with the Egyptians in Rhodes to the negotiations Neville Chamberlain had conducted with Adolf Hitler in Munich in 1938. He recalled that "our sages said that in order to stay on good terms it is permissible to attend a gentile funeral, but in Rhodes we are attending a Jewish funeral," and he declared that "we can rise up this very day and inherit the earth."[14]

Mapam's Moshe Sneh reacted by saying that Mapam intended "to build a bridge between the two parts of the land, with the chance of creating, in the future, a united country, through a brotherhood of both peoples," instead of "the abyss of partition," espoused by Mapai, which diminished "the possibility of uniting the country."[15] A few days later, Mapam ceased discussing the fate of the West Bank in an effort to obscure its support for the establishment of a Palestinian state there and evade the accusation that it was willing to shed Jewish blood in order to transfer the territory from Arabs to other Arabs. General Yigal Allon, a Mapam leader, summarized its approach: "Peace? Yes, willingly, with the inhabitants of the country. With invaders? No!"[16] Both Mapam and Herut called for the withdrawal of the foreign armies from western Palestine and advocated that Israel not participate in peace talks in Rhodes that were based on the current situation on the ground, and both promised that their way would guarantee "real peace."[17]

The issue of war and peace was foremost on the election and public agendas as election day approached. It stemmed directly from the reality of the time and reached its peak in a series of mass rallies throughout the country on the weekend of January 14–15. On Friday night, about five thousand people thronged to the Esther Cinema in Tel Aviv and the adjacent Dizengoff Square to listen, directly and through loudspeakers, to speeches by Generals Yitzhak Sadeh and Yigal Allon, both of Mapam. Public attention that weekend was primarily devoted to the "heavy guns" (as the senior politicians were commonly known)—Ben-Gurion, Shertok, Begin, and Israel Rokach, among others—who spoke at various gatherings throughout the city.[18] The most significant speech was that of the foremost Israeli Defense Forces (IDF) general in the war of independence and commander of the southern front, Yigal Allon. In retrospect, one might argue that his remarks, which were clearly directed against Ben-Gurion's leadership image, set the trajectory for his subsequent military and political careers: "Our achievements in the battlefield did not come to us through miracles, nor were they the result of *someone's Napoleonic genius*; rather, they occurred because an entire collective became its own leader. This victory is not the fruit of [efforts by] ministers or great commanders. It is the victory of our soldiers, the victory of the people, of bottom-of volunteerism, *of a healthy feeling that preceded the political wisdom* and replaced many things: training, arms, equipment."[19]

Davar queried whether the "image of the army" that Mapam had in mind was such "that every officer would be like a Chinese or Mexican general, and carry out a policy for himself and for his party."[20] Following the description in *Al Hamishmar* to the effect that Allon "blushed like a rose" when Yaacov Riftin (Mapam's political secretary) enumerated his virtues before the audience at Esther Cinema, *Herut* mockingly asked whether Mapam intended to turn IDF commanders into "pinup girls"—beauties in bathing suits who flamboyantly decorated the pages of magazines read by English and American soldiers.[21]

More detrimental to Allon's career was the reprimand issued by Ben-Gurion at a meeting of the IDF General Staff, which he instructed chief of staff Yaakov Dori to convey to all the senior commanders, down to the level of battalion commander. Ben-Gurion ordered that, although any soldier or commander had the right to participate in election campaigning and could even criticize or disparage whomever he wanted, "an army commander is not allowed to discuss, at public or non-public gatherings, military commands issued to him," even while wearing civilian clothes. Such an act is "a severe breach of the integrity of the army and a grave violation of the General Staff orders regarding its code of conduct."[22]

In the two weeks leading up to election day, northern front commander Moshe Carmel, Givati Brigade commander Shimon Avidan, and Harel Brigade commander Yosef Tabenkin, as well as Sadeh and Allon, took part in roughly a dozen public gatherings convened by Mapam and made a significant contribution to its campaign. Concurrently, Ben-Gurion, as defense minister, seized the opportunity to publicize his own party's position among army commanders. At a meeting with Mapai followers on the day following his announcement to the General Staff, one unidentified participant complained that "in some units, the members of the party are oppressed by the commanders, and many of them have to hide their views."[23]

At this forum, Ben-Gurion referred to Mapam's political position with unprecedented blatancy: "The notion that we would kill ourselves over the establishment of an Arab state in part of the country baffles me. No! We are not willing to do that!" He doubted that Mapam itself was actually willing to do so, charging that "they say this because they are sure that as the minority they will not have to follow through on what they say." He concluded, "Not one soldier, not one drop of blood, not one *prutah* [the smallest denomination of currency]."[24]

ELECTION DAYS

The period preceding elections to the Constituent Assembly was marked by a lack of enthusiasm. It seemed to be characterized by overt reluctance, by the sentiment conveyed in the rhetorical question: "Is all this fuss worth it, while our boys are still at their postings?" Two prominent articles captured this phenomenon. A December 3 editorial in *Haaretz* sarcastically noted that of the four thousand Jewish immigrants who had entered the country a week earlier, only three did not belong to any party—the babies born aboard the ship, "and there is a strange feeling, that the Yishuv, with its leaders, is fleeing to the familiarity of election campaigning in order to avoid feeling the enormity of the historic mission assigned it."[25] *Haaretz* called for a cessation of the "amusing verbal struggle" over the advantages of capitalism versus socialism, which in any case would not change the political balance of power, and for the focus to shift instead to the common task of absorption and settle-ment. From the point of view of its editor, Gershom Schocken, a prominent spokesman of the Progressive Party, the advocates of private enterprise had "a few other strong cards, aside from votes in the elections," on which to draw in shaping the socioeconomic character of the State of Israel; namely, their financial power and abilities.[26]

The competition for voters centered on two main target audiences: new immigrants and soldiers. From the party perspective, these were large-scale, simultaneously well-defined and amorphous groups. New immigrants were being housed in absorption camps or were in the process of moving to tem-porary or permanent places of residence around the country. Some of the soldiers were serving at the front, while others had various logistical or in-structional responsibilities.

Each group—soldiers and new immigrants, respectively—made up a large proportion of voters with direct experience of the upheavals of war and the transformation of the Yishuv into a state, more so than any other group in the nascent Israeli society. The tension between the mundane matters that weighed on all voters and influenced their choice, on the one hand, and the sense of living at a crucial crossroads in the history of the Jewish people, on the other, affected these groups more than any other.

In the margins of the election campaigning, and apparently as a relic of past practice, politicians and parties would bring up the "past sins" of their opponents. Herut's militant image bothered Aharonovich, who claimed that they were engaging in "diabolical incitement" among new immigrants and Oriental Jews; he even voiced concern that former Etzel members might use force to disrupt election day or attack institutions of the workers' parties.[27] Ben-Gurion replied that "any attempt to use force will be mercilessly sup-pressed."[28] This mood reflected the tension and uncertainty surrounding Is-rael's assimilation of the democratic process, although, as it turned out, there was not even one instance necessitating police involvement. The dispute over "who drove the British out of Palestine" did occasionally surface during ad-dresses delivered by speakers across the political spectrum, but it did not play a key role in the elections.[29]

Even the old slur comparing Revisionism with fascism seemed to have lost much of its force. Still, a particularly provocative example did appear in a propaganda leaflet titled *Niv Hahayal* ("The Soldier's Expression"), distrib-uted by Mapai in early January, in which pictures of Begin and Benito Musso-lini raising their arms were juxtaposed under the heading "The Same Shape—The Same Content." The pictures were captioned "Il Duce" and "The Leader Begin" respectively, and in the Yiddish version, for soldiers who could not read

Hebrew, the parallel terms were "Der Dutche" and "Der Führer." Herut members were enraged by the offensive publication, which reminded them that in the past, Ben-Gurion had called Vladimir Jabotinsky "Vladimir Hitler."

The same leaflet also aroused the anger of *Al Hamishmar*. On its front page, it reprinted a defamatory cartoon from the leaflet in which Mapam was seen locking the gates of Palestine before Jews and opening them to Arabs.[30] Its aim in reprinting the cartoon was to shame Mapai in the eyes of Labor voters. *Herut* and *Al Hamishmar* also used caricatures denigrating Mapai, depicting its leaders as riding on the heads of workers.[31] Thus mutual defamation in the daily newspapers and through posters on billboards evidently played a prominent role in the campaign.

THE ELECTION CAMPAIGN IN THE ARMY

Political and partisan issues merged with military ones and became an inseparable aspect of the events of the war of independence. Decisions about appointments, military maneuvers, the exercise of authority, strategic considerations, force structure, the reorganization of units, and methods of combat and training sparked major controversies and clashes. The most notorious disputes surrounded the dismissal of the head of the Haganah, the "generals' rebellion," the *Altalena* affair, and the dismantlement of the Palmach.[32] Unsurprisingly, the tension between the army and the political arena had a significant impact on elections to the Constituent Assembly, particularly given that on the eve of elections, Israel had about one hundred thousand serving soldiers, who constituted roughly 20 percent of registered voters (without counting their family members).

At a meeting with Mapai youth on August 7, 1948, Ben-Gurion identified "the conquest of the army" by Mapai—that is, instilling the general spirit and values of the party as the unified army of the people, the backbone of the entire nation, and the bearer of the vision of redemption—as one of the party's three goals, alongside serving among the masses and nurturing the young generation.[33] Nevertheless, Ben-Gurion's attempts to attract the military vote seemed clumsy and ill-prepared.

There was great apprehension in Mapai regarding the elections among army personnel. Yehiel Duvdevani, head of the party's military affairs department, asserted at a Mapai Bureau meeting on October 28 that "our situation in the army is catastrophic—there won't be votes for Ben-Gurion in the army. If we take action, we can salvage the situation."[34] Aharonovich maintained that it was essential to explain to the soldiers "why the blanket, which did not arrive on time, need not outweigh the state, which did arrive on time" thanks to the Mapai leadership, and that "the military equipment also arrived on time," through Ben-Gurion's initiative, thus enabling the IDF to achieve its victories. His words reflected the salient impression among enlisted Mapai activists—namely, that enlisted Mapam members instantly exploited any logistical shortcoming in order to tarnish the reputation of the defense minister (i.e., Ben-Gurion).[35]

Within a few weeks, these concerns began verging on hysteria. Aharonovich warned, "The IDF defeated the Arabs, and may defeat the Party of the Workers of Palestine [Mapai]." He noted that the military command "is mostly . . . in the hands of Mapam." Duvdevani added that three of the four regional front commanders were Mapam members (Carmel in the north, Zvi Ayalon in the center, and Allon in the south), as were nine of the fourteen brigade commanders. He informed his colleagues that before the bureau meeting, he had met with Ben-Gurion and asked him to replace the head of the IDF personnel division, General Moshe Tzadok, who was nonpartisan, with "a person who understands matters." He had also suggested that each regional front headquarters include two Mapai loyalists. In his opinion, the choice was between "relying on a miracle, and inviting our ministers here [to the Mapai Bureau], together with Yaakov Dori [the chief of staff], in order to try and save something." Duvdevani was joined by Shraga Nosovitzky (Netzer), a Mapai leader, who insisted that the party's ministers and four or five "top military commanders" be summoned to an urgent meeting of the bureau, adding that "if Dori is a member of the party, he has to come to the Bureau meeting." Countering the party activists' militancy, Isser Ben-Zvi, the security expert for Hever Hakvutzot (the kibbutz movement affiliated with Mapai) who was familiar with the results of previous clashes over senior command-level appointments, stated, "I do not believe that you imagine that we can, before the elections and for the sake of the elections, change the command echelon of the army. Even if Ben-Gurion and Dori had the best intentions in this matter, they could not succeed." Lubianker asserted that Mapai had an interest in conducting propagandist activity in the army and that politicians should be allowed to appear before the soldiers. He rebuked Duvdevani for presenting a such gloomy picture of the party's standing in the army and suggesting that a company or platoon commander who identified with Mapam would use the pretext of a military task to keep soldiers from voting. The meeting ended without any concrete resolution. A summary by Aharonovich—"In the matter of the army we are up against the wall. Such a thing has never happened to us"—reveals the willingness, even among senior Mapai activists, to focus on partisan and political considerations that had nothing to do with professional matters or the quality of wartime military command. This finding clashes with the widely held scholarly view of such practices as a malady more typical of Mapam.[36] Bitterly, Aharonovich warned, "We cannot accept the possibility that the elections to the Constituent Assembly of the State of Israel will be determined by one party, which, because of certain circumstances, gained decisive control over various command echelons and uses it [this control] for its own benefit and to the detriment of others." He demanded that the Defense Ministry take measures to ensure balanced elections in the army.[37]

Ben-Gurion believed that the fear of Mapam "taking over" the army, which numbered about one hundred thousand soldiers, was exaggerated. In his view, such concerns were primarily relevant to the infantry corps, which constituted about a quarter of the combat forces (27,375 soldiers), and to the artillery corps (3,958 soldiers), but not to the other services. He rejected Aharonovich's proposal that Mapai convene a conference of soldiers, arguing that "this means organizing a party within the army."[38] Presumably, however, he was no less bothered by the possibility that such an action would justify a similar move on Mapam's part.

The charged nature of concerns surrounding military votes manifested, to some extent, in the pessimistic mood that prevailed among Mapai activists. They felt that they were in a fundamentally inferior position vis-à-vis this sector of the population, which they perceived as inaccessible. The sensitivity of the issue became blatantly evident during discussions on the use of propaganda in the army, the technical arrangements for voting, and the format for active or passive participation by soldiers and officers in election campaigning. On September 22, 1948, Ben-Gurion appointed a committee tasked with proposing how the Defense Ministry should deal with election propaganda in the army and with participation by soldiers and officers in election campaigning. But the committee was unable to reach a decisive conclusion, and the political manipulations continued.[39]

The issue was then brought before the government, the Provisional State Council security committee, and, finally, the full council. Contrary to Ben-Gurion's position, Dori and Yigael Yadin, head of the IDF operations division, objected to allowing party representatives to appear before enlisted personnel. This was also the decision reached by the security committee, following a stormy debate that left the representatives of Mapai and Mapam in the minority. At a meeting of the Provisional State Council on November 25, the delegates from Mapai, Mapam, and Maki (the Communist Party) mustered their best rhetorical arguments: the Jewish soldier is a conscientious person who fulfills a national mission; myriads of brothers and sisters who stand in battle should not be fenced in; they are not being allowed to read posters, as if they were savages; this is thrusting a wedge between the army and the civilians; and "Why do you patronize the IDF, which mostly belongs to the workers' movement? Who gave you that right, that privilege?" The main thrust of these assertions was that left-wing parties should be allowed to campaign freely within the IDF, where presumably their potential political power far exceeded that of right-wing parties.

The balance was tipped by the decisive stance articulated by David Zvi Pinkas, a savvy Mizrachi parliamentarian and head of the security committee: "Just imagine an assembly of soldiers, in which one of the soldiers yells at a Mapam commander who is speaking, 'Get out!'" and how would a military base look if its walls were covered with slogans like "'Begin out!' [or] 'Ben-Gurion out!' (to use 'parliamentary expressions'). This would destroy military discipline, which means destroying morale, destroying the army."[40]

In this spirit, a prohibition was issued against oral election propaganda in army camps and against posting any partisan publication in the camps, except for the parties' platforms and lists of candidates, which could be posted on special billboards designated for that purpose. Ben-Gurion, who was evidently reluctant to support the use of election propaganda in army camps, did so primarily to seem responsive to requests by party activists, who shouldered the daily burden of the election struggle. During the Provisional State Council, debate on the matter was uncharacteristically silent.

However, the attempts to prevent any election propagandizing by army personnel failed, as these were "the heroes of the people and not of the party." Likewise, efforts to at least limit the personnel allowed to propagandize to the rank of major or below (based on the rationale that senior commanders were prohibited from "being involved in politics") also failed. The rule adopted instead, following Ben-Gurion's approach, provided that soldiers and officers be allowed to participate in election campaigning as long as they were not wearing their uniform at the time, there was no mention of their rank, and they only engaged in such activity on their own time.[41]

In contrast to the practice in future elections, soldiers on active duty were permitted to run as candidates for the Constituent Assembly, provided that their military service would end if they were elected. A last-minute attempt to retract this condition, on the grounds that military discipline would still oblige the elected soldier to protect military secrets, was rejected by the government out of hand. "The [Constituent] Assembly will meet on a regular basis. So, if he is a battalion commander, who will do his work? Will he get a replacement?" asked Ben-Gurion, with unmasked derision.[42]

Instead of oral propaganda, once a week over the course of four weeks, the competing parties were allowed to distribute about fifty thousand items of propaganda through the army's administrative system. On January 20, 1949, the IDF newspaper, *Bamahane*, published a special issue with the parties' platforms, excluding those of the Arab parties, which did not supply them, and the Lehi platform, which, although sent by the Fighters' List, had not been approved for publication. Soldiers voted using the identity cards they had received and their army personnel numbers. The army set up about two hundred polling booths throughout the country, where soldiers were stationed. No more than seven hundred soldiers voted at each polling booth to avoid the formation of long lines that might have disrupted military activity. The voting process entailed double envelopes to ensure the right to vote while maintaining the confidentiality of the actual vote.

ELECTION DAY AND THE RESULTS

Following Ben-Gurion's suggestion, the government decided to designate election day as an official holiday. It did so primarily to alleviate the administrative challenges of distributing the remaining identity cards and of busing voters from their homes to distant polling places. This set a precedent, which remains in force, and thus the "credit" for this holiday goes to Ben-Gurion. The parties' representatives agreed that schools would not hold classes because many served as polling places. The polls opened at 6:00 a.m. and remained open until midnight to allow as many people as possible to vote.[43]

The election provided a watershed moment, a culmination of the rapid political and security developments underway since late 1945. It signaled the beginning of a transition to the routine of a sovereign state that was leaving its revolutionary days behind, even though, as the forthcoming massive aliyah, new settlements, and austerity policy would attest, revolutionary times fade only gradually. As had happened in advance of fateful moments in the past, Ben-Gurion fell ill, and he remained in bed from January 24.[44] Unlike the previous two days of festivity in the Yishuv's history—November 29, 1947, and May 14, 1948—this occasion was a proper holiday, with no casualties on the following morning. Ezriel Carlebach, editor of *Maariv* and a gifted public speaker, eloquently described this "holiday of Israeli maturity":

> We, who are too close to the act, cannot fathom the greatness of this holiday. We, who hold the ballot in our hands, following official, practical instructions, tend to forget the value of this slip of paper we are holding. How many generations and peoples were killed and destroyed for this piece of paper, which now rests in pile before us, free for the taking? How many revolutions did the world undergo until it came to recognize the right of every person, in every nation, to shape its regime? How great is the deed we carry out today, as both the president and a young woman who only yesterday came on aliyah each have an equal vote, as all people are equal in their civil rights, all are created in the image of the same God. . . . And if such a holiday is a tremendous achievement

for any nation, for us it is all the more so. For the first time in the history of the oldest of peoples, its members go to the polls—free. For the first time they can experience their actual creation—a Jewish state, which grants *all* the rights to the Jew, by virtue of being a Jew.[45]

Tears, wonderment, and recitations of "Shehehyanu" (a blessing for special occasions) were an inseparable part of the first Israeli state election. The festive atmosphere was everywhere.[46] An editorial in *Haaretz* noted that the grumbling and resentment characteristic of Yishuv-era elections were absent. As if alluding, perhaps inadvertently, to itself, the newspaper added that "even the harshest critics do not ignore, deep in their hearts, the miracle of the momentous events" that had occurred during the eight months since the establishment of the state.

Qualified voters for the Constituent Assembly were identified based on the census of November 8, 1948. Of the 782,000 residents of the state (713,000 Jews and 69,000 non-Jews) at the time, 506,567 were identified as qualified voters. Of this number, 418,268 were civilians, though some did not receive their identity cards in time. About 90 percent of those who had identity cards actually voted. In the military sector, about 75,000 soldiers (88 percent) voted. Altogether, 440,095 people voted in the elections, accounting for 87 percent of all registered voters. The number of votes needed to gain a seat in the Constituent Assembly was 3,592.[47]

Below are the election returns for the parties that passed the threshold number of votes:

Table 5.1. Results of Israel's 1949 Constituent Assembly election by party

Name of List	Number of Valid Votes	% of Total Votes	Number of Seats
Mapai	155,274	35.7	46
Mapam	64,018	14.7	19
United Religious Front	52,982	12.2	16
Herut Movement	49,782	11.5	14
General Zionists	22,661	5.2	7
Progressive Party	17,786	4.1	5
Sephardic and Oriental Jews	15,287	3.5	4
Maki	15,148	3.5	4
Nazareth Democratic List	7,387	1.7	2
Fighters' List	5,363	1.2	1
WIZO and Union of Women for Equal Rights	5,173	1.2	1
Yemenites' Association	4,399	1	1

The distribution of votes among soldiers was as follows:

Sephardic List	1,251	United Religious Front	5,644
Fighters' List	1,355	Herut Movement	11,151
Progressive Party	2,106	Mapam	5,767
Maki	2,488	Mapai	31,158[48]
General Zionists	2,644		

Following the election, Ben-Gurion commented that although many members of Mapai had assumed that "the party is boycotted in the army," he had not believed this. In fact, Mapai received 40 percent of the votes among soldiers, 5 percent more than its share of the total population. He concluded that "the work that began in the army before the elections should continue not only in connection with the elections."[49]

James McDonald summarized the significance of the election results for his superiors in Washington: First, the elections were free and orderly. Second, there was "no major surprise" in the outcome or Mapai's victory. Third, with a note of self-congratulation, he observed that Herut's poor showing in the election validated his view that there was no reason to transform Begin into a "martyr" by preventing him from visiting the United States. Finally, McDonald regarded the fact that the Communists had received less than 4 percent of the vote as putting an end to "the widespread alarmist stories about Communist penetration in Israel."[50] By way of David R. Wahl, who had come to survey the elections for *Israel Speaks*, McDonald conveyed the following message to Abraham Feinberg and effectively to all of Israel's supporters among Truman's White House staff: "The President's policy of independence from Britain had been brilliantly successful and if adhered to would bring peace."[51] His conclusions offered a mix of concrete, voter-backed validations for the path taken, in combination with false hopes that even he, almost certainly, did not believe.

The election results also, finally, allowed Truman to grant Israel de jure recognition. On January 31, the president signed a declaration to this effect in the presence of three figures: his close friend Jacobson and the two B'nai B'rith leaders, Frank Goldman and Maurice Bisgyer. Truman used seven pens for the occasion. Three were gifted to these figures as personal souvenirs, and the remainder were sent to Weizmann, Feinberg, David Niles, and Stephen Wise—each pen having a carefully chosen political addressee in respect of the historical narrative relayed previously. A few days later, Feinberg sent a letter of thanks to Truman, expressing his pride as an American in light of the president's approach to Israel, his determination that its people receive "a fair deal," and his leadership in instilling democracy in parts of the world that had not known it.[52] While these remarks might have seemed like "hot air" flavored with a touch of obsequiousness when they were made, the test of time has confirmed their validity. There were also some who reacted in anger. Jacob Blaustein, who succeeded Joseph Proskauer as president of the American Jewish Committee, fumed in a letter to presidential aide Matthew Connelly: How could his organization have been excluded from this important ceremony and considered unworthy of a commemorative pen, given its constructive work toward resolution of the Palestine problem and its status as the foremost representatives of US Jewry?[53] In this context, one might also note Blaustein's personal financial contribution to the president's election. Clearly, the issue was not a shortage of pens or incidental administrative negligence but rather a scale of decisive contributions. Following the elections, and invoking a scale not of contributions but of political hostility, Ben-Gurion concluded that the time had come to be rid of the "founding father" who followed Dewey and opposed Henry Morgenthau and Henry Montor. Accordingly, he instructed his fellow Mapai leaders, Eliezer Kaplan and Berl Locker, who were set to depart for a meeting of the Jewish Agency's US section to discuss the future of state-agency ties, that "Silver and Neumann should be removed."[54] And this, indeed, is what happened.

Summarizing the results of both the Constituent Assembly election and the Histadrut election, which took place a few weeks later, Aharonovich observed that rather than "immersing oneself in the jungle" of numerical analyses of the returns, one should focus on the essence: the results, he averred, gave Mapai a historic opportunity "to determine the destiny of the working class in Israel for a whole generation, and to shape the nature of the state for a whole generation."[55] In a radio speech to the citizens of Israel delivered on the eve of the election, Ben-Gurion said that "the voters are those who laid the foundations of the State of Israel," and expressed his hope that the elected government would, for the sake of "eternal memory," publish the registry of voters, "so that our children and grandchildren, and all subsequent generations, will know who were the founders and first architects of the state."[56]

His hope has yet to be realized. The Provisional State Council, the first parliamentary body of the State of Israel, operated for eleven months, and its history has not yet been the subject of a systematic scholarly examination. The council served as a bridge between the era of the Yishuv, which essentially operated on a voluntary basis under British Mandate patronage, and that of the newborn state, where law would rule. The debates in the Provisional State Council, an important source of grounding and resilience for the fledgling State of Israel, demonstrated that alongside military victories, decision-making could take place democratically and in accordance with binding rules adopted consensually by representatives across a diverse political spectrum.

The council's most important achievement was undoubtedly its success in ensuring the transition, in accordance with democratic rules, from systems of voluntary rule to a legal, functioning regime. A crucial junction, perhaps even the climax, of its activity was the process that led to elections to the Constituent Assembly.

A hint of the atmosphere that characterized the proceedings of the Provisional State Council throughout its existence is evident in a description that appeared in the newspaper *Herut*. Although humorous in tone, the description accurately conveys the novelty of life in Israel as a parliamentary state: "In the past, when a Zionist activist came from the Diaspora to Eretz Israel for a visit, Jewish Agency officials would take him to a kibbutz, so he could personally witness how 'class-conscious' cows were being milked. Now, however, guests from abroad rush to the 'parliament' in Tel Aviv, to breathe the air of a real Jewish state." There, the writer did not fail to add, they have the privilege of observing, from the height of the gallery, the yarmulke on Zorach Warhaftig's head, "which is about the size of a 10-*grush* coin."[57]

On February 14, 1949, Ben-Gurion wrote in his diary: "At three o'clock I went to Yeshurun Synagogue, to listen to the prayers, as I had promised Rabbi Berlin [leader of the Mizrachi Movement] yesterday. This was my first time being present in a synagogue during services in Eretz Israel. At four o'clock the Constituent Assembly opened."[58]

One of the main objectives of the Constituent Assembly was to prepare a constitution for the new state. Two days after it convened, the members of this new body decided to change its name to the First Knesset. Rather than work on the adoption of a constitution, the members of the First Knesset opted to serve as a legislative body that focused on routine affairs and the passage of ongoing legislation in accordance with day-to-day needs. Ben-Gurion led the Israeli political campaign to refrain from drafting a written constitution. The historiography contains various explanations for his position, with different points of emphasis. What is evident, however, is that from his perspective, the young democracy did not need a constitution and that as a leader, he preferred to operate without one. His certainty that the Jewish state could maintain a democratic way of life even without a written constitution has been validated by the test of time. The fierce disputes that encumbered the new state's nation-building—such as questions of international orientation, the place of religion in public life, the role of the socialist outlook in Israel as a sovereign state, and the mass absorption of immigrants from

Islamic countries and of Holocaust survivors from Europe, among other issues—were debated without any pretense of establishing binding rules for generations to come.[59] The parliamentary system whereby the government is subordinated to the Knesset and must earn its confidence has remained in force to this day. On the other hand, on the very day that the Israeli parliament began to negate the necessity of a constitution—February 16, 1949—it also established one of the foundational pillars of the Israeli political system: the presidency.

"A Statesman in Winter": The First President

Throughout the military confrontation with Arab states and the internal political struggle leading up to elections, Weizmann's presence was marginal to imperceptible. The State of Israel seemed to be doing fine without him. He skirted the myriad pressures that stemmed from intense involvement in the battlefields, election results, and, later, the massive immigrant absorption effort with modesty and a focus on the day-to-day matters of newly achieved sovereignty. Precisely for this reason, his somewhat external vantage point offers instructive insights into the Israeli reality at the time, coming as it does from the perspective of a "tribal elder" with vast political experience in Jewish and Zionist affairs. During this period, Weizmann was also engaged in creating an independence-era presidency out of whole cloth as he gradually approached his twilight years, having passed the baton of leadership to his successors.

On September 29, 1948, Shertok flew from Israel to Geneva to take part in the UN General Assembly session in Paris. He was accompanied by the supervisor of the Aliyah Department, who earlier that day had conducted Weizmann and his wife Vera's citizenship swearing-in ceremony, with Shertok and Nahum Goldmann in attendance. A day earlier, Weizmann had sent notice to the government in London, relinquishing his and his wife's British citizenship. At 5:00 a.m. on the following day, the Weizmanns landed at the Tel Nof Airbase (south of Rehovot), where they disembarked from what is considered El Al's first flight. The modest reception ceremony included Weizmann's foremost loyalists in Mapai—Kaplan, Sprinzak, and David Remez. From there, the presidential convoy departed for Weizmann's home at the Sieff Institute in Rehovot.[60]

On the evening of September 30, the Provisional State Council also held a ceremony in honor of Weizmann at the Tel Aviv Museum on Rothchild Boulevard, in the same hall where Israel proclaimed independence on May 14. In retrospect, this could have been an appropriate occasion to have him sign Israel's declaration of independence—a matter over which Weizmann and his close associates would frequently voice displeasure in those days and in their memoirs.[61] At a personal level, the key sentence in Weizmann's speech before the council was that this time, he had come to Israel "(perhaps for the last time without returning abroad), in order to live here and stay here." Notwithstanding the months of intense hostilities and large numbers of casualties, Weizmann reiterated that his guiding principle was that "Zion will be redeemed by justice, and her returnees by righteousness" (Isaiah 1:27). Ben-Gurion, who spoke before him, made an unequivocal political commitment before those present when he stated that Weizmann had earned many official honors in his life: former president of the Zionist Organization, former president of the Jewish Agency, and now "president of the State Council, and I am sure that he will be president of the state."[62]

There were a few practical matters on Weizmann's agenda during his first months in Israel as president of the Provisional State Council: first, understanding Israel's new and evolving reality as a sovereign state coping simultaneously with the burden of war, the establishment of its diplomatic status, the absorption of mass numbers of immigrants, and the formation of official institutions; second, clarifying his standing and potential to influence Israel's reality and politics; and third, fulfilling the representative duties stemming from the natural aspirations of various localities and entities to enjoy his attention and esteemed presence. Weizmann's first official visit was to Kibbutz Givat Brenner, near Rehovot, a week after his arrival. In his address to hundreds of kibbutz members, he stated, "I have heard of intentions to concentrate large numbers of immigrants in the city. We must fight this trend. Our mission is the village and rural work. We have built many towns and cities, from Pithom and Ramses [in ancient Egypt] to the present. Now we must skillfully learn the craft of building large villages. I wish to see the village affect the city, and this is possible in a small country like ours, where villages are located near cities."[63] Weizmann's long-held view of the centrality of agriculture and settlement in shaping the "new Jew" and the "new society"—shedding the mark of exile in favor of modernization and progress—was not necessarily in line with the kibbutzniks' personal aspirations for their collective home. Nonetheless, his audience was undoubtedly pleased and touched by his remarks. On this matter of principle, Weizmann's position was similar to that of Ben-Gurion, although he lacked the energy that the latter had to struggle against powerful new trends in the kibbutz movements.[64]

In terms of symbolism, it was Weizmann's December 1 visit to Jerusalem that generated the most resonance. At a festive reception at the National Institutions building, chief Ashkenazi rabbi Yitzhak HaLevi Herzog joyously recalled Menachem Ussishkin's remarks during the debate over partition in 1937. Speaking before a protest assembly, Ussishkin had charged, "In their imagination, they [partition supporters, and Weizmann foremost] already envision the state and the president's top hat." Now, continued the rabbi, "we do not see the top hat, but we do see the president." Weizmann promised the city's officials and community leaders that the road to the Western Wall would be opened and that Israel would resist the establishment of an international regime over the new city. In response to their calls for Jerusalem to be declared Israel's capital, however, he was as moderate as ever, cautioning patience and advising, in characteristic style, "Let us not be hasty. Let us leave something for the Messiah, son of David, to do in the city." Weizmann then visited the Jerusalem commander, Lt. Gen. Moshe Dayan, and told him that "had your father [Shmuel, a friend of Weizmann] not built Nahalal, you would not be defending Jerusalem now."[65] At the same time, Weizmann supported placing the holy sites, and perhaps even the entire Old City, under an international regime. He believed that if these areas remained in Abdullah's hands, they would not be accessible to followers of all the religions. Weizmann further held that the Constituent Assembly should not be convened in Jerusalem, so as "not to annoy the geese [the United States, Britain, and the Vatican]" and because the Jordanian Legion might open fire on the participants. Ben-Gurion categorically dismissed his concerns at that time and a year later when he declared Jerusalem as Israel's capital. Writing in his diary, Ben-Gurion noted when Weizmann had called him and admitted that he had "reached the conclusion that he was wrong and I was right about Jerusalem."[66] When Weizmann tried to push the boundaries set by Ben-Gurion, the latter was quick to thwart his efforts. In mid-November, having learned that Weizmann was about to telegraph Truman about weapon supplies, Ben-Gurion wrote to Weizmann's political adviser, Leo Cohen, politely yet unequivocally informing him that "the president of the State Council should be advised that he cannot raise issues concerning the State of Israel with the US president—without the government's knowledge."[67] Even Weizmann had to admit, however indirectly, that he lacked the power to change his standing. In a letter to his English Jewish friend, Sir Simon Marks, he offered the following description of the political situation:

> I have been watching the work of the young Government, and although many things seem somewhat amateurish and hesitant, they have done extremely well on the whole under very difficult circumstances. B.G. as Prime Minister and Minister of Defense has proven a great success. Whether he will be the same success in peace time I am not prepared to say; he reminds me somewhat of Winston [Churchill] who is good in war and less so in peace.

However, it is too early to draw any conclusions. He is thoughtful, calm, resolute and a man of enormous courage. I think he enjoys the support of all parties and rightly so.[68]

Beyond the veil of pride over Israel's achievements, the powerful images Weizmann invoked also convey an admission of his own political and physical weakness relative to Ben-Gurion. Six weeks after his arrival, Weizmann wrote to British MP Richard Crossman, a close associate, that he was "still walking like in a dream." The main novelty in Weizmann's eyes—and not only his—related to the country's demographics. As he wrote to former British minister Leopold Amery, "I must admit that I have not yet got used to the fact that one can travel from Beer-Sheva to the North without meeting either an Englishman or an Arab."[69] On the Palestinian issue, Weizmann cultivated an image as a moral individual who abhors violence. At the political level, however, he maintained the fundamental distrust of the country's majority population and the Palestinian national movement that he had felt at the time of the 1917 Balfour Declaration and the 1937 Peel Commission partition plan. He still believed, in 1948, that population transfer was the appropriate solution.[70] Weizmann's first meaningful visit to Israel's new landscape took the form of a five-day tour of Haifa, Nahariya, Tiberias, and Nahalal, which began on November 10. Amid all the planned encounters, it was apparently a spontaneous occurrence at the Haifa Port that most touched him. While he was visiting the naval fleet, an immigrant ship coincidentally arrived in port. Its 490 passengers, squeezed onto the deck, erupted in cheers of "Long live President Weizmann" and burst out singing "HaTikva" ("The Hope"—Israel's anthem), accompanied, on the pier, by the president's entourage and hosts.[71]

The concrete conclusions Weizmann drew from the initial period of his Provisional State Council presidency are evident in a letter to James de Rothschild (son of the renowned philanthropist), whom he sought to enlist as an investor in expediting the settlement of immigrants. This was the most revealing letter he composed during the entire war of independence. The conclusion that emerges from it is that despite the image of moderation Weizmann strove to cultivate in his frequent criticism of the militarism that typified Israeli youth and the belligerence that characterized Ben-Gurion's policies, he, too, regarded the outcome of this conduct as the realization of Zionist yearnings, both overt and latent. Millions of dunams lie vacant, covered by weeds, he informed Rothschild. These include arable tracts in areas where Jews had never bought land, such as the Ramlah-Latrun region. It is doubtful that the Arabs will return to work these lands, he wrote. Aside from the seventy thousand or so Arabs who remained in Israel, "the Arab population has to all intents and purposes disappeared," he concluded without a hint of regret. Some would return once the hostilities ended, Weizmann surmised, but the rich effendis and landless peasants could easily resettle in Syria, Iraq, Egypt, and Transjordan. "So an opportunity is open to us which will really not arise for the near few centuries if ever. Our present trouble is that most of our young men are in the army and the newcomers . . . are apparently not very willing to come on the land; they will have to be gently persuaded to do so if they want to build up a reasonable existence for themselves." With one stroke of his pen, Weizmann outlined the vision of settlement, territorial takeover, and population dispersion that would guide Israeli policy for its first decade, leading to the establishment of hundreds of kibbutzim, moshavim, and development towns across the width and breadth of the country. Like many other Israeli leaders, Weizmann was impervious to the unbearable difficulties new immigrants faced in trying to adapt to the agricultural realities of the new land. Nor was he sensitive to the torments of acclimation dictated by the "melting pot" model, which had a searing impact on their lives and their consciousness, leaving its mark at both the personal and cultural levels. One sentence, omitted from the final version sent to Rothschild—perhaps so as not to dissuade the esteemed philanthropist from investing—indicates how attuned Weizmann was to the forthcoming challenges: "The financial situation is not the main difficulty, it is more the moral state of the newcomers who are not infused with the *chalutz* [pioneer] spirit like the previous generation." From Weizmann's elitist, patronizing perspective, the long-term goal was to create a modern Western state. It required adopting a completely non-empathic attitude toward the immigrants' tribulations, an attitude informed by the assumption that in time they, too, would enjoy the fruit of this forced endeavor. Weizmann told Meyer Weisgal, who reviewed the draft letter to Rothschild, that with proper preparations, it would be possible to create the conditions for the absorption of 250,000 new immigrants in 1949.[72]

Weizmann believed that the Negev should be a key destination for the settlement of these immigrants, and from late 1947, this territory was foremost on his political agenda. In the Israeli political arena, Weizmann stood alongside Ben-Gurion at the forefront of opposition to any Israeli concession in the Negev. On countless occasions throughout 1948, whether at the domestic level or in diplomatic contacts with British or American officials, Weizmann took the unequivocal position that the Negev should not be conceded "at any price." He regarded the Negev as a cornerstone of the political understanding reached with President Truman, a key facet of which was the United States' de facto recognition of Israel immediately upon its establishment.[73] Weizmann disdainfully likened the troublesome US State

Department officials seeking to deny Jews the right to control the Negev to "children pulling out a young plant in order to look at the roots" and equated them with British Colonial Office officials who followed the same practice. In fact, he charged, they could switch places across the Atlantic Ocean, and no one would notice.[74]

Behind closed doors, however, Weizmann conducted himself differently. Like Israel's other top officials, he supported the imperative of East–West neutrality against the background of escalating interbloc polarization. He also declared so publicly at a press conference in early October immediately after arriving in Israel.[75] On November 5, he met with the US envoy, McDonald, who documented the encounter in his diary but, in his report to his superiors, omitted Weizmann's vehemence: should the UN impose sanctions on Israel (following Operation Yoav), Weizmann charged, he would support the conquest of the West Bank as far as the Jordan River; moreover, Israeli forces were capable of reaching Damascus within an hour if they wished. Weizmann emphasized that Israel identified with the West and was interested in close ties with the United States because it was a democratic state with a Western character. Israel believed that this was the only way to develop and remain free, Weizmann told McDonald. Similarly, he promised his confidant, Justice Felix Frankfurter, that the Constituent Assembly elections would make clear how unsubstantial the procommunist leanings in Israel were. Amid the crisis that broke out following the IDF's advance toward El-Arish in early January 1949 and its downing of five British planes, Weizmann asserted in a *New York Times* interview that, in contrast to Soviet-aligned countries, Israel has no "red planes" and no Soviet citizens in its armed forces.[76] Once again, Weizmann took advantage of his personal relationship with Truman to underscore Israel's realist position in the interbloc conflict. In a letter dated January 9, 1949, he clarified the circumstances of Israel's unusual conduct toward the end of Operation Horev and warmly thanked the American president for agreeing to participate in an event in his honor and on behalf of the Weizmann Institute of Science, scheduled to take place in New York on February 19.[77] This was another miraculous moment in the relationship between the two presidents during 1947–1949. The link between their mutual trust at the individual and leadership levels and Israel's political commitment to the United States manifested unequivocally and tangibly—amid that crisis—in the form of Weizmann, who for a time was the linchpin of US–Israel relations. That link was the main factor in senior Mapai leaders' decision to appoint Weizmann as "head of the state."[78] Its value in terms of Jewish territorial and political gains during the war of independence proved once again to be decisive. This fundamental fact was no doubt evident to Mapai leaders when, soon thereafter, they had to decide on the state's first president.

On December 10, 1948, Weisgal informed Weizmann that Truman (whom he dubbed "your friend, Herschel") had agreed to be the only speaker at the annual fundraising event for the Sieff Institute, to take place in New York. "It is unprecedented in the history of American Presidents," Weisgal pointed out enthusiastically, as no American president had ever come to a fundraising event or granted such an honor to a private individual, yet here the motif was "a salute to the President of Israel." The event was planned for late January or sometime in February, he added, and "there is only one thing missing. THAT'S YOU!" This was another grand production initiated by Weisgal, which appeared to be taking shape with Feinberg's aid and thanks to his contacts and ability to persuade the American president. "You got de facto recognition from Herschel on the 14th of May. You can, in my opinion, get de jure recognition from him when you come here," Weisgal skillfully played on Weizmann's heartstrings. The visit would last a week, he promised, adding another, though unconfirmed, promise: to arrange for Weizmann to be flown from Israel to New York and back on "the President's personal plane, the Sacred Cow."[79] That promise was quickly taken off the table, for aside from any logistical difficulties that may have emerged behind the scenes on the American side, the ceremonial protocol did not allow for the president of an independent state to be flown on the official aircraft of another state's president to meet with the latter. As an alternative, it was agreed that Weizmann and his entourage would fly to England and continue from there to New York on the luxury liner *Queen Elizabeth*.[80] Naturally, this would prolong Weizmann's absence from the country.

On December 30, 1948, Vera Weizmann wrote to Weisgal, carefully enumerating her doubts surrounding the trip. She asked whether there was any possibility Truman would officially invite Weizmann to visit the United States, despite the political complications and declaratory significance of doing so, as opposed to merely inviting him for a weekend together, given that this would raise unwanted speculation in the political arena. Her concern was that this would create an unbridgeable gap between Truman's affection for Weizmann at the personal level and the US commitment to Israel. She also requested that the opinions of several American Zionist figures close to Weizmann be solicited to assess whether he should make the trip. Weizmann directly solicited an opinion from Justice Frankfurter (who in fact supported his taking the trip). As reasonable justification for traveling, Weizmann listed four potential achievements: completion of the discussions necessary to receive the requested loan, de jure American recognition of Israel,

American pressure on the French and British to gradually recognize Israel's existence, and the persuasion of American officials that there was no basis for concern over the impact of procommunist elements in the Israeli political arena. The unstated aim of this visit—a goal that all its organizers understood implicitly—was large-scale fundraising for the Weizmann Institute of Science in the months leading up to its inauguration. While Weizmann was still pondering how to proceed, a date was set for the event—February 19, 1949. On January 5, 1949, the White House issued an official press release announcing that Truman was scheduled to speak at a ceremonial dinner in honor of Weizmann sponsored by the American Committee for the Weizmann Institute of Science, to be held at the Waldorf-Astoria in New York.[81]

Concurrently, McDonald approached the State Department, presumably at Weizmann's urging, to ask that Israel be allowed to purchase a Skymaster, which would be used for the president's travel and thereafter by El Al for purely civilian purposes. This entire project was, however, overshadowed from the outset by the risk that, for health reasons, Weizmann's personal physician would not approve such a long midwinter trip. On January 20, Weizmann called Weisgal in New York and informed him that for health reasons—an acute attack of his neurological disorder and Vera having come down with the flu—his physician would not grant authorization for him to travel, and the visit would have to be postponed. Deeply upset, Weisgal wrote back on the following day, saying that if he did not have a wife and three children, and if he had just a little bit more courage, he would put an end to his life by jumping into the Hudson River.[82] On February 2, the White House issued a formal statement announcing that, for health reasons, the visit would be postponed to the spring, adding that Weizmann's health would not prevent him from participating in the opening session of the Constituent Assembly.[83] Weizmann's presence at the Constituent Assembly suggested that the trip had been delayed for political reasons, but it would later become evident that Weizmann's poor health would have genuinely prevented him from traveling to the United States at that time.

The "money meter" that guided Weisgal was not fully synchronized with Israel's "political meter." When Weisgal began formulating his plans, Israel was still in the midst of war. Now the war had ended, elections were pending, and Weizmann's schedule was subordinated to the legal process of completing Israel's transformation into a democratic state. The pretext of health considerations, as the reason for postponing the event to April, gives archival researchers a glimpse into the extent of Vera Weizmann's involvement in the presidential agenda. Our detailed account of the "Truman speech" affair serves mainly to shed light on the complexities, from Weizmann's perspective, of transitioning from the customs of the Zionist Movement and the Yishuv to the norms of sovereignty by which an independent state is expected to abide. An opportunity to raise funds and bask in the glory of public esteem seemed secondary in importance to his appointment to this coveted position—president of the State of Israel.

The dramatic event that Weisgal labored to produce coincided with Operation Horev, which concluded on January 7, 1949, heralding the end of the war of independence. The quiet on the fronts allayed any final doubts about holding Constituent Assembly elections on the scheduled date, January 25. In any event, they were to be followed within a few weeks by the first gathering of the new parliamentary body and soon thereafter by the election of a state president. Next, the president would select a candidate to form a government, drawing on his consultations with parliamentary party representatives. A dispute that broke out in the Provisional State Council on January 13, 1949, illustrates the tight timetable and the symbolic importance of Weizmann's presence in the country. The issue at hand was who would have the honor of opening the Constituent Assembly—the oldest delegate or the council president? Most of the constitutional committee members supported granting this privilege to the oldest delegate on the grounds that the elections would mark the end of the Provisional State Council, including its committees and president, and it was fitting that no one know in advance who would open the Constituent Assembly. The controversy generated a rare meeting of the minds between the Revisionist Movement and Mapam. Weizmann's opponents on both the right and the left—long-standing adversaries (from the early 1920s) as well as new ones (since the Twenty-Second Zionist Congress in 1946)—refuted his right to open the Constituent Assembly. Grabovsky, a Mapai delegate and central, albeit forgotten, figure in the formulation of legislation during Israel's first year, vehemently defended Weizmann as the recipient of this honor:

> We are not talking about the opening of a permanent parliament, for a second or third [session], but about opening the State of Israel's Constituent Assembly, for the first time in Israel's history. This assembly symbolizes the transition from one era to another: from the era of Zionism that lasted two generations to the era of independent statehood. And the right belongs to that man, who serves today as the president of the Provisional State Council—specifically Professor Dr. Chaim Weizmann, for he is the president of the Provisional State Council and the man who throughout his life has stood at the national helm of the Zionist movement—[he is] entitled to open the Constituent Assembly for the first time in Israel's history. And there is no need to rely on a vague law, or some custom, whereby one of the elders, an anonymous person no one knows, should open the assembly.[84]

He was joined by Warhaftig, chairman of the constitutional committee, who heatedly pointed out that anyone who wanted to "adopt the gentiles' constitution" would run into problems because there were many countries and many constitutions, and one could find a precedent for any approach: "In some countries the oldest delegate opens [the assembly] and in some countries the president of the previous house does so." Ben-Gurion, for his part, stated during a preliminary government discussion that if the oldest delegate were an Arab, then he would have to open the assembly. He was actually, and manipulatively, playing innocent, for even if one could ascribe Ben-Gurion's observation to a coherent constitutional doctrine that exalted equality, his intention was to deny the symbolic importance of the status being granted to Weizmann. The prime minister did not bother to put his position to the vote. The vote in the Provisional State Council was 15–7 in favor of having the council president open the Constituent Assembly.[85]

Only in early February 1949 did the Provisional Government formulate its position regarding the "president of the state." The tone and terms of the discussion were dictated by Ben-Gurion:

> As to the authority of the president—in my view this mission is an anachronism and there is no need for it. We are building a state in 1949, not in the eighteenth century, when the concept of a monarchy still existed. Aside from America, no president in any country has a function. In America—the president is the government. He is the executive body. But if this is not our situation—then the presidency is certainly unnecessary and would generate financial waste and confusion. It is a product of the past. But there is a special situation here: in my view Dr. Weizmann is worthy of being the head of state and he deserves this honor. If Theodor Herzl were alive today we would grant him this honor, the supreme honor in the state, but in truth this is definitely an unnecessary institution, and we should therefore keep the definition of the presidential duties to a minimum and not place too much weight on the matter.[86]

Ben-Gurion's definitive stance, which of course he refrained from voicing publicly, determined the character of the presidency in those days and for the decades that followed. By virtue of Israel's victory on the battlefield and Mapai's sweeping victory in the Constituent Assembly elections, the "founding father" succeeded in excluding Weizmann from the center stage of Israeli politics. A few days later, Ben-Gurion stated at a government meeting, "What is the role of the president? It is inconceivable that there would be two governments. The presidency is a purely symbolic institution."[87] This approach informed the Knesset's delineation of the president's four duties on February 16: signing treaties with other countries after their ratification by the Knesset, appointing the Israeli diplomatic representatives recommended by the authorized minister, receiving the credentials of diplomatic representatives from other countries, and exercising the authority to pardon criminals or commute their sentence.[88]

Meanwhile, Weizmann's health was improving at a distressingly slow pace. On the morning of February 14, 1949, the day of the Constituent Assembly's first session, Ben-Gurion urged the other government members to decide who would chair the discussion after Weizmann's opening speech. Having met with Weizmann the day before, he reported that his "state of health is very poor."[89] Weizmann had prepared for the speech in consultation with his advisers and, seeking to acknowledge the grandeur of the occasion, had asked McDonald to send him a copy of Abraham Lincoln's historical speech at his second presidential inauguration ceremony (March 4, 1865). That is, Weizmann planned to deliver an address with epic and historic elements, one that would leave an imprint. In practice, it was a flowery speech devoid of any substantive message or point. Those present were moved by the significance of the event, held at the Jewish Agency compound in Jerusalem. Some shed tears, and Weizmann's voice broke at times, but the barrenness of his remarks and the lack of any effort by his loyalists to instill the speech in collective memory meant that it was soon shelved and forgotten. It was only Weizmann's mention of the Jewish people's leaders toward the end of his remarks that sparked any real reaction. In listing the movement's guides and the founders of the Zionist enterprise, he named Herzl, Ussishkin, Rothschild, Max Nordau, Nachum Sokolov, Ahad Ha'am, Haim Nachman Bialik, Eliezer Ben-Yehuda, and Louis Brandeis. This naturally drew a response from the followers of Revisionism, who were aggrieved by the omission of Jabotinsky, among others. The list also omitted leaders of the Religious Zionist Movement, the liberal bourgeois civic circles, members of the Old Yishuv [pre-Zionist Movement], Sephardim, and women.[90]

Two days later, on February 16, the Knesset discussed the election of the state's first president (deliberations began five minutes before midnight, and the vote itself took place on February 17). Running against Weizmann, doctor of chemistry, was Professor Joseph Klausner, a scholar of Hebrew literature and messianism who was identified with right-wing circles on the Zionist political spectrum. If Weizmann did any work behind the scenes to ensure his election, these remain undocumented. Presumably, he relied primarily on Mapai ministers' personal indebtedness toward him, as expressed in writing and publicly. Another source of public support would have been the chapters of his autobiography, which Haaretz began to publish on December 31, 1948. The appearance of chapters from his book Trial and Error provided a convenient, respectable, nonbelligerent alternative to campaigning. In the internal wrangling leading up to the vote, Gruenbaum, as representative of the General Zionists, and Rabbi Meir Berlin, as representative of the Religious Zionists, were mentioned as candidates. The latter even drew support from secular Mapam, in furtherance of its ongoing struggle against the Western world's dominance over the newly founded Israel. Yet neither candidate put his name to the vote. The deliberations that preceded the vote were insubstantial. The Mapai delegate remained silent, Mapam's delegate, Eliezer Frei (Peri) made it clear that although his party would vote for Weizmann, this should not be interpreted as an expression of support for his political outlook, and Herut's delegate, Aryeh Ben-Eliezer, argued that Weizmann did not symbolize the aspiration to "a life of liberty and independence." Weizmann drew the support of eighty-three Knesset members, versus fifteen votes for Klausner, and became the first president of the State of Israel.[91]

On February 17, 1949, Weizmann was sworn in as the first president of Israel at a ceremony in the Knesset. Ben-Gurion was ill and did not attend. The first letter Weizmann wrote after his appointment was to Clark Clifford, the politician to whom—to the best of my understanding—Weizmann was most indebted for having achieved this post. Clifford had also been deeply involved in the political process leading up to Israel's proclamation of statehood, the Export-Import Bank loan, and the United States' de jure recognition. Weizmann had made a similar gesture after his election as president of the Provisional State Council: the first letter he wrote after receiving the news was to Rosenman, whom he described as having contributed "so much" to the "happy results during the past few days." Although he did not go into detail, it was clear that he was referring to the founding of the state, US recognition of it, and his own appointment. It was no coincidence that these were the first people to whom he wrote, or that he chose to close his letter to Clifford, which included a copy of his autobiography as a sign of appreciation, with the phrase "Zion will be rebuilt in justice."[92] This expression became a code of sorts during his later years, providing an intimate glimpse into the conceptual and political worldview he had formed during his decades of statesmanship in the service of the Zionist vision.

Weizmann's brief speech following his inauguration included two messages. The first was personal: "Great is the task entrusted me. But I am only flesh and blood and, God forbid, may fail in my deeds; please do not regard me as an intentional sinner." The second message related to Jewry as a whole: "I know that anything done, or anything not done, in this country will cast its light or shadow over our entire people."[93] Even if his modesty seemed disingenuous, considering his rich public career, this political message was both instructive and appropriate for the launch of parliamentary life in Israel, as was his admission of the impact of Israel's conduct on the lives of Diaspora Jewry. An editorial in *Davar* on the following morning stated, "The election of the republic's president at the Constituent Assembly symbolized to the nation and the world the permanence and stability of the State of Israel, which have become decisive, triumphant, recognized facts. The character of the elected president conveys to the nation and the world: this state, even in its permanence and stability, will not be a stagnant state."[94] In hindsight, it seems that, excluding the declaration of Jerusalem as Israel's capital in late 1949, Israel's first presidential inauguration marked the state's last all-inclusive moment of national joy. Henceforth, Weizmann's influence would steadily erode in conjunction with his poor health. On November 19, 1951, he was elected for a second term as Israel's president. His swearing-in took place a week later in his home, as his health prevented him from reaching the Knesset yet the law required that he be sworn in within seven days of his election. On the following day, Weizmann turned seventy-seven. Marking the occasion, as a virtuoso in the art of letter writing, Weizmann wrote to Dewey Stone a few days later, on November 29, 1951 (the fourth anniversary of the UN Partition Plan resolution). In what would turn out to be his last significant letter, of the tens of thousands he had composed throughout his life, he wrote: "The only redeeming of a birthday for a man of my age is perhaps this: The Years which have taken their toll of me have added the loot to the value of whatever achievement in which I may have share. In this respect, national institutions are much better off than human beings; their endurance is greater. Thus, I willingly shift the weight of this birthday from my frail shoulders onto the solid framework of the Weizmann Institute of Science."[95] The leader was transferring the mantle of his leadership, values, and influence over Israel and the Jewish people onto the figurative shoulders of the academic research institute bearing his name. His intermediary for this transition was Stone, who, we recall, had launched the process that led to the formation of a personal alliance between Truman and Weizmann in March 1948. Subsequently, Weizmann's health continued to decline steadily, until he could no longer fulfill his duties.

Over the course of 1952, the daily press occasionally reported on either an improvement or a deterioration in Weizmann's health, but it was clear to all that his days were numbered. Weizmann passed away on November 9, 1952, and was laid to rest a few days later near his home at the Weizmann Institute of Science in Rehovot. "It was with neither hysterical crying nor confused commotion that the masses received the news of the president's death," stated the IDF magazine *Bamahane*, "but rather in speechless silence." Hundreds of thousands paid their respects when his coffin was displayed in the garden of his home. An editorial in *Haaretz* concluded that "the masses' tribute parade . . . was intended less for the president as an exalted officeholder, and directed more towards the sublime and revered personality of Chaim Weizmann."[96] As part of the parting ritual, the press began publishing a series of anecdotes illuminating the departed president's character and leadership for the younger generations. The most popular of these, which became entrenched in Israel's collective memory, was the one about his handkerchief being the only place he could stick his nose—as a metaphor for his exclusion from political affairs. In retrospect, however, this may not have been the most significant of those anecdotes. Writing to Martin Buber in October 1951 to thank him for sending a message of recovery, Weizmann seized the opportunity to share the most instructive insight from his final days: "Our nation has great virtues and more so shortcomings, and the problem is that we think our shortcomings are a tremendous virtue." On a more personal note, he observed with respect to Buber and, in effect, himself: "If a shortcoming is a virtue—then a Jew such as yourself must truly be worried."[97] Weizmann passed away content, for he had lived to see the fulfillment of his political dream and the budding realization of his scientific dream, but most likely, he was also worried, quite worried.

CONCLUSION

"We are in the midst of a great constructive revolution, the climax of Jewish history. We have fought a war, established a State; we are building it, but we have not yet peace," declared David Ben-Gurion at the Jerusalem Conference in September 1950. The purpose of this gathering was to raise $1.5 billion within three years to complete and absorb the mass Jewish immigration.[1] Israel's war of independence has become entrenched in both collective memory and historiography as what historian David Tal succinctly termed "Ben-Gurion's war"—a concept that encapsulates the entire period of the state's establishment in all its aspects and contexts.[2] In one very clear sense, as this study found, it was not "Ben-Gurion's war"—namely, the 6–4 vote that never took place. Shalom Rosenfeld predicted that when the minutes of the People's Administration meeting of May 12, 1948, become publicly available, "they will provide boundless material for playwrights and poets."[3] Since then, playwrights and screenwriters have found other muses to inspire their art. Author Moshe Shamir immortalized the story of his brother Eliyahu (Elik), a Palmach fighter who fell on January 22, with the words "Elik was born of the sea." Equally valid, then, is the observation offered by Israel Kolatt, a founding scholar of historical research on the Yishuv as an Israeli academic discipline: "The practical outcome of Weizmann's policy has emerged in the form of the State of Israel."[4] In 1957, at an assembly commemorating the fortieth anniversary of the Balfour Declaration at the Weizmann Institute of Science, Moshe Shamir observed that, indeed, caution, moderation, and humility had always guided Chaim Weizmann, "like a melody of the soul." And yet, he added, this was "always up to a certain point, up to the point that seemed to him, in each and every case, as *decisive*; from that point forward he was a man of bold decisions, a man of struggle, constantly aware, with all the sorrow, and pain, and lack of alternative, that 'a state is not handed on a silver platter.'"[5] The story of Weizmann in and around 1948, as presented here, provides validation and substantive weight for Shamir's assertion.

The conclusion that emerges from the description and analysis offered throughout this study is that there were numerous fundamental issues over which fierce struggles erupted, disrupting as well as paving the way to independence. Moreover, the vibrant political life that characterized the transition from Yishuv to state contributed in various ways to the structure of the democratic regime that took shape in Israel during the years 1947–1949. When it came to these issues, Ben-Gurion's political cohorts did not view him as a legend in his own time, and he knew both success and failure in his confrontations over the political agenda. Decisions on other fundamental matters, such as a constitution and borders, were postponed until later days—which are slow in coming. The willingness to refrain from deciding on certain fundamental issues stemmed mostly from an interest in prioritizing the consolidation of a stable political community, one that would cultivate a sense of collective civil responsibility. The Zionist state consciousness had gradually taken root in the Yishuv community over the course of three decades under the British Mandate. One of the keys to the transition from a voluntary society to a sovereign state was the society's recognition of the importance of participating in political life, alongside the necessity of political processes that include competition and choice, for the maintenance of functional, agreed-upon public institutions.[6]

Amid Israel's war of independence, Ben-Gurion was hopeful about the future: "I can quite imagine a Jewish state of ten million" Jews. Would they be able to reside within the borders designated by the UN, pondered the interviewer, to whom Ben-Gurion replied, "I doubt it."[7] There was no doubt, however, surrounding a more prosaic matter of governance: on February 13, 1949, the day before the Constituent Assembly convened, two political institutions of the Yishuv were disbanded—the Assembly of Representatives and the National Council, which had not functioned for several months. National Council president Yitzhak Ben-Zvi had intended to formally dissolve them in June 1948, during the first truce, but the *Altalena* incident triggered a storm that left no room for concluding ceremonies. The Assembly of Representatives' final session closed with a one-sentence speech by the National Council Executive chairman, David Remez: "Like a river flowing into the sea, this evening the Assembly of Israel flows into the State of Israel, which will exist forever."[8] Any impression that this marked the end of Remez's career as a national leader was not universally shared. Ten days later, in a telegram to the attention of Harry Truman and George Marshall, James McDonald reported that he had visited Weizmann in Rehovot two days earlier and that Weizmann had predicted that Remez would almost certainly succeed Ben-Gurion if the latter failed to form Israel's first government. McDonald conveyed Weizmann's assessment that Remez was exceptionally intelligent and kind-hearted, even if he had not been endowed with the "obvious personal leadership" that Ben-Gurion projected. Moshe Shertok was a possible candidate, he added, but his chances were lower. McDonald noted in his diary that Weizmann regarded Shertok as "an extremely able technician, but as one who was not always wise on larger issues."[9] Weizmann's unfounded assessments reflected the degree of his familiarity with and engagement in contemporaneous Israeli politics.

Remez passed away in May 1951 without having reached the top of the political pyramid. Sharett (formerly Shertok) would be the one to succeed Ben-Gurion when the latter resigned and relocated to Sde Boqer in late 1953. In any event, Mapai's status was and remained unshakable during the transition from Yishuv to state. Just before assuming the position of party secretary in October 1948, Zalman Aharonovich wrote that both the right and the left were calling it the "ruling party" and describing it as "a power that is taking control, ruling, and governing using the attributes of governance: material wealth, tremendous organization, an aggressive majority, and the like." In truth, he admitted, Mapai was lacking in what he termed "spiritual assets"—especially since the unexpected death of Berl Katznelson—and it enviously observed its sister on the left, Mapam, sweepingly enlisting the cultural elite. Aharonovich went on to conduct a historical moral inventory for Mapai in terms of its core values and conduct since the formation of the first two workers' parties in Palestine in 1905 (HaPoel HaTzair and Poalei Zion) and up to the moment of independence: "The fact is," he argued, "that if our party took control, it did so not as a majority [rov] but as a rabbi [rav]—as a guide for the workers' movement and the Yishuv, for the Zionist movement and the people, and they have no basis for disappointment with this leadership, which is the one that brought you this far."[10] On this final point, he was right even from a retrospective assessment devoid of ideational or other interests. Seven decades later, we can also confirm the observation offered by the Labor Movement's sharpest and wittiest publicist, Yitzhak Lufban, who assessed in early 1948 that "the Jewish state, when it emerges, will be analogous to a clock situated inside a glass bell, with its inner workings and gears visible to all. Moreover, this is likely to be a magnifying glass with a one-directional quality, which will amplify every flaw and fault and minimize every virtue of ours."[11]

In December 1950, Abraham Feinberg delivered a present to Truman on behalf of Ben-Gurion: not a bell, which symbolizes American independence, but a gun and bullets.[12] In May 1948, Weizmann had chosen a different type of gift for Truman when he visited Washington after Israel's establishment, the United States' recognition of it, and his own election, with the United States' blessing, as president of the Provisional State Council: a Torah.[13] Looking back years later, Mapam leader Meir Yaari apparently donned a poet's hat in admitting the disappointment felt in 1948, when "our statesman received most of their tools [weapons] and political support from the East, but their heart was in the West."[14] Feinberg tried to bring Truman to Israel in 1955 for "Weizmann Day"—November 2—marking three years since his death. The former president was unable to attend because his wife had to undergo dental work, but Feinberg did succeed in bringing him to a ceremony in New York where Feinberg received a medal from B'nai B'rith on November 27, 1960.[15] That date happened to be Weizmann's birthday as well. At other times, Feinberg would also play a central role in fundraising for the construction of the nuclear reactor in Dimona, discreetly moderating between Presidents John Kennedy and Lyndon Johnson, on the one hand, and Israel's leaders, on the other, and in Israel's receiving a "not red" light for military action in June 1967.[16] But these are stories for another time, as each era produced its own gifts. For our purposes, it seems that Weizmann's and Ben-Gurion's gifts help explain Dean Rusk's reply, when asked in the early 1990s, how he would conduct himself if he had to oversee current US policy in the Middle East. Rusk, among the most measured and insightful of the American statesmen, who labored for decades in search of a solution to the Arab-Israeli conflict, answered that he would conduct himself as he had at the time: "on my knees in prayer."[17]

NOTES

Introduction

1. Provisional State Council, minutes, 13 January 1949, *People's Council*, 10; Yadin, "Transition Law," 79–80. On Ben-Gurion, see Shapira, *Father*; Segev, *State*.

2. Tal, "Declaration of Independence," 566.

3. UN General Assembly, Resolution 181, Partition Plan, A/RES/181(II) (29 November 1947); Mapai Central Committee, minutes, 8 January 1948, Labor Party Archives (hereafter cited as LPA).

4. Avineri, "A Leader's Place."

5. Bareli, "Between Party Politics."

6. Gelber, "Development." See also Tal, *War in Palestine*; Gelber, *Independence and Nakba*; Morris, *1948*; Bar-On, *In the Forefront of the Fiercest Battles*.

7. Tzahor, *Israel's Political Roots*, 11–20; Shapira, "Elements of the National Ethos," 255; Sharef, *Three Days*.

8. On Weizmann, see Golani and Reinharz, *Founding Father*.

9. Golani, *Last Commissioner*, 298–300.

10. Zionist General Council, minutes, 22 August 1948, Ben-Gurion Archives (hereafter cited as BGA). On Silver, see Shiff, *Defeated Zionist*.

11. See, for example, Ganin, "US View"; Ben-Zvi, *From Truman to Obama*.

12. Weizmann to Truman, 12 December 1945, in Weizmann, *Letters*, vol. 22, 80–81.

13. Ezriel Carlebach, "Independence in Exile in New York," *Maariv*, 11 May 1951.

1. The Path to Sovereignty

1. Bullock, *Ernest Bevin*, 359–363; General Zionist Council, minutes, 28 December 1946, Central Zionist Archives (hereafter cited as CZA); Ofer, *Enemy and Rival*, 218–219. Bevin had long been considering referring the question of Palestine to the UN and in fact notified Abba Hillel Silver of this option as early as November 14, 1946. Louis, *British Empire*, 444–445.

2. Ben-Gurion to Paula Ben-Gurion, 14 February 1947, BGA; Ben-Gurion's Diary, 15 February 1947, BGA; Cohen, *Palestine*, 203–223.

3. The United Nations Special Committee on Palestine (UNSCOP) was established on May 14, 1947.

4. "'Partition!' Says the Majority of the UN Commission," *Davar*, 1 September 1947; Freundlich, *From Destruction to Resurrection*, 98–129. An ad hoc committee established by the UN General Assembly to discuss the question of Palestine, on the basis of UNSCOP recommendations, reduced the transition period from two years to one year. This committee also reduced the territory allocated to the Jewish state relative to the Arab state, from 62:38 to 55:45 (percent).

5. National Council Executive, minutes, 11 September 1947, J1/7267, CZA. Warhaftig, who had immigrated to Palestine a few weeks earlier, became the new HaPoel HaMizrachi representative to the National Council Executive. *Mizrachi* as used here was an acronym for the phrase "religious center."

6. Mapai Secretariat, minutes, 11 October 1947, 18 November 1947, LPA.

7. Shapira, "A Political History of the Yishuv," 8–15.

8. Bareli and Gorny, "Unity and Participation," 127–167.

9. Mapai Secretariat, minutes, 18 September 1947, LPA.

10. Mapai Council, minutes, 8 August 1947, LPA; Zionist General Council, minutes, 26 August 1947, BGA.

11. Assembly of Representatives, 2 October 1947, in Ben-Gurion, *Chimes of Independence*, 382–384; Fifth Zionist Conference of Keren HaYesod, in Ben-Gurion, *Chimes of Independence*, 438.

12. "Questions of the Hour: An Emergency Higher Committee," *Haboker*, 16 October 1947; "Yishuv Leadership Authorized to Establish Jewish State for Entire Nation," *Haboker*, 21 October 1947; "Permanent Representation to Local Authorities Established," *Haboker*, 28 October 1947; Mapai Secretariat, minutes, 21 October 1947, LPA.

13. "The Internal Debate," editorial, *Haaretz*, 22 November 1947; "National Council Assembly," editorial, *Haaretz*, 11 November 1947; Yosef Sapir, "State, Not Strife," *Haaretz*, 6 November 1947; M. Kramer, "Reply to Mr. Sapir," *Haaretz*, 7 November 1947.

14. Warhaftig, "Memoranda on the Constitutional Problems of the Jewish State," Memorandum A, 9 October 1947, in *A Constitution for Israel: Religion and State*, 442.

15. Warhaftig, *A Constitution for Israel*, 185–187; Mapai Secretariat, minutes, 11 October 1947, LPA.

16. National Council Plenum, minutes, 25 November 1947, J1/7241, CZA.

17. Ben-Gurion's Diary, 30 November 1947, BGA.

18. "Notice from D. Ben-Gurion," *Davar*, 30 November 1947; Jewish Agency Executive, minutes, 7 December 1947, CZA.

19. Jewish Agency Executive, minutes, 30 November 1947, CZA; Mapai Secretariat, minutes, 30 December 1947, LPA. Lake Success, New York, was the temporary seat of the UN headquarters until 1951.

20. National Council Executive, decisions, 30 November 1947, 1 December 1947, J1/7268, CZA.

21. Histadrut Executive Committee, minutes, 3 December 1947, Lavon Institute for Labour Movement Research (hereafter cited as Lavon Institute); Mapai Central Committee, minutes, 3 December 1947, LPA (emphasis added).

22. Mapai Central Committee, minutes, 3 December 1947, LPA.

23. Central Bureau of Statistics, *Immigration to Israel, 2007–2010* (Jerusalem: CBS, 2012), 28.

24. Mapai Secretariat, minutes, 6 January 1948, LPA.

25. Mapai Central Committee, minutes, 3 December 1947, LPA.

26. Truman to Morgenthau, 2 December 1947, Morgenthau Papers, Box 776, Weizmann File, Franklin D. Roosevelt Presidential Library (hereafter cited as FDRL); on Morgenthau, see Levy, *Henry Morgenthau, Jr.*

27. Jewish Agency Executive, minutes, 7 December 1947, CZA.

28. David Ben-Gurion, "Our Efforts and Our Victims—Labor Pains of the State of Israel," *Davar*, 2 January 1948.

29. Gelber, *Independence and Nakba*, 60–70. The data on casualties is taken from remarks by Ben-Gurion, Mapai Secretariat, minutes, 8 January 1948, LPA.

30. Mapai Secretariat, minutes, 8 January 1948, LPA (emphasis added).

31. Ze'ev Sharef, interviewed by Yigal Dunitz, 12 August 1975, Oral Documentation Division, BGA.

32. Security Committee, minutes, 13 January 1948, Security Committee File, BGA.

33. "Words of Repentance at Mapai Security Gathering," 15 January 1948, BGA; Ben-Gurion, "Towards a Turning Point," 15 January 1948, in *As Israel Fought*, 36–37.

34. Mapai Secretary Zeev Isserson (On) to Associates, 14 January 1948, BGA; "In the Secretariat," *Hapoel Hatzair*, 20 January 1948.

35. Mapai Secretariat, minutes, 16 January 1948, BGA. The minutes are not on file at the LPA.

36. Ben-Gurion, *Army and Security*, 23–28; Ben-Gurion, *Uniqueness and Destiny*, 19–22.

37. Mapai Secretariat, minutes, 16 January 1948, BGA.

38. Ben-Gurion's Diary, 17 January 1948, BGA.

39. "Decisive Defeat for Gush Etzion Attackers," "Arab Losses Outnumber Ours Tenfold," staff columnist, "In the Fighting over Gush Etzion," *Davar*, 16 January 1948; "Loyalty and Friendship," editorial, *Davar*, 18 January 1948.

40. Israel Cohen, "The Yishuv in Battle," *Hapoel Hatzair*, 20 January 1948; "The Battle Escalates," editorial, *Davar*, 23 January 1948.

41. Buber, Magnes, and Senator to press offices, 27 January 1948, BGA.

42. Ben-Gurion, "Problems of Security and Defense," Ohel Shem Cultural Center, Tel Aviv, 27 January 1948, BGA.

43. Ben-Gurion, "Profile of the Jewish Defender," *Ashmoret*, 4 March 1948.

44. Security Committee, minutes, 10 February 1948, Security Committee File, BGA.

45. These observations relate in particular to Ben-Gurion's efforts to impose his outlook on the security establishment and in the conduct of the war, an issue that has received comprehensive and detailed examination in the scholarship. See Shapira, *Army Controversy*; Gelber, *Why Was the Palmach Disbanded?*

46. Shertok to Reuven Zaslani and Ze'ev Sharef, 30 January 1948, in Yogev, *Documents*, 266–267; Shertok to Ben-Gurion, 6 February 1948, in Yogev, *Documents*, 312; Jewish Agency Executive, minutes, 9 February 1948, S44/565, CZA.

47. Ben-Dror, *Ralph Bunch*, 44–49. The Commission members were Denmark, Czechoslovakia, Panama, Bolivia, and the Philippines—a composition of unimposing international status by any measure.

48. "Eliezer Kaplan: Don't Hope to Find 'Moderate' Jews," *Haaretz*, 10 February 1948.

49. Remez to Ben-Gurion, 2 February 1948, J1/14155, CZA. On Agudat Israel's steadily increasing participation in political efforts to establish a Jewish state in 1948, see Ehrenvald, *Haredim*, 30–36, 87–90.

50. National Council Plenum, minutes, 16 February 1948, J1/8029, CZA.

51. Ibid.; National Council Executive, minutes, 9 February 1948, 11 February 1948, J1/6589, CZA.

52. Security Committee, minutes, 10 February 1948, Security Committee File, BGA.

53. National Council Plenum, minutes, 16 February 1948, J1/8029, CZA.

54. Sprinzak to Naomi and Zvi, 20 February 1948, in Sprinzak, *Letters*, vol. 3, 18.

55. Jewish Agency Executive, minutes, 1 February 1948, CZA; Jewish Agency Executive, minutes, 15 February 1948, 7900/24, Israel State Archives (hereafter cited as ISA).

56. Sprinzak to Naomi and Zvi, 20 February 1948, in Sprinzak, *Letters*, vol. 3, 18.

57. Ben-Gurion's Diary, 11 February 1948, BGA. On Myerson's fundraising efforts, see Medzini, *Golda*, 175–185, 198–199; Goldstein, *Golda*, 237–245.

58. Editorial, *Davar*, 17 February 1948.

59. Natan Alterman, "American Jewish Delegation," The Seventh Column, *Davar*, 20 February 1948 (my translation).

60. Histadrut Executive Committee, 4 March 1948, Lavon Institute.

61. Ben-Gurion to Shertok, 12 February 1948, in Yogev, *Documents*, 332–333; Freundlich, *From Destruction to Resurrection*, 207.

62. Shertok to Ben-Gurion, 18 February 1948, BGA; Ben-Gurion's Diary, 27 February 1948, BGA.

63. Histadrut Executive Committee, minutes, 31 December 1947, Lavon Institute.

64. "Elkana" [Haganah news service] to "Amitai" [Ben-Gurion], Memorandum No. 2, 16 February 1948, BGA; Ben-Gurion, remarks at a gathering of the Mobilization Fund, 17 February 1948, BGA; Ben-Gurion's Diary, 17 February 1948, BGA.

65. Ben-Gurion to Shertok, 27 February 1948, in Ben-Gurion, *War Diary*, vol. 1, 266; Ben-Gurion's Diary, 27 February 1948, BGA.

66. Henry Montor to Ben-Gurion, 2 July 1945, BGA; Teveth, *Kin'at David*, vol. 4, 519–531; Rosen, *American Treasure*. On the Sonneborn Institute, see also Slater, *Pledge*, 78–83, 106–107, 116–117; Penslar, *Jews and the Military*, 239–244.

67. Ben-Gurion to Kaplan, 14 December 1947, BGA; Ben-Gurion to Myerson, 11 February 1948, BGA; Ben-Gurion to Meyerov, 5 April 1948 (emphasis in the original), 11 April 1948, BGA; Ben-Gurion to Shertok, 16 April 1948, in Yogev, *Documents*, 648.

68. Shertok to Ben-Gurion, 13 February 1948, in Yogev, *Documents*, 336; Ben-Gurion to Shertok, 13 February 1948, in Yogev, *Documents*, 339.

69. Shertok to Kaplan and Ben-Gurion, 29 February 1948, BGA. See also the telegrams of 18 February 1948, 20 February 1948, 1 March 1948, in Yogev, *Documents*, 359, 367, 403.

70. Ben-Gurion's Diary, 18 February 1948, 27 February 1948, BGA; Kaplan to Ben-Gurion, 2 March 1948, BGA. The minutes of the Jewish Agency Executive meeting of February 27 could not be located.

71. National Council Plenum, minutes, 1 March 1948, J1/7242, CZA; "The Establishment of the Provisional Government Council," *Davar*, 3 March 1948.

72. Remez to Ben-Gurion, 3 March 1948, S44/566, CZA. According to Lehi, its attack was in retaliation for British soldiers having assisted in causing an explosion near national institutions in Jerusalem on February 22, killing forty-nine Jews.

73. Ibid.

74. Ben-Gurion to Shertok and Myerson, 3 March 1948, BGA; Ben-Gurion's Diary, 3 March 1948, BGA; Sharef to Ben-Gurion, 17 December 1947, Emergency Committee File, BGA. The minutes of the Jewish Agency Executive meeting of March 3 could not be located.

75. Ben-Gurion's Diary, 3 March 1948, BGA; Mapai Secretariat, decision, 3 March 1948, File of Minutes from Secretariat Meetings, LPA.

76. Mapai Central Committee, minutes, 6 March 1948, LPA; Ben-Gurion's Diary, 6 March 1948, BGA; Women's Organizations to Ben-Gurion, 10 March 1948, BGA; Ben-Gurion to Women's Organizations, 29 March 1948, BGA; Ben-Gurion to Shertok and Myerson, 14 March 1948, in Yogev, *Documents*, 460.

77. Ezriel Carlebach, "Battle Diary," *Maariv*, 8 March 1948.

78. Ben-Gurion to Shertok and Myerson, 14 March 1948, in Yogev, *Documents*, 459–460.

79. American Section of the Jewish Agency Executive to Ben-Gurion, 22 March 1948, in Yogev, *Documents*, 489–490.

80. Ben-Gurion's Diary, 22 March 1948, BGA.

81. Ben-Gurion to Shertok, 23 March 1948, in Yogev, *Documents*, 496; National Council Executive, decisions, 23 March 1948, J1/8099, CZA; "Jewish Government: Statement by the Jewish Agency and the National Council," 7900/24-A, ISA.

82. Ben-Gurion to Shertok, 23 March 1948, in Yogev, *Documents*, 496 (as noted, the UN Partition Plan mentioned a "Provisional Council of Government," not a provisional government as referenced by Ben-Gurion); Ben-Gurion's Diary, 22 March 1948, 25 March 1948, BGA; Jewish Agency Executive, decisions of 22–25 March 1948, BGA. Records of those discussions have not been located.

83. Eilam, "Historians and the Declaration of Statehood," in *What Happened Here*, 178.

84. Mapai Secretariat, minutes, 20 March 1948, LPA.

85. Ibid.; Ben-Gurion's Diary, 25 March 1948, BGA; "Summary of Mapai Political Committee Meeting with Our Members in the Jewish Agency Executive and the National Council Executive," 24 March 1948, 2-26-1948-6, LPA.

86. Ben-Gurion to Shertok, 28 March 1948, BGA; Gelber, *Independence and Nakba*, 110–113.

87. Remez to Ben-Gurion, 22 March 1948, 29 March 1948, S44/566, CZA; Israeli Galili and Yigal Yadin to Yohanan Ratner, 26 March 1948, BGA; Ben-Gurion's Diary, 28 March 1948, BGA.

88. Ben-Gurion to Mapai Bureau, 30 March 1948, S53/2092, CZA (emphasis in the original); Avizohar and Bareli, *Now or Never*, 391–393.

89. Remez to Mapai Bureau, 1 April 1948, in Avizohar and Bareli, *Now or Never*, 393–395.

90. Frister, *Uncompromising*, 357; Zvi Maimon (Ben-Gurion's personal secretary, writing what was clearly a dictated letter on his behalf) to the World Confederation of General Zionists, 29 March 1948, BGA (the source for the first remark by Ben-Gurion); Ben-Gurion to Zalman Schocken, 27 April 1948, BGA (the source for the second remark by Ben-Gurion).

91. Chaim Berman, Walter Eytan, Leo Cohen, and Eliyahu Sasson to Shertok, 28 March 1948, in Yogev, *Documents*, 526; Leo Cohen to Ben-Gurion, 29 March 1948, BGA.

92. Golani, *British Mandate*, 45–46; Gelber, *The Emergence*, 109. On Operation Nachshon, see Gelber, *The Emergence*, 106–130; Milstein, *History*, 242–296.

93. Summary of Military Situation, 1 April 1948, BGA.

94. Gelber, *Independence and Nakba*, 111, 119.

95. Untitled document, 4 April 1948, BGA. The speakers' names are indicated by initials.

96. Ibid.

97. Security Committee, minutes, 1 April 1948, 4 April 1948, Security Committee File, BGA; Israel Rokach and G. Felt to Ben-Gurion, 4 May 1948, and Ben-Gurion to Rokach and G. Felt, 4 May 1948, Security Committee File, BGA; Shapira, *Army Controversy*, 24–25.

98. Yitzhak Ben-Zvi to Jewish Agency Executive, 5 April 1948, in Yogev, *Documents*, 559–561; Gelber, *The Emergence*, 115.

99. Zionist General Council, minutes, 6 April 1948, CZA. See Jewish Agency Statistics Department, "Summary of Casualties from the Hostilities during December 1947 And January–March 1948," May 1948, S25/7732, CZA.

100. Zionist General Council, 6 April 1948, CZA.

101. Shertok to Ben-Gurion (two telegrams), 11 April 1948, in Yogev, *Documents*, 604–605.

102. "Declaration by the Zionist General Council," 12 April 1948, in Tsoref, *Zalman Shazar*, 311–312; Shachar, *Dignity*, 42–47.

103. "Behind the Scenes of the Zionist General Council: The Full Megillah," *Hamashkif*, 13 April 1948.

104. Jewish Agency Executive, minutes (two sessions), 11 April 1948, CZA; Mapai Political Committee, decisions, 24 March 1948, LPA; "Zionist General Council Session Adjourned," *Davar*, 13 April 1948; *Haaretz*, editorials, 3 March 1948, 14 April 1948; Avizohar and Bareli, *Now or Never*, 364–365. On Deir Yassin, see Tauber, *Deir Yassin*. On the Revisionists' efforts to join the provisional government, see Weitz, *From Underground to Political Party*, 98–100.

105. Jewish Agency Executive, minutes (evening session), 11 April 1948, CZA.

106. "Internal Yishuv Inquiries," *Davar*, 9 March 1948; Jewish Agency Executive, minutes, 14 April 1948, CZA; "May the Torah of Israel Be the Foundation of the State of Israel," *Hatzofeh*, 19 April 1948; "Chief Rabbi Herzog on the Jewish Government," *Hatzofeh*, 18 April 1948; D. Levenstein and Y. Abramowicz (Agudat Israel representatives) to Dobkin, 23 April 1948, CZA; Ehrenvald, *Haredim*, 90.

107. Bareli, "Mapai during the War," 188–189.

108. Weizmann, "Plea to Accept Partition Plan," 287.

109. Summary of joint meeting of Mapai Political Committee, members from the United States, and members of the Mapai Bureau, 17 April 1948, 2-26-1948-6, CZA; Yud-Gimel meeting, minutes, 18 April 1948, *People's Administration*, 9.

110. "I Read It—I Wrote It Down," *Maariv*, 19 April 1948; "Partition of the Country + Allocation of Portfolios =?," *Hamashkif*, 20 April 1948.

111. Shertok to Ben-Gurion (two telegrams), 11 April 1948, in Yogev, *Documents*, 604–605.

112. "The People's Council," editorial, *Davar*, 4 May 1948; People's Administration, minutes, 18 April 1948, 12–13.

113. People's Council, minutes, 4 May 1948, 6.

114. "Powers and Functions of Yud-Gimel and Lamed-Zayin," *Davar*, 21 April 1948.

115. Ben-Gurion to Mapai Bureau, 18 April 1948, in Avizohar and Bareli, *Now or Never*, 399–400.

116. Ben-Gurion to People's Administration members, 19 April 1948, BGA; People's Administration, minutes, 3 May 1948, 12 May 1948, 55–57, 157–160; Shapira, *Army Controversy*, 28–49.

117. Mapai Central Committee, minutes, 6 March 1948, LPA (emphasis added).

2. The "Red Shadow" and
Weizmann's Involvement

1. "C. Weizmann—President of the State Council," *Davar*, 17 May 1948; Provisional State Council, 16 May 1948, 4–5.

2. Ben-Gurion, "Preface," 5.

3. Weizmann, *Trial and Error*, 573; Cohen-Levinovsky, "Presidents," 496.

4. See Eban, "Tragedy and Triumph."

5. Rose, *Weizmann*, 434–446.

6. Ibid., 279–280; Horowitz, *In the Heart of Events*, 24; Kimchi, *First President*, 105.

7. Rose, *Weizmann*, 445.

8. "A Detail: Weizmann and Partition," *Davar*, 21 November 1947.

9. Weisgal, *So Far*, 263; Weizmann, *The Impossible*, 231. See also Orian, *Forgotten Founder*, 736.

10. Nimrod, *War or Peace*.

11. Ibid., 172.

12. See, for example, Snetsinger, *Jewish Vote*; Ganin, *Truman*; Grose, *Israel*; Cohen, *Truman and Israel*; Benson, *Truman*; Ottolenghi, "Harry Truman's Recognition of Israel"; Radosh, *Safe Haven*; Judis, *Genesis*, 283–319.

13. Weizmann, *Trial and Error*, 573–589.

14. Cohn to Vera Weizmann, 14 August 1952, Weizmann Archives (hereafter cited as WA); Cohn to Weisgal, 3 November 1952, WA; Jacobson to Cohn, 30 March 1952 (published as Eddie Jacobson, "Two Presidents and a Haberdasher—1948," *American Jewish Archives*, April 1968, pp. 4–15), Z5/3141, CZA (hereafter cited as Jacobson Letter); Cohn, "Report on Dr. Weizmann's Visit to the USA (February–May 1948)," Z5/3141, CZA (hereafter cited as Cohn Report).

15. See Weisgal, *So Far*, 261–262.

16. Ben-Gurion to Weizmann, 22 August 1937, in Ben-Gurion, *Memoirs*, vol. 4, 422–424 (my emphasis); Goldstein, *Path to Hegemony*, 124–167. For the relations between Weizmann and Ben-Gurion in different periods, see, for example, Gorny, *Partnership*; Teveth, *Kin'at David*, vol. 3, 64–70, 120–150, 201–209, and so on; Shapira, "Weizmann and Ben-Gurion."

17. Ben-Gurion to Weizmann, 28 October 1946, BGA.

18. Slutsky, *History of the Haganah*, vol. 3, 897; Weizmann to Shertok, 27 June 1946, in Weizmann, *Letters*, vol. 22, 228–229, 231 (the letter was not sent until January 20, 1947).

19. Weizmann, "The Appeal That Failed," 16 December 1946, Twenty-Second Zionist Congress, in Litvinoff, *Papers*, series B, vol. 2, 642–651; Rose, *Weizmann*, 418–420.

20. Ben-Gurion to the Chairman of Permanent Committee of the Zionist Congress, Zalman Rubashov, 20 December 1946, in Ben-Gurion, *Towards the End of the Mandate*, 288–296; Zionist General Council, minutes, 28 December 1946, CZA; Teveth, *Kin'at David*, vol. 4, 852–885.

21. Jewish Agency Executive, 29 December 1947, CZA.

22. Ben-Gurion's Diary, 27 June 1935, BGA.

23. See Weizmann's letters to Frankfurter, 7 January 1947, 1 May 1947; to Weisgal, 7 January 1947, 20 January 1947, 27 March 1947; to Ginsburg, 10 January 1947, 16 March 1947; to Rokach, 16 January 1947; to Sprinzak, 29 January 1947; to Kaplan, 23 January 1947, 27 March 1947, in Weizmann, *Letters*, vol. 22, 214–217, 223–224, 232, 234–235, 240, 274–275, 294, 296, 329; Gorny, *Partnership*, 202.

24. Weizmann to Henry Morgenthau Jr., 13 January 1947, in Weizmann, *Letters*, vol. 22, 221–222; Weizmann to Weisgal, 13 January 1947, in Weizmann, *Letters*, vol. 22, 223. The remaining two-thirds of the UJA funds were allocated to the Joint Distribution Committee and Jewish communities in the United States.

25. Weizmann to Sprinzak, 29 January 1947, in Weizmann, *Letters*, vol. 22, 241; Weizmann to Kaplan, 23 January 1947, 27 March 1947, in Weizmann, *Letters*, vol. 22, 234–235, 294.

26. Weizmann to Kaplan, 27 March 1947, in Weizmann, *Letters*, vol. 22, 292; Weizmann to Morgenthau, 1 May 1947, WA; Teveth, *Kin'at David*, vol. 3, 416–418.

27. Sprinzak to Pinhas Lubianker and Benjamin West, 23 January 1947, S53/2058, CZA.

28. Weizmann to Shertok, January 1947 [no precise date], in Weizmann, *Letters*, vol. 22, 237; Weizmann to Kaplan, 29 June 1947, in Weizmann, *Letters*, vol. 22, 353–354; Gorny, *Partnership*, 201.

29. Weizmann to Weisgal, 23 March 1947, in Weizmann, *Letters*, vol. 22, 296.

30. Jewish Agency Executive, minutes, 26 April 1947, LPA.

31. Mapai Central Committee, minutes, 8 June 1947, 18 June 1947, CZA; Cohen-Levinovsky, "Presidents," 503.

32. "Weizmann's Speech before UN Committee," *Davar*, 9 July 1947.

33. Ganin, *Truman*, 138–142; Cohen, *Truman and Israel*, 159–160; Radosh, *Safe Haven*, 261–265; Cohen-Levinovsky, "Presidents," 504–507.

34. Jewish Agency Executive, US section, minutes, 13 October 1947, Z5/2372, CZA.

35. Neumann to Morgenthau, 27 October 1947, Morgenthau Papers, Box 776, Neumann File, FDRL; Weizmann to Albert K. Epstein, 10 November 1947, in Weizmann, *Letters*, vol. 23, 27–28; Sprinzak to Hannah Sprinzak (his wife), 20 November 1947, in Sprinzak, *Letters*, vol. 3, 12; Rose, *Weizmann*, 427–428.

36. Mapai Central Committee, minutes, 16 December 1947, LPA.

37. "The Jews Are Ready to Govern—Weizmann," *Davar*, 2 December 1947; editorial, *Davar*, 2 December 1947. A verbatim record of Weizmann's remarks could not be located.

38. Silver to Arthur Lourie (director of the Secretariat of the American section of the Jewish Agency Executive in New York), 21 January 1948, in Yogev, *Documents*, 215; Jewish Agency Executive, minutes, 25 January 1948, CZA; Jewish Agency Executive, US section, minutes, 25 February 1948, BGA; Orian, *Forgotten Founder*, 640–653; Shiff, "Abba Hillel Silver and David Ben-Gurion," 395–396. On Truman's lukewarm attitude toward Silver, see, for example, Cohen, *Truman and Israel*, 66–67; Benson, *Truman*, 95–97. On the US embargo, see Ilan, *Origin*, 76–106.

39. Jewish Agency Executive, minutes, 25 January 1948, CZA.

40. House of Commons Debates, *Hansard*, 22 January 1948, vol. 446, col. 384, 388; "Bevin Threatens Russia and Announces Western Europe's Cohesion," *Davar*, 23 January 1948.

41. See Linton to Brodetsky, 25 January 1948, in Yogev, *Documents*, 224–225; Epstein to Myerson, 19 January 1948, in Yogev, *Documents*, 187–196; Shertok to Ben-Gurion, 19 January 1948, in Yogev, *Documents*, 187; Israel Goldstein (acting chairman of the American Zionist Emergency Council in Silver's absence) to Jewish Agency Executive, US section, 19 January 1948, in Yogev, *Documents*, 190–192; Jewish Agency Executive, summary of meeting, 22 January 1948, BGA.

42. Ben-Gurion and Bevin, meeting, 12 February 1947, in Ben-Gurion, *Towards the End of the Mandate*, 354–356.

43. Ben-Gurion to Bevin, 14 February 1947, BGA.

44. Bialer, "Documents," 539.

45. Jewish Agency Executive, minutes, 11 May 1947, CZA; Shertok to Myerson, 11 August 1947, S25/3985, CZA (emphasis in the original); Freundlich, *From Destruction to Resurrection*, 85–87, 146–147.

46. Ro'i, *Soviet Decision Making*, 136–137n34, 221n23.

47. Mapai Bureau, minutes, 6 March 1949, LPA; Bialer, *Between East and West*, 35.

48. Mapai Central Committee, minutes, 3 December 1947, LPA; Bialer, *Between East and West*.

49. "The Watchman," *Time*, 16 August 1948.

50. Bialer, "Top Hat, Tuxedo and Cannons," 647–667.

51. Zionist General Council, minutes, 7 April 1948, BGA.

52. Louis, *British Empire*, 495–508; Eilat, *Struggle*, vol. 2, 531.

53. See Ro'i, "Deterioration of Relations"; Freundlich, "Soviet Outpost."

54. "Little Accident," *Time*, 15 March 1948.

55. Kennan, memorandum, 19 January 1948, *Foreign Relations of the United States* (hereafter cited as FRUS), 1948, vol. 5, 546–554; Kennan to Marshall, 20 January 1948, FRUS, 1948, vol. 5, 546; Policy Planning Staff, 22 February 1948, FRUS, 1948, vol. 5, 619–625; Miscamble, *Kennan*, 93–99; Eilat, *Struggle*, vol. 2, 519–525, 538–539; Louis, *British Empire*, 498–502.

56. Ben-Gurion's Diary, 13 February 1948, BGA.

57. Kennan, 28 January 1948, in *Diaries*, 210–211.

58. Clifford to Truman, memorandum, 8 March 1948, FRUS, 1948, vol. 5, 690–696; Eilat, *Struggle*, vol. 1, 213–214; Cohen, *Palestine*, 350–354; Ganin, *Truman*, 157–160. On Clifford, see, for example, Frantz and McKean, *Friends*.

59. Jewish Agency, New York, memorandum, 30 January 1948, in Yogev, *Documents*, 267–276.

60. Weizmann, *Trial and Error*, 575–576; Eban, "Tragedy and Triumph," 353–354; Lourie to Weizmann, 26 January 1948, 67/6-FO, ISA; Shertok to Ben-Gurion, 26 January 1948, in Yogev, *Documents*, 237; Ben-Gurion's Diary, 30 January 1948, BGA; Kurzman, *Genesis*, 90–93.

61. Vera Weizmann's Diary, 4 February 1948, WA.

62. Herbert L. Matthews, "London Insists Communists Were Bound for Palestine," *New York Times*, 1 February 1948; "Shertok Denies British Charge of Communists on Refugee Ships," *New York Times*, 2 February 1948.

63. Joint Intelligence Committee, "Illegal Jewish Immigration from Pan York and Pan Crescent," 23 January 1948, Co 537/3880, National Archives, London (hereafter cited as NA); Cunningham to the Secretary of State for the Colonies, 19 January 1948, Co 537/3954, NA; Bergman, "Unexpected Recognition," 159–161.

64. Bergman, "Unexpected Recognition," 159–161.

65. Secretary of State for the Colonies to Commissioner of Jewish Camps, Cyprus, 3 February 1948, Co 537/3954, NA; Matthews, "Britain Confirms Smuggling of Reds," *New York Times*, 5 February 1948.

66. "Information Received by Marshall," *New York Times*, 5 February 1948; Hahn, *Caught in the Middle East*, 29.

67. "Zionist Denounces U.S. Arms Embargo," *New York Times*, 7 February 1948; Epstein to Marshall, 4 February 1948, in Yogev, *Documents*, 293; Zalman Lifshitz, memorandum, 15 February 1948, in Yogev, *Documents*, 342–343.

68. Epstein to Jewish Agency Executive, 5 March 1948, in Yogev, *Documents*, 427.

69. I. F. Stone, "The Mood in America on the Palestine Question: Unfounded Fears in the State Department," *Davar*, 16 January 1948. The article originally appeared in the illustrated American periodical *Picture Magazine*.

70. See, for example, "British Foreign Office Is the Source of the Conspiracy," *Davar*, 4 February 1948; "No U.S. Comment on Refugee Red Scare," *Palestine Post*, 6 February 1948.

71. Joint Intelligence Committee, "Short Term Intentions of the Soviet Union in Palestine," 13 February 1948 Co 537/3880, NA; Epstein to Ben-Gurion, 4 February 1948, in Yogev, *Documents*, 292.

72. Marshall, memorandum, 12 May 1948, FRUS, 1948, vol. 5, 975.

73. Marshall to Lovett, 25 November 1947, FRUS, 1947, vol. 5, 1288; Benson, *Truman*, 85; Louis, *British Empire*, 480–481, 495–508.

74. Weizmann to Truman, 28 November 1947, in Weizmann, *Letters*, vol. 23, 45.

75. Shertok to Ben-Gurion, 11 February 1948, in Yogev, *Documents*, 332; Histadrut Executive Committee, minutes, 31 December 1947 to 1 January 1948, Lavon Institute.

76. Histadrut Executive Committee, minutes, 14 January 1948, Lavon Institute.

77. Mapai Secretariat, minutes, 5 April 1948, LPA; Heller, *Birth of Israel*, 36.

78. "Moscow Fiercely Attacks Weizmann," *Maariv*, 9 April 1948.

79. Gideon Ruffer (Rafael) to Ze'ev Sharef, 10 February 1948, in Yogev, *Documents*, 325.

80. Cohen, *Palestine*, 348–349; Forrestal, 18 February 1948, in *Forrestal Diaries*, 376; James V. Forrestal Papers, *Diaries*, 18 February 1948, used with the permission of Princeton University Library.

81. Marshall to Lovett, 19 February 1948, FRUS, 1948, vol. 5, 633; Cohen, *Palestine*, 350–366.

82. Isaacson and Thomas, *Wise Men*, 451–452.

83. Ganin, *Truman*, 138–142, 167–168, 179; Cohen, *Truman and Israel*, 159–160, 182–198; Benson, *Truman*, 120–121, 133–146; Freundlich, *From Destruction to Resurrection*, 227–231.

84. Joseph and Stewart Alsop, "Matter of Fact: Object Lesson," *New York Herald Tribune*, 25 March 1948; "The End of Partition," *Time*, 29 March 1948.

85. "The Jewish State Will Indeed Come to Be!" *Haaretz*, 21 March 1948.

86. "As Long as Jews Live in This Country They Will Be Free" (statement by Remez), "The Jewish State Exists and Will Exist If We Defend It" (statement by Ben-Gurion), *Davar*, 21 March 1948.

87. "Marshall Said to Explain U.S. Shift on Partition as Step to Aid Peace," *New York Times*, 25 March 1948.

88. Shertok, Epstein—Marshall, Lovett, meeting report, 26 March 1948, in Yogev, *Documents*, 509–521 (the quote appears on p. 517).

89. Shertok to Lovett (on the day after their meeting), 22 February 1948, in Yogev, *Documents*, 372; Shertok, Epstein—Marshall, Lovett, meeting report, 26 March 1948, in Yogev, *Documents*, 519–520; Epstein, memorandum to Jewish Agency Executive on his meeting of March 26 with Henderson, 29 March 1948, in Yogev, *Documents*, 528–531.

90. Epstein to Ben-Gurion, 29 March 1948, BGA; Shertok to Ben-Gurion, 30 March 1948, BGA.

91. Forrestal, diary entry, 4 April 1948, FRUS, 1948, vol. 5, 797–798.

92. Forrestal to Marshall, 19 April 1948, FRUS, 1948, vol. 5, 832–833; Rusk, memorandum on conversation with Truman, 30 April 1948, FRUS, 1948, vol. 5, 877–879; Cohen, *Palestine*, 363–365.

93. Freundlich, *From Destruction to Resurrection*, 238–247.

94. Shertok, report on meeting with Lovett and Rusk, 9 April 1948, in Yogev, *Documents*, 593, 595.

95. Abraham Feinberg, speech, 25 November 1947, WA; "2,000 at Weizmann Dinner Cheer First President of Jewish State," *New York Times*, 26 November 1947.

96. Ibid.; "Vote on Palestine Cheered by Crowd," *New York Times*, 30 November 1947; "Fund Aid Stressed by Zionists Here," *New York Times*, 8 December 1947; "For Jewish State Expected to Clinch Decision to Set Up Permanent Conference," *Jewish Telegraphic Agency*, 1 December 1947.

97. "'Americans for Haganah' Organized in the United States," *Jewish Telegraphic Agency*, 3 July 1947. On Feinberg, Dewey Stone (discussed next), and Edmund Kaufmann (discussed below), see Cohen, *Truman and Israel*, 70–73. On American Jewish involvement in founding and managing the Weizmann Institute of Science, see Cohen, *Laboratory*, 115–155.

98. *A Story of Daring and Dedication in the Dramatic Events Leading to the Establishment and Development of the State of Israel and the Weizmann Institute of Science Published in Tribute to Dewey D. Stone and Harry Levine on the Occasion of the Birthday Dinner* (pamphlet), 16 December 1970, New York, 8–10; Hammer, "David Stone"; Eban, "Dewey David Stone"; Kaplan to Stone, 31 January 1946, P-529, Box 3, Folder 15, Dewey Stone Collection, Jewish Heritage Center at New England Historic Genealogical Society, Boston (hereafter cited as JHC); Cohen, *Truman and Israel*, 70–71; Rosen, *American Treasure*, 156–157. On the purchase of weapons in the United States, see also Ilan, *Origin*, 72–108.

99. "ZBT Frat Honors Dewey Stone and Frank Goldman," *Jewish Advocate*, 26 February 1948; Stone to Bisgyer, 3 August 1970, P-529, Box 3, Folder 15, Dewey Stone Collection, JHC (hereafter cited as Stone Letter).

100. Ibid.; Weizmann to Truman, 10 February 1948, in Weizmann, *Letters*, vol. 23, 86; Bisgyer, *Challenge*, 190.

101. Jacobson to Matthew Connelly, 26 January 1948, Connelly to Jacobson, 27 January 1948, Papers of Edward Jacobson, Correspondence File, Correspondence—White House Aides, 1946–1952, Box 1, Harry S. Truman Presidential Library, Independence, Missouri (hereafter cited as HSTL); "In Washington Yesterday," *New York Times*, 30 January 1948.

102. See Jacobson Letter; Cohen, *Truman and Israel*, 163–172, 182–187; Adler, *Roots*, 198–224, 432n59.

103. Jacobson Letter; Stone Letter: Bisgyer, *Challenge*, 188–196.

104. See, for example, Ganin, *Truman*, 159–163; Cohen, *Truman and Israel*, 188–198; Orian, *Forgotten Founder*, 678–691; Cohen-Levinovsky, "Presidents," 514–518; Brecher, *American Diplomacy*, 5–32.

105. Jacobson Letter; Ganin, *Truman*, 168.

106. "Weizmann: 'The Jewish People Will Double Down Efforts to Ensure Its Political Liberty,'" *Davar*, 23 March 1948; "Weizmann Scores U.S. Trustee Plan," *New York Times*, 26 March 1948.

107. Weizmann to Doris May, 23 March 1948, in Weizmann, *Letters*, vol. 23, 92.

108. Ibid. Weizmann to Frieda Goldschmidt, to Bergmann, 2 April 1948, in Weizmann, *Letters*, vol. 23, 96–97.

109. Frankfurter to Weizmann, 6 April 1948, WA; Weizmann to Sigmund Gestetner, 7 April 1948, in Weizmann, *Letters*, vol. 23, 98.

110. Weizmann to Truman, 9 April 1948, FRUS, 1948, vol. 5, 807–809 and in Weizmann, *Letters*, vol. 23, 99–101.

111. Weizmann to Frankfurter, 13 April 1948, in Weizmann, *Letters*, vol. 23, 104.

112. Ben-Gurion's Diary, 21–22 December 1941, BGA.

113. Eilat, *Struggle*, vol. 2, 674–675.

114. Hammer, "David Stone," 7–8.

115. Kaufmann to Rosenman, 10 April 1948, Papers of David K. Niles, Box 29, Israel File, January–February 1948, HSTL.

116. Clifford, *Counsel*, 53–55, 77; Vera Weizmann's Diary, 8 March 1948, WA; Epstein to Rosenman, 8 March 1948, in Yogev, *Documents*, 440.

117. Donovan, *Conflict*, 376; Eilat, *Struggle*, vol. 2, 567–568.

118. Jacobson Letter.

119. Austin to Marshall, 15 April 1948, FRUS, 1948, vol. 5, 823–824.

120. Weizmann, *Trial and Error*, 579.

121. Austin to Marshall, 15 April 1948, FRUS, 1948, vol. 5, 823–824.

122. See Eilat, *Struggle*, vol. 2, 675–676; Freundlich, *From Destruction to Resurrection*, 236–237; Orian, *Forgotten Founder*, 712.

123. Benson's position, while emphasizing different aspects, is essentially comparable to mine. Benson, *Truman*, 152.

124. "Austin Visited Weizmann," *Maariv*, 18 April 1948; Dan Pines, "America Urges, Presses . . . ," *Davar*, 5 May 1948.

125. Weizmann, *Trial and Error*, 577.

126. Kurzman, *Genesis*, 211. For Weizmann's other requests, see his letter to Rosenman, 19 April 1948, in Weizmann, *Letters*, vol. 23, 109–110.

127. Ben-Gurion to Shertok and Myerson, 14 March 1948, in Yogev, *Documents*, 462; Jewish Agency Executive, American section, 20 March 1948, Z5/2384, CZA.

128. Jewish Agency and National Council, statement, *Davar*, 24 March 1948; see also *Davar*'s main headline on that date.

129. *Davar*, 24 March 1948.

130. Cohn Report; Adler, *Roots*, 212, 434n88.

131. Weizmann to Weisgal, 20 April 1948, 12/90/235, Weizmann Institute Archives, Rehovot (hereafter cited as WIA); Weizmann to Bergmann, 14 April 1948, in Weizmann, *Letters*, vol. 23, 106.

132. Weisgal to Weizmann, 17 April 1948, in Weisgal, *So Far*, 256–259; Bergmann to Vera Weizmann, 18 April 1948, 12/90/235, WIA.

133. Weizmann to Bergmann, 20 April 1948, in Weizmann, *Letters*, vol. 23, 111.

134. Cohn Report.

135. Provisional Government, minutes, 16 May 1948, ISA; Eban, *An Autobiography*, 110. According to Eban, Weizmann informed him of this on the day after his meeting with Rosenman.

136. Eban, "Tragedy and Triumph," 310. On Truman's deliberations in this context, see Louis, *British Empire*, 515.

137. Kaufmann to Rosenman, 24 April 1948, WA. The archives contain another letter dated April 24, 1948, from Kaufman to Rosenman, which is less polished and appears to be a rough draft.

138. Eilat, *Struggle*, vol. 2, 577–578; Weizmann to Frankfurter, 23 February 1948, in Weizmann, *Letters*, vol. 23, 87.

139. Nahum Goldmann, "Report on Meeting with Lovett," 28 April 1948, Z6/2759, CZA.

140. Jessup to Rusk, 4 May 1948, FRUS, 1948, vol. 5, 897.

141. Ovendale, *Britain*, 286–287.

142. Louis, *British Empire*, 518–521; Gorny, *Ambiguous Tie*, 192–193.

143. Rusk, *As I Saw It*, 149–150; Rusk, memorandum on conversation with Truman, 30 April 1948, FRUS, 1948, vol. 5, 877–879; Rusk, memorandum to Lovett, 3 May 1948, FRUS, 1948, vol. 5, 886–889; Jewish Agency Executive, US section, meeting with the Zionist Emergency Council, minutes, 27 April 1948, Z5/2386, CZA.

144. Bergmann to Vera Weizmann, 5 May 1948, 12/90/235, WIA.

3. The Decisive Moments

1. The main sources and studies on this topic are Sharef, *Three Days*, 97–99; Bar-Zohar, *Ben-Gurion*, vol. 2, 732–742; Teveth, *HaDerech LeIyar*, 242–252 (this is the source of the expression "a hair's breadth"); Tzahor, *Vision*; Feldstein, "Three Days in May 1948," 361–365; Nimrod, *War or Peace*, 170–178; Sharett, "Moshe Sharett"; Eilam, *What Happened Here*, 150–181; Bareli, "Mapai during the War," 199–201.

2. Sharef, *Three Days*, 97–99.

3. Slutsky, *History of the Haganah*, vol. 3, pt. 3, 1792; Ben-Gurion, *War Diary*, vol. 1, 412n6; Ben-Gurion, *War Diary: Supplement*, 6.

4. Bialer, "David Ben-Gurion and Moshe Sharett," 69. Bialer later became a professor of international relations at the Hebrew University of Jerusalem.

5. Nimrod, "Scarecrow: The Hidden Circumstances of the Declaration of Independence," in *Mifgash BaTzomet*, 127–141; Nimrod, *War or Peace*, 176–177.

6. Clifford, handwritten notes found in the Clifford Papers, dated 4 May 1948, editorial note, FRUS, 1948, vol. 5, 906.

7. Marshall, report on meeting with Magnes, 4 May 1948, FRUS, 1948, vol. 5, 901–904.

8. Proskauer to Shertok, 27 April 1948, in Yogev, *Documents*, 684–686; Shertok to Ben-Gurion, 28 April 1948, 3 May 1948, 4 May 1948, in Yogev, *Documents*, 692–693, 720, 726–727; Jewish Agency, US Section to Jewish Agency, Palestine, 7 May 1948, in Yogev, *Documents*, 746–747; Kaufman, "Zionists and Non-Zionists," 387–390.

9. Proskauer to Ben-Gurion, 30 April 1948, in Yogev, *Documents*, 705–706; Shertok to Ben-Gurion, 30 April 1946, in Yogev, *Documents*, 707.

10. Shertok to Ben-Gurion, 2 May 1948, 95/1-FO, ISA; Shertok to Ben-Gurion, 4 May 1948, in Yogev, *Documents*, 726; Vera Weizmann's Diary, 13 May 1948, WA; Eilat, *Struggle*, vol. 2, 718–723, 729–730; Orian, *Forgotten Founder*, 720–722.

11. Shertok to Ben-Gurion, 4 May 1948, in Yogev, *Documents*, 727. For a sympathetic account of Shertok's conduct during this period, see Sheffer, *Sharett*, 353–377 (on this issue, see p. 366).

12. David Hacohen to Ben-Gurion, Remez, Sprinzak, Myerson, and Kaplan, 7 May 1948, BGA.

13. Clifford, *Counsel*, 5–6.

14. Rusk to Marshall, 6 May 1948, FRUS, 1948, vol. 5, 920–923; Eilat, *Struggle*, vol. 2, 728.

15. Vera Weizmann's Diary, 13 May 1948, WA.

16. Eilat, *Struggle*, vol. 2, 730; Rusk to Marshall regarding his meeting with Shertok and Silver, 6 May 1948, FRUS, 1948, vol. 5, 917–920.

17. Shertok to Marshall, 7 May 1948, FRUS, 1948, vol. 5, 929–930; Rosenman to Clifford, 9 May 1948, Goldmann to Rosenman, 10 May 1948, Clifford Papers, Box 18, Palestine, Correspondence, File 1, HSTL; Vera Weizmann's Diary, 13 May 1948, WA (describing Weizmann's expectations of Shertok); Ganin, *Truman*, 184, 218n74.

18. "Shertok Meets with Marshall before Leaving for Eretz Israel," *Yedioth Ahronoth*, 10 May 1948.

19. Ben-Gurion to Shertok, 8 July 1942, BGA.

20. Provisional Government, minutes, 16 May 1948, ISA.

21. Shertok, meeting with Marshall, Lovett, and Rusk, 8 May 1948, in Yogev, *Documents*, 760, 769; Marshall to US Consul in Jerusalem, 9 May 1948, FRUS, 1948, vol. 5, 945.

22. Shertok, meeting with Marshall, Lovett, and Rusk, 8 May 1948, in Yogev, *Documents*, 767. Cf. Ottolenghi, "Harry Truman's Recognition of Israel," 986–987.

23. "On the Formation of the State in Practice and by Military Might," Shertok's remarks at a people's assembly in Tel Aviv, *Davar*, 16 May 1948.

24. Jewish Agency, US Section, minutes, 10 May 1948, Z5/2388, CZA.

25. Eilat, *Struggle*, vol. 2, 752–753.

26. Ibid., 754.

27. Ibid., 723.

28. Lourie to Shertok, 11 May 1948, in Yogev, *Documents*, 776.

29. Nimrod, *War or Peace*, 178.

30. Sharef, *Three Days*, 97.

31. See, for example, Donovan, *Conflict*, 383–385.

32. Lourie to Shertok, 11 May 1948, in Yogev, *Documents*, 777.

33. Clifford, memorandum on conversation with Rusk, 8 May 1948, FRUS, 1948, vol. 5, 935–936; Rusk, Jessup, and Ross, transcript of telephone conversation, 11 May 1948, FRUS, 1948, vol. 5, 967; Hamby, *Man of the People*, 415.

34. Lourie to Shertok, 12 May 1948, in Yogev, *Documents*, 782.

35. Jewish Agency, US Section, minutes, 17 May 1948, Z5/2390, CZA.

36. Epstein, Nathan, Ginsburg, and Gass to Ben-Gurion, 15 May 1948, BGA.

37. Marshall, memorandum, 12 May 1948, FRUS, 1948, vol. 5, 975. On the historiography of this meeting, see Fetter, "'Showdown in the Oval Office.'" Fetter does not address the contexts discussed here.

38. McCullough, *Truman*, 614.

39. In this context, see Grose, *Israel*, 290.

40. See, for example, Donovan, *Conflict*, 381–382; Ganin, *Truman*, 185–189.

41. See, for example, "Russian Bloc Seen Recognizing Jews," *Washington Post*, 12 May 1948.

42. Marshall, memorandum, 12 May 1948, FRUS, 1948, vol. 5, 974–975; editorial note, FRUS, 1948, vol. 5, 976.

43. Clifford, *Counsel*, 15.

44. Cohen, *Truman and Israel*, 214–215.

45. Clifford, *Counsel*, 18, 21. For Lovett's version of his conversations with Clifford, see FRUS, 1948, vol. 5, 1005–1007.

46. Clifford, *Counsel*, 19; Eilat, *Struggle*, vol. 2, 768–773.

47. Marshall, memorandum, 12 May 1948, FRUS, 1948, vol. 5, 973–974 (emphasis added). For the UP news item, see "Marshall Message Reported," *New York Times*, 12 May 1948.

48. "The Watchman," *Time*, 16 August 1948. Isaac Deutscher's renowned biography of Leon Trotsky, *The Prophet Armed*, would only be published in 1954.

49. Two days earlier, Gruenbaum returned to his regular work as a member of the Jewish Agency (after having resigned on March 23), and began serving as a member of the People's Administration.

50. Nimrod, *War or Peace*, 173; People's Administration, 3 May 1948, 24–31.

51. See, for example, the main headlines in the newspapers *Davar, Haaretz, Hamashkif, Hatzofeh, Haboker*, 10 May 1948.

52. David Lazar, "What Does Shertok Bring?" *Maariv*, 10 May 1948 (emphasis added).

53. "Religious Judaism Will Not Allow the Sanctity of the Sabbath to Be Disregarded in Security Bodies," *Hatzofeh*, 9 May 1948; Histadrut HaPoel HaMizrachi to Ben-Gurion, 6 May 1948, BGA; Ben-Gurion to Baret, 13 May 1948, BGA (emphasis in the original).

54. Zionist General Council, minutes, 7 April 1948, BGA.

55. Summary of minutes from meetings of the Jewish Agency, US Section, with the Political Advisory Committee, 3–4 May 1948, Z5/43, CZA; Shertok to Ben-Gurion, 4 May 1948, in Yogev, *Documents*, 727; Ben-Gurion, telegrams to Shertok, 6 May 1948, BGA.

56. Ben-Gurion's Diary, 16 May 1948, BGA.

57. The choice of the term "coalition" to describe the political alliance between the two at that time is based on the actual terminology Ben-Gurion and Sharett used. See their correspondence of 26 March 1954, 4 April 1954, 8 April 1954, BGA; Sharett, *Personal Diary*, vol. 3, 742, vol. 6, 1544–1546, 1554–1555, 1594–1601.

58. Vera Weizmann's Diary, 13 May 1948, WA.

59. Eban, "Tragedy and Triumph," 310–311. Vera Weizmann's version, the most credible one, is that Weizmann telephoned Shertok while the latter was at the airport. Weizmann, *The Impossible*, 231; Sharef, *Three Days*, 193.

60. Kurzman, *Genesis*, 214.

61. Ross, memorandum of telephone conversation, 9 May 1948, FRUS, 1948, vol. 5, 941.

62. People's Administration, minutes, 12 May 1948, 57; Douglas (US ambassador to London) to Marshall, 13 May 1948, cited in Cohen, *Palestine*, 357; Nimrod, *War or Peace*, 161–178.

63. People's Administration, minutes, 12 May 1948, 40–44; Mapai Central Committee, minutes, 11 May 1948, LPA.

64. People's Administration, minutes, 12 May 1948, 45–46 (emphasis added).

65. Ibid.; Shertok, meeting with Marshall, Lovett, and Rusk, 8 May 1948, in Yogev, *Documents*, 769; Marshall, memorandum, 12 May 1948, FRUS, 1948, vol. 5, 973.

66. People's Administration, minutes, 12 May 1948, 65–67.

67. Ibid., 71–76.

68. Ibid., 87.

69. National Council Executive, minutes, 12 May 1948, J1/7269, CZA.

70. Fishman to Ben-Gurion, 12 May 1948, BGA; Shabtai Teveth files, People's Administration, BGA.

71. Mapai Central Committee, minutes, 11 May 1948 (the date was incorrectly amended by hand to read 12 May 1948), CZA.

72. People's Administration, minutes, 12 May 1948, 106. See also 57, 59.

73. "The Jewish State and Its Provisional Government to Be Established upon Termination of the Mandate," *Davar*, 13 May 1948.

74. "Shertok: 'Now—or Never!'" *Haboker*, 14 May 1948; "Zionist to Set Up State on Schedule," *New York Times*, 14 May 1948.

75. Bar-Zohar, *Ben-Gurion*, vol. 2, 732–735. Cf. Sharett, "Moshe Sharett and the Declaration of Independence," 282–288.

76. People's Administration, minutes, 12 May 1948, 110–111.

77. Ibid., 112–114.

78. Moshe Gurari, "The Labor Pains of the Declaration of Independence: BG Edits Sharett's Version," *Davar*, 11 May 1973.

79. People's Administration, minutes, *Provisional State Council*, 14 May 1948, 19.

80. "On the 'Attendees' at the Proclamation Ceremony and on the Status," letter to delegates, 26 May 1948, 2–932-1948-47A, p. 6, LPA.

81. Dobkin, remarks, Mapai Secretariat, minutes, 13 June 1948, CZA.

82. "From Day to Day: The State of Israel—from Sacred to Secular," *Haaretz*, 16 May 1948.

83. Lovett, memorandum on conversations, 17 May 1948, FRUS, 1948, vol. 5, 1005–1007.

84. Abba Eban, "Israel and America," remarks at a dinner in honor of President Truman, Washington D.C., 26 May 1952, *Voice of Israel* (New York, 1957), 86. This is a paraphrase of Jeremiah 2:2.

85. "From Day to Day: The State of Israel—from Sacred to Secular," *Haaretz*, 16 May 1948.

86. Forrestal, 14 May 1948, in *Forrestal Diaries*, 440.

87. Rusk, letter to the Historical Office, 13 June 1974, FRUS, 1948, vol. 5, 993.

88. "Ocean Flight Canceled," *New York Times*, 9 May 1948; "Shertok in the Country," *Hatzofeh*, 12 May 1948.

89. Weisgal to Reva Ziff, 12 May 1948, 12/90/235, WIA. Ziff was Weizmann's secretary. The message was necessary to ensure that Weizmann was available and ready for a phone call from Weisgal.

90. People's Administration, minutes, 12 May 1948, 59.

91. "E. Kaplan: An Entire People Is Fighting—with Body and Capital," *Davar*, 16 May 1948 (emphasis added).

92. Reuven [Zaslani] to Weisgal, 13 May 1948, BGA. A year later, Zaslani established the Mossad, Israel's national intelligence agency.

93. Weisgal to Zaslani, 13 May 1948, BGA. The telegram stated, "SPOKE TO ZAKEN NEW YORK YESTERDAY WILL COOPERATE FULLY stop Deem it most important your chief send him appropriate message Waldorf Astoria on the fifteenth STOP Awaiting word from you Dorchester regards. Meyer."

94. Ben-Gurion, Kaplan, Myerson, Remez, and Shertok to Weizmann, 14 May 1948, 2391/67-FO, ISA (emphasis added).

95. Ibid.

96. "Weizmann Elected Head of Council," *Washington Post*, 17 May 1948; "The First President," *Jewish Chronicle*, 21 May 1948.

97. "May 15," *Jewish Chronicle*, 14 May 1948.

98. "David Ben-Gurion to the Yishuv: The State of Israel Calls on Every Jew to Fulfill His Duty Loyally," *Davar*, 16 May 1948.

99. Provisional State Council, 16 May 1948, 5.

100. Provisional Government, minutes, 16 May 1948, ISA.

101. "C. Weizmann—State Council President," *Davar*, 17 May 1948. The quote is taken from Ben-Gurion's remarks as published in *Davar*.

102. Sprinzak to Weisgal, 18 May 1948, Weisgal to Sprinzak, 25 May 1948, Box 356, 12/90/58, WIA.

103. "Truman Acts Soon after New Nation Is Created," *Washington Post*, 15 May 1948. According to Max Lowenthal's diary, the unsigned article was authored by White House correspondent Ferdinand Kuhn.

104. Max Lowenthal's Diary, 15 May 1948, Box 8, Folder 62, University of Minnesota Archives.

105. "The US Government Recognized Our State," *Davar*, 16 May 1948.

106. Marshall to Lovett, 24 May 1948, FRUS, 1948, vol. 5, 1036–1037; Lovett to Truman, 26 May 1948, FRUS, 1948, vol. 5, 1051–1053; Slonim, "The 1948 American Embargo," 509–512; Feinberg, opening remarks at a reception for Weisgal, Waldorf Astoria, 27 May 1948, WA.

107. Douglas to Marshall, 25 May 1948, FRUS, 1948, vol. 5, 1046–1047.

108. Eban, "Weizmann," 128.

109. Editorial, *Davar*, 17 May 1948.

110. Eban to Shertok, 21 May 1948, *Documents*, vol. 1, 58–59; James Reston, "US-British Rift on Palestine Feared as Benefit to Russia," *New York Times*, 21 May 1948.

111. Provisional State Council, 16 May 1948, 7.

112. Twenty-Second Zionist Congress, minutes, 16 December 1946, 345; Weizmann to Ben-Gurion, 17 May 1948, in Weizmann, *Letters*, vol. 23, 122.

113. "Flag of Israel to Fly at Waldorf Here Soon," *New York Times*, 18 May 1948; Weizmann to Shertok, 23 July 1948, in Weizmann, *Letters*, vol. 23, 183.

114. See, for example, Cohen, *Truman and Israel*, 188–222; Ottolenghi, "Harry Truman's Recognition of Israel," 963–988.

115. "Weizmann Visits Truman; Loan and Arms Indicated," *New York Times*, 26 May 1948; Shertok to Epstein, 27 May 1948, *Documents*, vol. 1, 86.

116. Ezriel Carlebach, "War Diary," *Maariv*, 26 May 1948.

117. Weizmann to various personalities, in Weizmann, *Letters*, vol. 23, 124–126, 131, 142, 149, 162.

118. McDonald, *Envoy*, 43–44, 51, 62.

119. Weizmann to Weisgal, 30 July 1948, 2 August 1948 (the letter of July 30 was sent as a nonbinding draft alongside the letter of August 2, which was intended to replace it; the quotes

in the text are from the draft letter), in Weizmann, *Letters*, vol. 23, 191–192, 197–199; Weizmann to Shertok, 2 August 1948, Weizmann, *Letters*, vol. 23, 197; Bergmann to Weisgal, 11 August 1948, 12/90/59, WIA; Morris, "Weizmann and the Arabs," 196–199; Crossman, "The Prisoner," 325–336. Weizmann's mention of "Balkan-style conduct" was a reference to the small-scale armed clashes that preceded World War I.

120. Shertok to Eban, 8 August 1948, 2391/71-FO, ISA; Eban to Shertok, 11 August 1948, 67/6-FO, ISA.

121. Shertok, remarks before the committee of five, 5 July 1948, in Sharett, *Speaking Out*, 225.

122. Shertok, remarks before Mapai Council, 18 June 1948, in Sharett, *Speaking Out*, 159.

123. "Had the Government Conceded to the Dissidents, It Would Have Destroyed the State," *Davar*, 25 June 1948 (references to the "sacred cannon" were removed from the Provisional State Council's official records but appeared with minor changes in the daily press); Histadrut Executive Committee, minutes, 23 June 1948, Lavon Institute.

124. "The Voice of Herut: On Swearing-In Day," 28 June 1948, 1/3/20/4K, Jabotinsky Institute.

125. Y. Bader, "They Crossed the Line," *Hamashkif*, 25 June 1948.

126. "Not a Fraternal War but a War against Pillagers of the People's Liberty," *Davar*, 24 June 1948.

127. Mapai Central Committee, minutes, 24 July 1948, LPA.

128. "Mifleget Poalei Eretz Yisrael Central Committee: We Must Be Prepared to Win the Final Battle," *Davar*, 25 July 1948.

129. Morris, *Palestinian Refugee Problem*, 348–354; Gelber, *Independence and Nakba*, 304.

130. Shapira, *Army Controversy*.

131. Provisional Government, minutes, 26 September 1948, ISA; Ben-Gurion's Diary, 26 September 1948, BGA; Shiloah to Shertok, 30 September 1948, *Documents*, vol. 1, 658.

132. Provisional State Council, 27 September 1948, 19–20 (emphasis in the original).

133. Ben-Gurion's Diary, 29 September 1948, BGA; Ben-Gurion to Dori, 29 September 1948, BGA; Dori to heads of branches and others, 7 October 1948, BGA. On the dismantlement of Palmach headquarters, see Gelber, *Why Was the Palmach Disbanded?* 211–240.

134. Shiloah to Shertok, 30 September 1948, *Documents*, vol. 1, 658.

135. Bar-Zohar, *Ben-Gurion*, vol. 2, 819.

136. Ben-Gurion's Diary, 5 October 1948, BGA; Ben-Gurion, *Resurgent State of Israel*, vol. 1, 294.

137. Ben-Gurion's Diary, 6 October 1948, BGA; Provisional Government, minutes, 6 October 1948, ISA.

138. Marshall, statement on Palestine, 21 September 1948, FRUS, 1948, vol. 5, 1415–1416; Douglas to Lovett, 12 November 1948, FRUS, 1948, vol. 5, 1570; Weizmann to Jacobson, 27 September 1948, in Weizmann, *Letters*, vol. 23, 211–212; Ben-Gurion's Diary, 6 October 1948, BGA.

139. On Operation Yoav, see Tal, *War in Palestine*, 376–400; Morris, *1948*, 320–338.

140. David Lazar, "The Path Is Clear," *Maariv*, 21 October 1948 (emphases in the original).

4. The Political Fog in the Lead-Up to Elections

1. See, for example, Cohen, *Truman and Israel*, 240–256. Fetter, "Forthcoming Three Months."

2. Entry for 2 December 1947, in Ferrell, *Diary of Eben A. Ayers*, 213–214.

3. Lovett to Truman, 26 May 1948, FRUS, 1948, vol. 5, 1051–1053; McClintock to Rusk, 1 July 1948, FRUS, 1948, vol. 5, 1178–1179; Weizmann to Truman, 26 May 1948, *Documents*, vol. 1, 83; Eban to Rosenman, 16 June 1948, *Documents*, vol. 1, 168–169; Eban to Goldmann, 22 June 1948, *Documents*, vol. 1, 202–203; Kaufmann to Niles, Papers of David Niles, Israel Files, Box 29, June–July 1948, HSTL; McDonald, *Envoy*, 15–17.

4. Lovett, memorandum of conversation with Epstein, 8 July 1948, FRUS, 1948, vol. 5, 1199; Epstein to Shertok, 8–9 July 1948, *Documents*, vol. 1, 302–303.

5. Ginsburg to Weizmann, 1 July 1948, 2414/26-FO, ISA; Ben-Gurion's Diary, 1 July 1948, BGA. See also Epstein to Shertok, 24 June 1948, *Documents*, vol. 1, 208.

6. Remarks by Shertok, minutes, Mapai Secretariat, 13 June 1948, LPA.

7. Ginsburg to Weizmann, 1 July 1948, 2414/26-FO, ISA; Marshall to Douglas, 13 August 1948, FRUS, 1948, vol. 5, 1308–1310; Douglas to Marshall, 27 August 1948, FRUS, 1948, vol. 5, 1354–1359. On the formulation of the second Bernadotte Plan and the struggle to undermine it, see Ilan, *Bernadotte*, 181–191; Ben-Dror, *Mediator*, 121–130, 140–144; Fetter, "Forthcoming Three Months," Part II, 202–206.

8. See, for example, Weizmann to Truman, 26 May 1948, in Weizmann, *Letters*, vol. 23, 128–130; Epstein and Gass to Kaplan, 2 June 1948, *Documents*, vol. 1, 114–115; Shertok to Marshall, 8 June 1948, *Documents*, vol. 1, 141; Epstein to Lovett, 3 August 1948, *Documents*, vol. 1, 447–449; Heydt et al. to Epstein, 31 August 1948, *Documents*, vol. 1, 566; Lovett to Truman, 11 August 1948, FRUS, 1948, vol. 5, 1300–1301; Marshall to Truman, 16 August 1948, FRUS, 1948, vol. 5, 1313–1315; Epstein to Shertok, 20 August 1948, *Documents*, vol. 1, 540; Weizmann to Truman, 6 September 1948, *Documents*, vol. 1, 571; Gass to Silver, 15 September 1948, 376/9-FO, ISA; Eilat, *Memoirs*, 114–121; Fetter, "Forthcoming Three Months," Part I, 252–256.

9. Knox to Marshall, 13 July 1948, M1390/1, NARA; Knox, letters to family members, 9 August 1948, 23 August 1948, 28 September 1948, Charles F. Knox Jr. Files, Box 1, Subject File, Correspondence, HSTL.

10. McDonald's Diary, 13 August 1948, in McDonald, *Envoy*, 61; McDonald to Marshall, 19 August 1948, FRUS, 1948, vol. 5, 1326–1327. See also Cohen, *Truman and Israel*, 240–247; Ganin, *Uneasy Relationship*, 158–163.

11. Marshall to Truman, 30 August 1948, FRUS, 1948, vol. 5, 1359; Marshall to Truman, 8 September 1948, FRUS, 1948, vol. 5, 1380; Jessup to Marshall, 6 August 1948, FRUS, 1948, vol. 5, 1291.

12. McDonald to Truman, 24 August 1948, FRUS, 1948, vol. 5, 1337–1339; Marshall to McDonald, 31 August 1948, 1 September 1948, FRUS, 1948, vol. 5, 1364, 1366–1368; McDonald, *Envoy*, 50.

13. McDonald to Truman, 12 September 1948, FRUS, 1948, vol. 5, 1392–1393; McDonald's Diary, 9–10 September 1948, in McDonald, *Envoy*, 112–114.

14. McDonald Marshall, 9 September 1948, FRUS, 1948, vol. 5, 1384–1386; McDonald's Diary, 8 September 1948, in McDonald, *Envoy*, 106–109.

15. Marshall to McDonald, 17 September 1948, FRUS, 1948, vol. 5, 1408.

16. Ibid., 1409; Stern, "A Party under Trial," 419–425.

17. Knox, letters to family members, 28 September 1948, 5 December 1948, Charles F. Knox Jr. Files, Box 1, Subject File, Correspondence, HSTL; Bar-On, *Of All the Kingdoms*, 36–42; Ben-Dror, *Mediator*, 121–130.

18. Horowitz, *In the Heart*, 16.

19. Ben-Gurion's Diary, 20 August 1948, BGA; Henry Montor, "Minutes of a Meeting to Discuss Financing," 21 June 1948, Morgenthau Papers, Box 776, Kaplan File, FDRL.

20. Henry Montor, "Minutes of a Meeting to Discuss Financing," 21 June 1948, Morgenthau Papers, Box 776, Kaplan File, FDRL; Horowitz, *In the Heart*, 13.

21. Henry Montor, "General Memorandum," 20 June 1949, 1886/21-P, ISA.

22. Ezriel Carlebach, "War Diary: The Threat to US Zionism," *Maariv*, 27 October 1948.

23. Ben-Gurion's Diary, 25 June 1948, 26 June 1948, 4 July 1948, BGA; Ben-Gurion to Kollek, 26 June 1948, BGA; Kollek to Morgenthau, 30 June 1948, Morgenthau Papers, Box 776, Teddy Kollek File, FDRL; Joseph, *The Faithful*, 220–222. A clandestine, circuitous route for the delivery of food and supplies to Jerusalem, which came to be known as the Burma Road, was constructed around this time.

24. Leila Yosef, untitled, cited in Helman, *The Story of the Yiftach-Palmach Brigade*, 74; Yosef, *Memoirs*, 89–90.

25. See Ganin, *Uneasy Relationship*, 54–94; Orian, *Forgotten Founder*, 784–829; Feldstein, *Gordian Knot*, 29–42.

26. *Americans for Haganah*, 10 November 1947, 15 December 1947 (in the course of 1948, the magazine changed its name to *Haganah Speaks* and toward the end of the year to *Israel Speaks*). For more on the magazine, see Penslar, *Jews and the Military*, 248–252.

27. Sonneborn to Feinberg, 16 February 1948, F41/47, CZA; Rosen, *American Treasure*, 182–185.

28. Jewish Agency Executive, US section, minutes, for 4 March 1948, 7 June 1948, 10 June 1948, CZA; Meeting of organizations active in Americans for Haganah, minutes, 29 March 1948, Z5/2385, CZA; Rosen, *American Treasure*, 174–187.

29. Kollek Shertok, 24 June 1948, 2389/2-FO, ISA; Feinberg to Silver, 16 June 1948, Silver Archives, Reel 36, File 879, BGA; "Americans for Haganah Will Not Quit While Needed," *Haganah Speaks*, 2 July 1948.

30. Interview with Samuel Rosenman, 15 October 1968, Oral History Interview, HSTL.

31. McCullough, *Truman*, 633.

32. Ben-Gurion to Kollek, 14 December 1947, BGA; Ben-Gurion to Feinberg, 13 July 1948, BGA; exchange of telegrams between Silver and Lourie, 25 June 1948, 30 June 1948, Silver Archives, Reel 36, File 879, BGA; "Opposition Meetings," *Davar*, 5 July 1948; Orian, *Forgotten Founder*, 785–789.

33. Feinberg to Sonneborn, 13 July 1948, 12–90 (154), WIA; "Dr. Silver Announces Americans for Haganah Will Suspend Activities Immediately," *Jewish Telegraph Agency*, 14 July 1948; "Americans for Haganah Announces Dissolution," *Jewish Telegraph Agency*, 19 July 1948; "'New Group Being Formed to Support Israel," *Haganah Speaks*, 16 July 1948; Jewish Agency Executive, US section, minutes, 22 July 1948, CZA.

34. Jewish Agency Executive, minutes, 18–19 August 1948, CZA; ZGC, minutes, 22 August 1948, 24 August 1948, BGA; Ben-Gurion to Locker, 6 November 1933, BGA; "Silver, Neumann, and Goldstein Align with the General Zionists' Platform in Israel," *Haboker*, 19 August 1948; Orian, *Forgotten Founder*, 630, 792–798; Feldstein, *Gordian Knot*, 29–33; Raphael, *Silver*, 173–175.

35. Provisional Government, minutes, 10 November 1948, ISA.

36. "Day to Day: Political Report Card," *Haaretz*, 3 September 1948.

37. See Meir Grabovsky, "After the ZGC Gathering," *Hapoel Hatzair*, 7 September 1948.

38. Ben-Gurion's Diary, 17 August 1948, BGA; Jewish Agency Executive, evening session, minutes, 19 August 1948, CZA.

39. Ganin, *Uneasy Relationship*, 54–59; Orian, *Forgotten Founder*, 792–799; Feldstein, *Gordian Knot*, 29–34; Raphael, *Silver*, 175–182.

40. Montor to Goldstein, 10 September 1948, S41/144/24, CZA; Goldstein to Montor, 27 September 1948, S41/144/24, CZA; Goldstein Kaplan, 30 September 1948, S41/144/24, CZA; see also the sources in the previous note.

41. McCullough, *Truman*, 678; Heard, *Costs of Democracy*, 262–267.

42. Truman to Kaufmann, 16 September 1948, F41/74, CZA; Daily Appointment Sheet for President Harry S. Truman, 9 September 1948, Connelly Files, Daily Presidential Appointments, 1945–1952, Daily Appointments, January–December 1948, HSTL. Given his position, Niles, who was on friendly terms with Kaufmann, probably drafted the letter, but friendship alone would not account for a letter such as this.

43. Interview with Feinberg, 23 August 1973, Oral History Interview, HSTL; Redding, *Inside the Democratic Party*, 167–169; McFarland and Roll, *Louis Johnson*, 137–144; Donovan, *Conflict*, 418–419; Frantz and McKean, *Friends*, 86. Louis Johnson, who agreed to chair Truman's fundraising campaign, often reminisced fondly about this formative meeting,

without distinguishing between the portion in which Truman spoke and the subsequent gathering at DNC headquarters. Each time he recounted the event, the number of participants grew. Initially, he recalled that sixty-five were invited and only forty attended. Later, he related that eighty were invited and only fifty attended (see the sources cited in McFarland and Roll).

44. Interview with Feinberg, 23 August 1973, Oral History Interview, HSTL. The legal limit for donations was $5,000 per person, and the official fundraising process adhered to this format. Johnson's vice chair for Truman's fundraising campaign was the Jewish plastics manufacturer Nathan Lichtblau. After Truman's victory, Lichtblau stated: "I don't want a job or anything. I work purely as an Amateur." "The Angels of the Truman Campaign," *Time*, 6 June 1949.

45. Daily Appointment Sheet for President Harry S. Truman, 10 September 1948, 15 September 1948, Connelly Files, Daily Presidential Appointments, 1945–1952, Daily Appointments, January–December 1948, HSTL.

46. Jewish Agency Executive, US section, minutes, 28 September 1948, CZA; Epstein to Shertok, 27–28 September 1948, *Documents*, vol. 1, 644–645; "Another Reversal—Another Betrayal," *New York Times*, 30 September 1948; Fetter, "Forthcoming Three Months," Part II, 203–204.

47. Jewish Agency Executive, US section, minutes, 28 September 1948, CZA; Joseph Shulman (secretary for the new committee) to Jewish Agency Executive, 27 September 1948, A123/78, CZA.

48. McCullough, *Truman*, 674, 679–680; Clifford, *Counsel*, 231; Ross, *Truman Victory*, 203–204.

49. Ross, *Truman Victory*, 175–176; Clifford, *Counsel*, 231; Holbrook and VanDeMark, interview with Clifford, 25 March 1988, Papers of Richard G. Holbrooke, Box 2, Files 1–2, HSTL; Jacobson to Truman, n.d., Papers of Edward Jacobson, Correspondence File, Correspondence with Harry S. Truman, 1948–1952, Box 1, HSTL. The lack of funding for radio broadcasts of Truman's campaign speeches was a recurring problem, for which the campaign always found a creative solution, from the Greek community in New York to various other sources. See Redding, *Inside the Democratic Party*, 230–235.

50. "Activities of Americans for Haganah, July 1947–December 1948," F41/5, CZA. The document is unsigned and undated. The table of contents suggests that the archival copy is incomplete or that the document itself was never completed. The content of the document and its similarity in style to other documents on file in this archive leave no doubt that the author was Wahl.

51. Haynes, Klehr, and Vassiliev, *Spies*, 207–212.

52. "Address in Oklahoma City," in *Public Papers*, 609–614.

53. McCullough, *Truman*, 694, 697, 680; "Papers Back Dewey," *New York Times*, 29 October 1948. Other candidates drew the residual support.

54. Eban to Weizmann, 24 September 1948, *Documents*, vol. 1, 637; Weizmann to Jacobson, 27 September 1948, in Weizmann, *Letters*, vol. 23, 211–212; Jacobson to Weizmann, 30 September 1948, Jacobson to Connelly, 30 September 1948, and Connelly to Jacobson, 5 October 1948, Papers of Edward Jacobson Correspondence File, Correspondence—Israel, 1947–1953, Box 1, HSTL; Marshall to Lovett, 30 September 1948, FRUS, 1948, vol. 5, 1446; Cohen, *Truman and Israel*, 245–247; Fetter, "Forthcoming Three Months," Part II, 204–205.

55. Dulles to Silver, 30 September 1948, 376/9-FO, CZA; Epstein Silver, 8 October 1948, *Documents*, vol. 2, 42–43; Shertok to Epstein, 10 October 1948, *Documents*, vol. 2, 45; Epstein to Silver, 14 October 1948, 376/9-FO, CZA. Silver would actually have preferred Senator Robert Taft from his own state of Ohio, with whom he was closely aligned, as a Republican presidential candidate, but this does not detract from the fact that he did not consider a Democratic candidate to be deserving of public support at that time. See Segev, *Ethnic Politicians*, 274–288.

56. Epstein to Shertok, 20 October 1948, *Documents*, vol. 2, 74; Shertok to Epstein, 21 October 1948, *Documents*, vol. 2, 74n1.

57. See, for example, Epstein, conversation with Lovett, 11 November 1948, *Documents*, vol. 2, 165–166.

58. Shertok to Epstein, 23 October 1948, *Documents*, vol. 2, 86.

59. Cohen, *Truman and Israel*, 250–256; Fetter, "Forthcoming Three Months," Part II, 206–212.

60. Morgenthau to Montor, 23 October 1948, Morgenthau Papers, Box 771, United Jewish Appeal File, FDRL; "Henry Morgenthau Visits Negba," *Al Hamishmar*, 26 October 1948; Moshe Brilliant, "A Home in the Negev Desert," *Palestine Post*, 29 October 1948.

61. Ben-Gurion's Diary, 25 October 1948, BGA.

62. "Moshav HaShachar—Between Tel Aviv and Jerusalem," *Davar*, 28 October 1948; Jewish Agency Executive, minutes, 24 October 1948, CZA.

63. Jewish Agency Executive meeting with ZGC, minutes, 26 January 1949, BGA.

64. "Address in Madison Square Garden," New York City, 28 October 1948, in *Public Papers*, 913; Redding, *Inside the Democratic Party*, 279–281. On the previous day, Wallace had addressed nineteen thousand enthusiastic supporters in the same venue. Ross, *Truman Victory*, 237.

65. Epstein to Shertok, 29 October 1948, *Documents*, vol. 2, 111; Morgenthau to Ben-Gurion, 4 November 1948, Morgenthau Papers, Box 771, United Jewish Appeal File, FDRL; "Taft Hits at Truman on Palestine Course," *New York Times*, 27 October 1948; Ross, *Truman Victory*, 237.

66. "Truman in Strongest Plea for Israel," *New York Times*, 29 October 1948; "US Press Describes Truman Speech as Extremely Enthusiastic," *Haaretz*, 1 November 1948.

67. "Day to Day: A Truman Victory and Our Issue," *Haaretz*, 4 November 1948; Snetsinger, *Jewish Vote*, 133–135; Donaldson, *Truman Defeats Dewey*, 205–206; Orian, *Forgotten Founder*, 811–812.

68. Donovan, *Conflict*, 419; Edward Jacobson, "I Want the American People to Know the Truth," *Kansas City Jewish Chronicle*, 29 October 1948, Papers of Edward Jacobson, Personal File, Box 1, HSTL.

69. "The Failure of the Masses," editorial, *Al Hamishmar*, 4 November 1948.

70. Truman to Weizmann, 29 November 1948, FRUS, 1948, vol. 5, 1634.

71. Cohen, *Truman and Israel*, 253–255.

72. Marshall, memorandum of conversation with Shertok, 13 November 1948, FRUS, 1948, vol. 5, 1577–1580; Shertok, report to the Israeli delegation to the UN General Assembly, 14 November 1948, *Documents*, vol. 2, 171–172.

73. Lovett to Marshall, 30 October 1948, FRUS, 1948, vol. 5, 1533–1534; Isaacson and Thomas, *Wise Men*, 19–32. See also Cohen, *Truman and Israel*, 256.

74. Douglas to Lovett, 29 October 1948, FRUS, 1948, vol. 5, 1530–1532. The telegram was simultaneously sent to Marshall as well—for his eyes only. Ibid., 1533. Marshall was in London from October 29 to November 1.

75. Bevin to UK ambassador to the UN, 21 May 1948, FO 800/487, NA; Holmes to Lovett, 22 December 1948, FRUS, 1948, vol. 5, 1680–1685; Louis, *British Empire*, 570.

76. "Anglo-American Dispute over Palestine," *Newsweek*, 6 December 1948; McDonald to Secretary of State, 14 December 1948, M1390/1, NARA. (Marshall was on extended sick leave following surgery to remove a kidney and had plans to resign. The telegram was essentially intended for Lovett and Truman.)

77. See, for example, FRUS, 1948, vol. 5, 1142, 1183, 1199, 1291–1292, 1361.

78. Forrestal, 12 October 1948, in *Forrestal Papers*.

79. Bialer, "Top Hat, Tuxedo and Cannons," 657–661.

80. Holmes to State Department, 29 December 1948, M1390/1, NARA. On Beeley's status, see Louis, *British Empire*, 455.

81. McDonald, *Envoy*, 140–141; Ben-Gurion's Diary, 25 November 1948, BGA.

82. McDonald to Niles, 26 December 1948, Papers of David K. Niles, Box 30, No. 1, Israel File, January–June 1949, HSTL.

83. McDonald to Secretary of State, 15 January 1949, M1390/1, NARA; David Miron, memorandum to Foreign Minister, 31 January 1949, 2414/26-FO, ISA; Michael Pragai, memorandum to Foreign Minister, 8 February 1949, 2414/26-FO, ISA; Heller, *Birth of Israel*, 45.

84. McDonald to State Department (two telegrams, the first of which was also intended for Truman and Lovett), 16 January 1949, Clifford Papers, Box 14, Telegrams and Cables, File 1, HSTL. McDonald advised that Clifford and Niles meet with Klaus to receive a firsthand report of his findings. Clifford further recommended that they consider having him meet with the president. McDonald to Clifford, 14 January 1949, Box 13, Palestine Correspondence, File 2, HSTL; McDonald to Niles, 15 January 1949, Papers of David K. Niles, Box 30, File 1, Israel File, January–June 1949, HSTL.

85. Meeting between Epstein and State Department officials, 21 December 1948, FRUS, 1948, vol. 5, 1678–1679; Epstein to Lovett, 22 December 1948, 374/1-FO, ISA.

86. McDonald to Secretary of State, 20 December 1948, FRUS, 1948, vol. 5, 1674–1676.

87. McDonald to Clifford, 22 December 1948, Clifford Papers, Box 14, Telegrams and Cables, File 1, HSTL.

88. "Today's Agenda," editorial, *Davar*, 20 December 1948.

89. Provisional Government, minutes, 15 December 1948, 19 December 1948, ISA. On Operation Horev, see Tal, *War in Palestine*, 433–458; Morris, *1948*, 350–374.

90. Uriel Heyd (first secretary of the Israeli legation to Washington) to Shertok, 30 December 1948, *Documents*, vol. 2, 319; McDonald, message to Shertok, *Documents*, vol. 2, 331–332.

91. McDonald to Secretary of State, 5 January 1949, FRUS, 1949, vol. 6, 614–615. See also Morris, *1948*, 365–369.

92. McDonald to State Department, 11 January 1949, 24 January 1949, Truman Papers, Box 158, Foreign Affairs—State of Israel, HSTL; McDonald's Diary, 10 January 1949, 22 January 1949, 20 February 1949, in McDonald, *Envoy*, 324–325, 346, 395.

93. McDonald to State Department, 18 January 1949, Clifford Papers, Box 14, Telegrams and Cables, File 2, HSTL; McDonald's Diary, 18 January 1949, in McDonald, *Envoy*, 337.

94. McDonald's Diary, 15 January 1949, in McDonald, *Envoy*, 334.

95. Editorial note, FRUS, 1949, vol. 6, 681; Bialer, *Between East and West*, 208.

96. McDonald to State Department, 24 January 1949, M1390/1, NARA; "Today's Agenda," editorial, *Davar*, 21 January 1949; "Attack of Friendliness," *Al Hamishmar*, 21 January 1949; "The Jewish Voter Will Prove His Maturity," *Herut*, 23 January 1949; Ezriel Carlebach, "War Diary: American Payment," *Maariv*, 20 January 1949.

5. The Parliament and the Presidency

1. Tzahor, "Mapai," 381–387; Weitz, *From Underground*, 185–238.

2. Tzahor, "The First."

3. Mapai Council, 12 January 1949, LPA. Dinur was minister of education during 1951–1955.

4. Provisional State Council, 18 November 1948, 8.

5. Provisional State Council, 25 November 1948, 7; Provisional Government, 6 October 1948, ISA; "The Elections—On the 25 of January," *Haaretz*, 26 November 1948.

6. "Today's Agenda," editorial, *Davar*, 26 November 1948.

7. Provisional State Council, 18 November 1948, 21.

8. See, for example, "In the Elections Battle," *Hatzofeh*, 7 January 1949; "In the Elections Battle," *Herut*, 7 January 1949.

9. "No Central Issue in the Elections War," *Haaretz*, 10 January 1949; "The Foreign Policy Events Are Shaping the Election Campaign," *Haaretz*, 12 January 1949.

10. Mapai Central Committee, 30 November 1948, LPA.

11. "The First Direct Israeli-Arab Negotiations Has Begun," *Davar*, 14 January 1949.

12. Mapai Council, 12 January 1949, LPA; "The Craftsman of Words on Mapai's Stage," *Yedioth Ahronoth*, 13 January 1949.

13. "The Voters Should Decide Whether to Continue the War," *Haaretz*, 13 January 1949.

14. "Menachem Begin in Gathering of Thousands in Tel Aviv on Saturday," *Herut*, 16 January 1949.

15. Moshe Sneh, "Questions vs. Questions," *Al Hamishmar*, 14 January 1949.

16. "War and Peace in a Cloud of Smoke," *Al Hamishmar*, 20 January 1949.

17. "The Opposition Answers Shertok's Question about Peace or Continued War," *Haaretz*, 16 January 1949; "Mapam's Decisions on the Conditions for Peace," *Davar*, 18 January 1949.

18. "Saturday of Elections Campaigning," *Davar*, 16 January 1949; "The Opposition Answers Shertok's Question about Peace or Continued War," *Haaretz*, 16 January 1949; "The Elections Propaganda Reaches Its Peak," *Haboker*, 17 January 1949.

19. "Masses from the Village and the City Heard Mapam's Views on the Soldier and the Working Man," *Al Hamishmar*, 16 January 1949; "I Didn't Disappoint You in the Past and I Won't Disappoint You in the Future," *Haboker*, 16 January 1949 (emphasis added).

20. "To the Voter," *Davar*, 17 January 1949.

21. "They're Coming!," *Al Hamishmar*, 18 January 1949; "'Pin-up Girl'. . . ," *Herut*, 20 January 1949.

22. Ben-Gurion's Diary, 17 January 1949, BGA; Shapira, *Yigal Allon*, 449.

23. Ben-Gurion's Diary, 18 January 1949, BGA; Ben-Gurion, "The Political and Military Battle," 18 January 1949, BGA.

24. Ben-Gurion, "The Political and Military Battle," 18 January 1949, BGA.

25. "From Day to Day: The Elections War and Its Nature," *Haaretz*, 3 December 1948.

26. "Economic Planning—Desirable but It's Important to Avoid Using It for Political Purposes," *Yom Yom*, 8 December 1948; "The Progressive Party Cards," *Al Hamishmar*, 12 December 1948; "Voters to Be Deluged by 200 Tons of Paper," *Maariv*, 13 December 1948.

27. Ben-Gurion's Diary, 16 January 1949, 22 January 1949, BGA.

28. Ibid. On the role of past events in the elections, cf. Tzahor, "Mapai," 383; Weitz, *From Underground*, 201–203.

29. See, for example, Yaakov Meridor's speech in "Kol Israel," *Herut*, 11 January 1949; "Shertok Speaks at a Soldiers' Meeting in Netanya," *Davar*, 23 January 1949.

30. "Niv Hahayal," LPA; "Mapai's Fair Elections Propaganda," "The Obscenity of Mapai's Niv," *Al Hamishmar*, 13 January 1949; "On the Sharp Tip of a Pen," *Herut*, 14 January 1949; "'Vladimir Hitler,'" *Herut*, 16 January 1949.

31. "In the Margins of Things," *Davar*, 18 January 1949.

32. See, for example, Shapira, *Army Controversy*; Gelber, *Why Was the Palmach Disbanded?*

33. Ben-Gurion's Diary, 7 August 1948, BGA.

34. Mapai Bureau, 17 August 1948, LPA (emphasis in the original).

35. Gathering of Mapai activists, 7 November 1948, IV-406-107, Lavon Institute; Ben-Gurion's Diary, 8 November 1948, BGA.

36. Mapai Bureau, 23 November 1948, LPA.

37. Zalman Aharonovich's Diary, 12–19 November 1948, IV-104-127-228, Lavon Institute.

38. Ben-Gurion's Diary, 18 December 1948, BGA.

39. Bar-Rav-Hai to Yaakov Dori, 17 September 1948, 126/6127/1949, IDF Archives; Ben-Gurion to member of the committee on election propaganda in the army, 22 September 1948, 263/580/1956, IDF Archives; Committee's report, 4 November 1948, 263/580/1956, IDF Archives.

40. Provisional State Council, 25 November 1948, 23.

41. Security Committee of the Provisional State Council, 12 November 1948, 19 November 1948, 10 December 1948, 435/11-K, ISA; Provisional Government, 1 December 1948, 5 December 1948, 8 December 1948, 9 December 1948, ISA; Provisional State Council, 25 November 1948, 15–28, 16 December 1948, 39–43, ISA; Ben-Gurion to Chief of Staff, 13 December 1948, 23 December 1948, BGA.

42. Provisional Government, 9 December 1948, ISA.

43. "Proposed Sabbatical on the Elections Day," *Haaretz*, 11 January 1949; Provisional Government, 19 January 1949, 23 January 1949, ISA.

44. Ben-Gurion's Diary, 23–28 January 1949, BGA.

45. Ezriel Carlebach, "Battle Diary: The Celebration," 25 January 1949, *Maariv* (emphasis in the original).

46. See, for example, "Today Israel Is Going to Choose Its First Legislature," *Haboker*, 25 January 1949; "Today's Agenda," editorial, *Davar*, 25 January 1949; "Elections Marked by Celebratory Atmosphere and Tremendous Participation," *Herut*, 26 January 1949.

47. Ben-Gurion's Diary, 2 February 1949, BGA; "Results of the Constituent Assembly Elections," *Official Newspaper*, no. 49, 7 February 1949; *Israel Government Year Book, 1950*, 7–8.

48. Knesset, minutes, 21 November 1949, *Knesset Records*, vol. 3, 127.

49. Mapai Central Committee meeting with party branch delegates, 16 March 1949, LPA.

50. McDonald to Secretary of State, 28 January 1949, M1390/1, NARA.

51. McDonald's Diary, 28 January 1949, in McDonald, *Envoy*, 356–357.

52. Hopkins (presidential aide) to Niles, 31 January 1949; Truman to Feinberg, 1 February 1949; Feinberg to Truman, 4 February 1949, Papers of David K. Niles, Box 30, No. 1, Israel File, January–June 1949, HSTL.

53. Solomon, *The Speech . . . February 15, 1948*, 157.

54. Ben-Gurion's Diary, 26 January 1949, BGA.

55. Mapai Central Committee meeting with party branch delegates, 16 March 1949, LPA.

56. Ben-Gurion, "To the Nation and to the Army," 23 January 1949, BGA.

57. "Who Will Stay and Who Will Be Absent . . . ," *Herut*, 16 January 1949.

58. Ben-Gurion's Diary, 14 February 1949, BGA.

59. Shapira, *Israel: A History*, 179–183; Harris, *The Israeli Law*, 61–63; Kedar, *David Ben-Gurion and the Foundation of Israeli Democracy*, 26–51.

60. Weizmann to British Home Secretary James Chuter Ede, 28 September 1948, in Weizmann, *Letters*, vol. 23, 212; Chaim Posner to Ze'ev Sharef, 1 October 1948, 2391/68-FO, ISA; "President Weizmann Arrived," *Maariv*, 30 September 1948.

61. Rose, *Weizmann*, 446.

62. Provisional State Council, 30 September 1948, 12–13.

63. "'Our Mission Is in the Village'—Weizmann at Givat Brenner," *Davar*, 8 October 1948.

64. See Tzur, "The Exodus."

65. Military Government Council in Jerusalem to Weizmann, 1 December 1948, WA; "Jerusalem Is and Will Remain Ours," *Haboker*, 2 December 1948; "From Nahalal to Jerusalem," *Palestine Post*, 2 December 1948.

66. Ben-Gurion's Diary, 14 December 1948, 16 December 1949, BGA; correspondence between Ben-Gurion and Weizmann, 15 December 1948, 16 December 1948, 22 December 1948, BGA; Weizmann to Amery, 21 March 1949, in Weizmann, *Letters*, vol. 23, 267–268.

67. Ben-Gurion to Leo Cohen, 16 November 1948, BGA.

68. Weizmann to Simon Marks, 24 October 1948, in Weizmann, *Letters*, vol. 23, 218.

69. Weizmann to Amery, 24 October 1948, in Weizmann, *Letters*, vol. 23, 215; Weizmann to Crossman, 10 November 1948, in Weizmann, *Letters*, vol. 23, 227.

70. Gorny, *The Arab Question*, 123–131, 138–142, 269–275, 380, and so on; Morris, "Weizmann and the Arabs."

71. Aryeh Nesher, "Dr. Chaim Weizmann Surveys the Israeli Navy," *Haaretz*, 12 November 1948.

72. Weizmann to Rothschild, 19 November 1948, WA (unsent draft); Weizmann to Weisgal, 23 November 1948, in Weizmann, *Letters*, vol. 23, 228; Weizmann to Rothschild, 1 December 1948, in Weizmann, *Letters*, vol. 23, 235–236.

73. See, for example, Weizmann, *Letters*, vol. 23, 145–148, 153, 158, 178, 209, 215, 222–224, and 247–248, among other examples. See also Asia, *Core of the Conflict*, 56–57, 67–68, 75–76.

74. Weizmann to Rosenman and Joseph Cohen, 12 July 1948, 21 July 1948, in Weizmann, *Letters*, vol. 23, 169, 179.

75. "Weizmann: Our State Will Be a Model for the World," *Haaretz*, 3 October 1948.

76. McDonald's Diary, 5 November 1948, in McDonald, *Envoy*, 224; McDonald to Lovett, 17 November 1948, FRUS, 1948, vol. 5, 1606–1607; Weizmann to Frankfurter, 31 December 1948, in Weizmann, *Letters*, vol. 23, 241–242; "Weizmann Warns British Course Will Lead to War," *New York Times*, 13 January 1949.

77. Weizmann to Truman, 9 January 1949, in Weizmann, *Letters*, vol. 23, 247.

78. Ben-Gurion, Kaplan, Myerson, Remez, and Shertok to Weizmann, 14 May 1948, 2391/67-FO, ISA.

79. Weisgal to Weizmann, 10 December 1948, WA; Feinberg to Weizmann, 23 December 1948, WA.

80. Weisgal to Weizmann, 23 December 1948, WA.

81. Vera Weizmann to Weisgal, 30 December 1948, WA; Weizmann to Frankfurter, 31 December 1948, in Weizmann, *Letters*, vol. 23, 241–242; Weizmann to Truman, 9 January 1949, in Weizmann, *Letters*, vol. 23, 247; "Truman to Speak at Event in Honor of Weizmann," *Davar*, 6 January 1949.

82. McDonald to State Department, 6 January 1949, 19 January 1949, Clifford Papers, Box 14, Telegrams and Cables, File 2, HSTL; Weizmann to Weisgal, 20 January 1949, in Weizmann, *Letters*, vol. 23, 252; Weisgal to Weizmann, 21 January 1949, WA.

83. "Truman Regrets Trip by Weizmann Waits," *New York Times*, 3 February 1949; "Weizmann Trip Postponed for Health Reasons," *Maariv*, 3 February 1949.

84. Provisional State Council, 13 January 1949, 7–9.

85. Ibid.; Provisional Government, minutes, 20 December 1948, ISA.

86. Provisional Government, minutes, 2 February 1949, ISA.

87. Provisional Government, minutes, 6 February 1949, ISA.

88. Knesset, minutes, 16 February 1949, *Knesset Records*, vol. 1, 52.

89. Provisional Government, minutes, 14 February 1949, ISA.

90. McDonald to Weizmann, 2 February 1949, WA; Knesset, minutes, 14 February 1949, *Knesset Records*, vol. 1, 5–7; "The One Missing," *Hamashkif*, 15 February 1949.

91. Knesset, minutes, 16 February 1949, *Knesset Records*, vol. 1, 48–49; "Who Will Be Israel's President?," *Hamashkif*, 15 February 1949; Herzl Rosenblum, "What Preceded the Election of Dr. Weizmann," *Yedioth Ahronoth*, 17 February 1949.

92. Weizmann to Rosenman, 17 May 1948, Weizmann to Clifford, 20 February 1949, in Weizmann, *Letters*, vol. 23, 122, 254–255; Epstein to Clifford, 24 January 1949, 2 February 1949, 347/1-FO, 377/11-FO, ISA.

93. Knesset, minutes, 17 February 1949, *Knesset Records*, vol. 1, 51.

94. "Today's Agenda," *Davar*, editorial, 18 February 1949.

95. Weizmann to Dewey Stone, 29 November 1951, in Weizmann, *Letters*, vol. 23, 308.

96. "Sunday, 9 November 1952," *Bamahane*, 13 November 1952; *Haaretz*, editorial, 12 November 1952.

97. Weizmann to Martin Buber, 28 October 1951, WA.

Conclusion

1. Ben-Gurion's opening address, Jerusalem Conference, 3 September 1950, BGA. The conference launched the establishment of Israel Bonds, securities sold by Israel to Diaspora Jews as a means of raising funds for large development projects (the National Water Carrier, Dead Sea Works, and Israel's seaports, among others).

2. Tal, "Israel's War of Independence."

3. Shalom Rosenfeld, "History Enfolded in a File . . . ," *Maariv*, 10 May 1951.

4. Kollat, "Chaim Weizmann's Rise to Leadership," 19; Shamir, *With His Own Hands*.

5. Moshe Shamir, "Chaim Weizmann in Our Generation's Eyes," 3 November 1957, WA (emphasis in the original).

6. Bareli and Kedar, *Israeli Republicanism*, 32–50.

7. "The Watchman," *Time*, 16 August 1948.

8. National Council Executive, minutes, 23 June 1948, J1/7077, CZA; Attias, *Book*, 426–427.

9. McDonald to Truman and Marshall, 23 February 1949, M1390/2, NARA; McDonald, *Envoy*, 395.

10. Z. Aharonovich, "On the Threshold," *Hapoel Hatzair*, 21 September 1948.

11. Y. Lufban, "The Attribute of Statehood," *Hapoel Hatzair*, 20 January 1948.

12. Truman to Feinberg, 20 December 1950, BGA. On November 1, 1950, two Puerto Rican independence activists attempted to assassinate Truman. One of Truman's bodyguards was killed, but the president was not harmed. This may have been the reason for choosing such a gift. When Ben-Gurion met with Truman in Washington on May 8, 1951, he gifted him with a menorah. This was Truman's birthday and a peak moment in his dispute with General Douglas MacArthur over the management of the Korean War.

13. Perhaps it would be more appropriate to draw a comparison not between Weizmann's and Ben-Gurion's gifts but between the conditions of prestate Israel during the crisis involving the esteemed General Marshall three years earlier and Israel's situation during the dramatic crisis involving the general this time. In each crisis, Truman's decision remains valid to this day.

14. Meir Yaari, "Is Security Being Turned into a Pickaxe?," *Al Hamishmar*, 18 April 1962.

15. Feinberg-Truman correspondence, 20 June 1955, 8 July 1955, 18 July 1955, 22 July 1955, 25 July 1955, 14 June 1960, 6 January 1961, Papers of Harry S. Truman, Post Presidential Papers, Secretaries Office Files, Feinberg Abraham File, Box 18, No. 1–2, HSTL.

16. Cohen, *Israel and the Bomb*, 70, 104, 315, 368n82; Segev, *1967*, 126–130, 321.

17. Rusk, *As I Saw It*, 153.

BIBLIOGRAPHY

ARCHIVES

Ben-Gurion Archives, Sde Boker (BGA)
Central Zionist Archives, Jerusalem (CZA)
Franklin D. Roosevelt Presidential Library, Hyde Park, New York (FDRL)
Harry S. Truman Presidential Library, Independence, Missouri (HSTL)
IDF Archives, Tel Hashomer
Israel State Archives, Jerusalem (ISA)
Jabotinsky Institute, Tel Aviv
Jewish Heritage Center at New England Historic Genealogical Society, Boston (JHC)
Labor Party Archives, Beit Berl (LPA)
Lavon Institute for Labour Movement Research, Tel Aviv (Lavon Institute)
National Archives, London (NA)
National Archives, Washington (NARA)
Princeton University Library
University of Minnesota Archives, Minneapolis, Minnesota
Weizmann Archives, Rehovot (WA)
Weizmann Institute Archives, Rehovot (WIA)

NEWSPAPERS (HEBREW)

Al Hamishmar
Ashmoret
Bamahane
Davar
Haaretz
Haboker
Hamashkif
Hapoel Hatzair
Hatzofeh
Herut
Maariv
Official Newspaper
Yedioth Ahronoth
Yom Yom

BOOKS AND ARTICLES

Adler, Frank J. *Roots in a Moving Stream: The Centennial History of Congregation B'nai Jehudah of Kansas City, 1870–1970*. Kansas City, MO: The Temple, Congregation B'nai Yehuda, 1972.

Asia, Ilan. *The Core of the Conflict: The Struggle for the Negev, 1946–1956*. Jerusalem: Yad Izhak Ben-Zvi, 1944 [Hebrew].

Attias, Moshe, ed. *Book of Documents about the Va'ad Leumi*. Jerusalem: Dfus RH Cohen, 1963 [Hebrew].

Avineri, Shlomo. "A Leader's Place in History: On the Leadership of David Ben-Gurion." In *Leaders and Leadership in Jewish and World History*, edited by Irad Malkin and Zeev Tzahor, 327–338. Jerusalem: Zalman Shazar Center, 1992 [Hebrew].

Avizohar, Meir, and Avi Bareli, eds. *Now or Never: Proceedings of Mapai in the Closing Year of the British Mandate*. Beit Berl, Israel: Berl Katznelson Center, 1989 [Hebrew].

Bareli, Avi. "Between Party Politics and Government Politics: Mapai's Leadership in the First Years of the State of Israel." *Israel*, no. 5 (2004): 31–62 [Hebrew].

———. "Mapai during the War of Independence: The End of Yishuv Politics and the Beginning of Israeli Politics." In *Politics in Wartime: Studies on the Civilian Society during the Israeli War of Independence*, edited by Mordechai Bar-On and Meir Chazan, 179–206. Jerusalem: Yad Izhak Ben-Zvi, 2014 [Hebrew].

Bareli, Avi, and Yosef Gorny. "Unity and Participation in a Modern Democracy: The Development of the Democratic-Republican Concept of Achdut Haavoda and Mapai." In *Israel and Modernity: In Honor of Moshe Lissak*, edited by Uri Cohen, Eliezer Ben-Rafael, Avi Bareli, and Ephraim Ya'ar, 127–167. Sde Boqer, Israel: Ben-Gurion Research Institute, 2006 [Hebrew].

Bareli, Avi, and Nir Kedar. *Israeli Republicanism*. Jerusalem: The Israel Democracy Institute, 2011 [Hebrew].

Bar-On, Mordechai. *In the Forefront of the Fiercest Battles: Research Essays on the History of Israel's War of Independence*. Modi'in, Israel: Effi Melzer, 2015 [Hebrew].

———. *Of All the Kingdoms: Israel's Relations with the United Kingdom during the First Decade after the End of the British Mandate in Palestine, 1948–1958*. Jerusalem: Yad Izhak Ben-Zvi, 2006 [Hebrew].

Bar-Zohar, Michael. *Ben-Gurion: A Political Biography*. Vol. 2. Tel Aviv: Am Oved, 1977. [Hebrew].

Ben-Dror, Elad. *The Mediator: Ralph Bunche and the Arab-Israeli Conflict, 1947–1949*. Sde Boqer, Israel: Ben-Gurion Institute, 2012 [Hebrew].

Ben-Gurion, David. *Army and Security*. Tel Aviv: Maarachot, 1955 [Hebrew].

———. *As Israel Fought*. Tel Aviv: Mapai, 1950 [Hebrew].

———. *Chimes of Independence: Memoirs (March–November 1947)*. Edited by Meir Avizohar. Tel Aviv: Am Oved, 1993 [Hebrew].

———. *Memoirs: 1937*. Vol. 4. Edited by Mordechai Nesiyahu and Eli Shaltiel. Tel Aviv: Am Oved, 1976 [Hebrew].

———. "Preface." In Weisgal and Carmichael, *Chaim Weizmann*, 1–7.

———. *The Resurgent State of Israel*. Tel Aviv: Am Oved, 1969 [Hebrew].

———. *Towards the End of the Mandate: Memories (June 1946–March 1947)*. Edited by Meir Avizohar. Tel Aviv: Am Oved, 1993 [Hebrew].

———. *Uniqueness and Destiny: Remarks on Israel's Security*. Tel Aviv: Maarachot, 1971 [Hebrew].

———. *War Diary: Supplement—Additions and Revisions*. Edited by Gershon Rivlin and Elhanan Oren. Tel Aviv: Ministry of Defense, 1984 [Hebrew].

———. *War Diary: The War of Independence, 1947–1949.* Edited by Gershon Rivlin and El-hanan Oren. Tel Aviv: Ministry of Defense, 1982 [Hebrew].

Benson, Michael T. *Harry S. Truman and the Founding of Israel.* Westport, CT: Praeger, 1997.

Ben-Zvi, Abraham. *From Truman to Obama: The Rise and Early Decline of American-Israeli Relations.* Tel Aviv: Yedioth Sfarim, 2011 [Hebrew].

Bergman, Elihu. "Unexpected Recognition: Some Observations on the Failure of a Last-Gasp Campaign in the U.S. State Department to Abort a Jewish State." *Modern Judaism*, no. 19 (1999): 133–171.

Bialer, Uri. *Between East and West: Israel's Foreign Policy Orientation 1948–1956*, Cambridge: Cambridge University Press, 1990.

———. "David Ben-Gurion and Moshe Sharett: Images and Decisions on the Eve of State-hood." MA thesis, Hebrew University of Jerusalem, September 1971 [Hebrew].

———. "Documents on Israeli-Soviet Relations, 1941–1953." *Iyunim Bitkumat Israel* 11 (2001): 534–542 [Hebrew].

———. "Top Hat, Tuxedo and Cannons: Israeli Foreign Policy from 1948 to 1956." In *The History of the Jewish Community in Eretz-Israel since 1882: Israel—The First Decade*, edited by Moshe Lissak, 634–701. Jerusalem: Bialik Institute, 2009 [Hebrew].

Bisgyer, Maurice. *Challenge and Encounter: Behind the Scenes in the Struggle for Jewish Survival.* New York: Crown, 1967.

Brecher, Frank W. *American Diplomacy and the Israeli War of Independence.* Jefferson, NC: McFarland & Company, 2013.

Bullock, Alan. *Ernest Bevin: Foreign Secretary, 1945–1951.* New York: Norton, 1983.

Central Bureau of Statistics. *Immigration to Israel, 2007–2010.* Jerusalem: CBS, 2012 [Hebrew].

Clifford, Clark, with Richard Holbrooke. *Counsel to the President: A Memoir.* New York: Random House, 1991.

Cohen, Avner. *Israel and the Bomb.* New York: Columbia University Press, 1998.

Cohen, Michael J. *Palestine and the Great Powers, 1945–1948.* Princeton: Princeton University Press, 1982.

———. *Truman and Israel.* Berkeley: University of California Press, 1990.

Cohen, Uri. *Laboratory, Research Institute, City of Science: From the Daniel Sieff Research Institute to the Weizmann Institute of Science, 1934–1949.* Jerusalem: Bialik Institute, 2016 [Hebrew].

Cohen, Uri, and Meir Chazan, eds. *Weizmann: The Leader of Zionism.* Jerusalem: Zalman Shazar Center, 2016 [Hebrew].

Cohen-Levinovsky, Nurit. "Presidents in 1948: Between Weizmann and Truman." In Cohen and Chazan, *Weizmann*, 495–525 [Hebrew].

Crossman, R. H. S. "The Prisoner of Rehovoth." In Weisgal and Carmichael, *Chaim Weizmann*, 325–356.

Donaldson, Gary A. *Truman Defeats Dewey.* Lexington: University Press of Kentucky, 1999.

Donovan, Robert J. *Conflict and Crisis: The Presidency of Harry S Truman, 1945–1948.* New York: Norton, 1977.

Eban, Abba. *An Autobiography.* London: Weidenfeld and Nicolson, 1977.

———. "Dewey David Stone: A Prototype of an American Zionist." In Kaganoff, *Solidarity*, 27–36.

———. "Tragedy and Triumph." In Weisgal and Carmichael, *Chaim Weizmann*, 249–313.

———. *Voice of Israel.* New York: Horizon, 1957.

———. "Weizmann during the Political Struggle of 1947–1948." In *A Statesman in Times of Crisis: Chaim Weizmann and the Zionist Movement, 1900–1948*, edited by Yosef Gorny and Gedalia Yogev, 120–130. Tel Aviv: Hakibbutz Hameuchad, 1977 [Hebrew].

Ehrenvald, Moshe. *Haredim during the Independence War.* Ben-Shemen, Israel: Modan, 2017 [Hebrew].

Eilam, Yigal. *What Happened Here.* Tel Aviv: Am Oved, 2012 [Hebrew].

Eilat, Eliahu. *The Struggle over the State: Washington, 1945–1948.* Vols. 1–2. Tel Aviv: Am Oved, 1982 [Hebrew].

———. *Through the Mists of Time: Memoirs.* Jerusalem: Yad Izhak Ben-Zvi, 1989 [Hebrew].

Feldstein, Ariel. *Gordian Knot: David Ben-Gurion, the Zionist Organization, and American Jewry.* Sde Boqer, Israel: Ben-Gurion Institute [Hebrew].

———. "Three Days in May 1948: A Fresh Look at the Historical Documents." *Iyunim Bitkumat Israel* 8 (1998): 354–374 [Hebrew].

Ferrell, Robert H, ed. *Truman in the White House: The Diary of Eben A. Ayers.* Columbia: University of Missouri, 1991.

Fetter, Henry D. "'Forthcoming Three Months Represent Best Remaining Opportunity for Accomplishment': Israeli Diplomacy and the 1948 US Presidential Election." Part I, *Israel Affairs* 15, no. 3 (2009): 246–260; Part II, *Israel Affairs* 16, no. 2 (2010): 201–218.

———. "'Showdown in the Oval Office': 12 May 1948 in History." *Israel Affairs* 14, no. 3 (2008): 499–518.

Forrestal, James. *The Forrestal Diaries.* Edited by Walter Millis. New York: Viking, 1951.

Frantz, Douglas, and David McKean. *Friends in High Places: The Rise and Fall of Clark Clifford.* Boston: Little, Brown, 1995.

Freundlich, Yehoshua, ed. *Documents on the Foreign Policy of Israel, Vol. 1, 14 May–30 September 1948.* Jerusalem: Israel State Archives, 1981.

———, ed. *Documents on the Foreign Policy of Israel, Vol. 2, October 1948–April 1949.* Jerusalem: Israel State Archives, 1984.

———. *From Destruction to Resurrection: Zionist Policy from the End of the Second World War to the Establishment of the State of Israel.* Tel Aviv: University Publication Industries, 1994 [Hebrew].

———. "A Soviet Outpost in Tel Aviv: The Soviet Legation in Israel, 1948–53." *Journal of Israeli History* 22, no. 1 (2003): 37–43.

Frister, Roman. *Uncompromising.* Tel Aviv: Zemorah-Bitan, 1987 [Hebrew].

Ganin, Zvi. *Truman, American Jewry and Israel.* New York and London: Holmes and Meier, 1979.

———. *An Uneasy Relationship: American Jewish Leadership and Israel, 1948–1957.* Syracuse: Syracuse University Press, 2005.

———. "The US View of the Establishment of Israel, 1945–1948." In *We Were as Dreamers: Selected Essays on the War of Independence,* edited by Yehuda Wallach, 201–248. Tel Aviv: Massada [Hebrew].

Gelber, Yoav. "Development of Research on the War of Independence." In *Politics at War: Studies on the Civilian Society during the Israeli War of Independence,* edited by Mordechai Bar-On and Meir Chazan, 11–35. Jerusalem: Yad Izhak Ben-Zvi, 2014 [Hebrew].

———. *The Emergence of a Jewish Army: The Veterans of the British Army in the IDF.* Jerusalem: Yad Izhak Ben-Zvi, 1986 [Hebrew].

———. *Independence and Nakba: Israel, the Palestinians, and Arab Countries, 1948.* Or Yehuda, Israel: Dvir, 2004 [Hebrew].

———. *Why Was the Palmach Disbanded? The Jewish Military Force in the Transition from a Yishuv to a State.* Tel Aviv: Schocken, 1986 [Hebrew].

Golani, Motti. *The British Mandate for Palestine, 1948: War and Evacuation.* Jerusalem: Zalman Shazar Center, 2009 [Hebrew].

———. *The Last Commissioner: General Sir Alan Gordon Cunningham, 1945–1948.* Tel Aviv: Am Oved, 2011 [Hebrew].

Golani, Motti, and Jehuda Reinharz. *The Founding Father: Chaim Weizmann, Biography, 1922–1952.* Tel Aviv: Am Oved, 2020 [Hebrew].

Goldstein, Yaakov. *The Path to Hegemony: Mapai—The Consolidation of Its Policy, 1930–1936.* Tel Aviv: Am Oved, 1980 [Hebrew].

Goldstein, Yossi. *Golda: Biography.* Beer Sheva: Ben-Gurion University Press, 2012 [Hebrew].

Gorny, Yosef. *The Ambiguous Tie: The British Labour Movement and Its Attitude to Zionism, 1917–1947.* Tel Aviv: Hakibbutz Hameuchad, 1982 [Hebrew].

———. *The Arab Question and the Jewish Problem.* Tel Aviv: Am Oved, 1985 [Hebrew].

———. *Partnership and Conflict: Chaim Weizmann and the Jewish Labour Movement in Palestine.* Tel Aviv: Am Oved, 1976 [Hebrew].

Grose, Peter. *Israel in the Mind of America.* New York: Alfred A. Knopf, 1983.

Hahn, Peter L. *Caught in the Middle East: U.S. Policy toward the Arab-Israeli Conflict, 1945–1961.* Chapel Hill: University of North Carolina Press, 2006.

Hamby, Alonzo L. *Man of the People: A Life of Harry S. Truman.* New York: Oxford University Press, 1995.

Hammer, Dewey Gottlieb. "David Stone: An Appreciation." In Kaganoff, *Solidarity,* 5–15.

Harris, Ron. *The Israeli Law—The Formative Years: 1948–1977.* Tel Aviv: Hakibbutz Hameuchad, 2014 [Hebrew].

Haynes, John Earl, Harvey Klehr, and Alexander Vassiliev. *Spies: The Rise and Fall of the KGB in America.* New Haven, CT, and London: Yale University Press, 2009.

Heard, Alexander. *The Costs of Democracy.* Chapel Hill: University of North Carolina Press, 1960.

Heller, Joseph. *The Birth of Israel, 1945–1949: Ben-Gurion and His Critics.* Gainesville: University Press of Florida, 2000.

Helman, Yudke, ed. *The Story of the Yiftach-Palmach Brigade.* Bat Yam, Israel: 1970 [Hebrew].

Horowitz, David. *In the Heart of Events.* Ramat Gan: Masada, 1975 [Hebrew].

Ilan, Amitzur. *Bernadotte in Palestine, 1948.* New York: St. Martin's, 1989.

———. *The Origin of the Arab-Israeli Arms Race.* London: Macmillan in association with St. Antony's College, Oxford, 1996.

Isaacson, Walter, and Evan Thomas. *The Wise Men: Six Friends and the World They Made—Acheson, Bohlen, Harriman, Kennan, Lovett, McCloy.* New York: Simon & Schuster, 1986.

Israel Government Year Book, 1950. Tel Aviv: Government Printer, 1950 [Hebrew].

Joseph, Dov. *The Faithful City: The Siege of Jerusalem, 1948.* New York: Simon & Schuster, 1960.

Judis, John B. *Genesis: Truman, American Jews, and the Origins of the Arab/Israeli Conflict.* New York: Farrar, Straus and Giroux, 2014.

Kaganoff, Nathan M., ed. *Solidarity and Kinship: Essays on American Zionism—In Memory of Dewey David Stone.* Waltham, MA: American Jewish Historical Society, 1980.

Kaufman, Menahem. "American Zionists and Non-Zionists in the Struggle for Jewish Statehood 1947–1948." In *Zionism and Its Jewish Opponents,* edited by Haim Avni and Gideon Shimoni, 375–393. Jerusalem: Hassifria Haziyonit, 1990 [Hebrew].

Kedar, Nir. *David Ben-Gurion and the Foundation of Israeli Democracy.* Bloomington: Indiana University Press, 2021.

Kennan, George F. *The Kennan Diaries.* Edited by Frank Costigliola. New York: Norton, 2014.

Kimchi, Yigal. *The First President: Chapters in the Life of Chaim Weizmann.* Tel Aviv: Ministry of Defense, 1994 [Hebrew].

Kollat, Israel. "Chaim Weizmann's Rise to Leadership." In *Avot U-Meyasdim,* 1–22. Tel Aviv: Hakibbutz Hameuchad, 1975 [Hebrew].

Kurzman, Dan. *Genesis 1948: The First Arab-Israeli War.* London: Vallentine, Mitchell, 1972.

Levy, Herbert. *Henry Morgenthau, Jr.: The Remarkable Life of FDR's Secretary of Treasury*, New York: Skyhorse, 2010.

Louis, William Roger. *The British Empire in the Middle East, 1945–1951*. Oxford: Clarendon, 1984.

McCullough, David. *Truman*. New York: Simon & Schuster, 1992.

McDonald, James G. *Envoy to the Promise Land: The Diaries and Papers of James G. McDonald, 1948–1951*. Edited by Norman J. W. Goda et al. Bloomington: Indiana University Press, 2017.

McFarland, Keith D., and David L. Roll. *Louis Johnson and the Arming of America: The Roosevelt and Truman Years*. Bloomington: Indiana University Press, 2005.

Medzini, Meron. *Golda: Golda Meir and the Vision of Israel: A Political Biography*. Tel Aviv: Miskal, 2008 [Hebrew].

Milstein, Uri. *History of Israel's War of Independence*. Vol. 4. Lanham, MD: University Press of America, 1998.

Miscamble, Wilson D. *George F. Kennan and the Making of American Foreign Policy, 1947–1950*. Princeton: Princeton University Press, 1992.

Morris, Benny. *The Birth of the Palestinian Refugee Problem Revisited*. Cambridge: Cambridge University Press, 2004.

———. *1948: A History of the First Arab-Israeli War*. New Haven, CT, and London: Yale University Press, 2008.

———. "Weizmann and the Arabs." In *Chaim Weizmann: Scientist, Statesman, and Architect of Science Policy*, edited by Benjamin Z. Kedar, 173–203. Jerusalem: Israel Academy for Sciences and Humanities, 2015 [Hebrew].

Nimrod, Yoram. *Mifgash BaTzomet: Jews and Arabs in Palestine—Recent Generations*. Ein HaHoresh and Oranim, 1984 [Hebrew].

———. *War or Peace? Formation of Patterns in Israeli-Arab Relations, 1947–1950*. Givat Haviva, Israel: Hamachon Lecheker Hashalom, 2000 [Hebrew].

Ofer, Pinhas. *Enemy and Rival: The Zionist Movement and the Yishuv between the Arabs and the British, 1929–1948*. Tel Aviv: Tcherikover, 2001 [Hebrew].

Orian, Noach. *The Forgotten Founder: A. H. Silver and the Political Campaign for the Establishment of Israel*. Tel Aviv: Hamama Safrutit, 2012 [Hebrew].

Ottolenghi, Michael. "Harry Truman's Recognition of Israel." *Historical Journal* 47, no. 4 (2004): 963–988.

Ovendale, Ritchie. *Britain, The United States, and the End of the Palestine Mandate, 1942–1948*. London: Royal Historical Society, 1989.

Penslar, Derek J. *Jews and the Military: A History*. Princeton: Princeton University Press, 2013.

People's Council, The Provisional State Council. Tel Aviv: 1948–1949 [Hebrew].

Public Papers of the Presidents of the United States: Harry S. Truman, Containing the Public Messages, Speeches, and Statements of the President, January–December 1948. Washington, DC: United States Government Printing Office, 1964.

Radosh, Allis, and Ronald. *A Safe Haven: Harry S. Truman and the Founding of Israel*. New York: Harper, 2009.

Raphael, Marc Lee. *Abba Hillel Silver: A Profile in American Judaism*. New York: Holmes and Meier, 1989.

Redding, Jack. *Inside the Democratic Party*. Indianapolis: Bobbs Merrill, 1958.

Ro'i, Yaacov. "The Deterioration of Relations: From Support to Severance." *Journal of Israeli History* 22, no. 1 (2003): 21–36.

———. *Soviet Decision Making in Practice: The USSR and Israel, 1947–1954*. New Brunswick, Canada: Transaction, 1980.

Rose, Norman. *Chaim Weizmann: A Biography*. New York: Penguin, 1986.

Rosen, Doron. *In Quest of the American Treasure: The Israeli Underground (the Haganah) Activity in the U. S. in 1945–1949*. Tel Aviv: Ministry of Defense, 2008 [Hebrew].

Ross, Irwin. *The Loneliest Campaign: The Truman Victory of 1948*. New York: New American Library, 1968.

Rusk, Dean. *As I Saw It: As Told to Richard Rusk*. Edited by Daniel S. Papp. New York: Penguin, 1991.

Segev, Tom. *1967: Israel, the War, and the Year That Transformed the Middle East*. Jerusalem: Keter, 2005 [Hebrew].

———. *A State at Any Cost: The Life of David Ben-Gurion*. London: Head of Zeus, 2019.

Segev, Zohar. *From Ethnic Politicians to National Leaders: American Zionist Leadership, the Holocaust and the Establishment of Israel*. Sde Boqer, Israel: Ben-Gurion Institute, 2007 [Hebrew].

Shachar, Yoram. *Dignity, Liberty and Honest Toil: Drafting the Israeli Declaration of Independence*. Sde Boqer, Israel: Ben-Gurion Institute, 2021 [Hebrew].

Shamir, Moshe. *With His Own Hands*. Merhavia, Israel: Hashomer Hatzair, 1951.

Shapira, Anita. *The Army Controversy, 1948: Ben-Gurion's Struggle for Control*. Tel Aviv: Hakibbutz Hameuchad, 1985 [Hebrew].

———. *Ben-Gurion: Father of Modern Israel*. New Haven, CT: Yale University Press, 2014.

———. "Elements of the National Ethos in the Transition to Statehood." In *Jewish Nationalism and Politics: New Perspectives*, edited by Jehuda Reinharz, Gideon Shimoni, and Yosef Salmon, 253–271. Jerusalem: Zalman Shazar Center, 1996 [Hebrew].

———. *Israel: A History*. Waltham, MA: Brandeis University Press, 2012.

———. "A Political History of the Yishuv, 1918–1939." In *The History of the Jewish Community in Eretz Israel since the First Aliya: The Period of the British Mandate*. Vol. 2, edited by Moshe Lissak, Anita Shapira, and Gavriel Cohen, 1–172. Jerusalem: Bialik Institute and the Israel Academy for Sciences and Humanities, 1994 [Hebrew].

———. "Weizmann and Ben-Gurion: Portraits in Contrast." In *The Individual in History: Essays in Honor of Jehuda Reinharz*, edited by ChaeRan Y. Freeze et al., 165–181. Waltham, MA: Brandeis University Press, 2015.

———. *Yigal Allon: Spring of His Life—A Biography*. Tel Aviv: Hakibbutz Hameuchad, 2004 [Hebrew].

Sharef, Ze'ev. *Three Days: 12, 13, 14 of May 1948*. Tel Aviv: Am Oved, 1959 [Hebrew].

Sharett, Moshe. *Personal Diary*. Tel Aviv: Maariv, 1978 [Hebrew].

———. *Speaking Out: Israel Foreign Ministers Speeches, May—December 1948*. Edited by Yaakov Sharett and Rina Sharett. Tel Aviv: Moshe Sharett Heritage Society, 2013 [Hebrew].

Sharett, Yaakov. "Moshe Sharett and the Declaration of Independence." In *A Statesman Assessed: Views and Viewpoints about Moshe Sharett*, edited by Yaakov Sharett and Rina Sharett, 277–295. Tel Aviv: Moshe Sharett Heritage Society, 2008 [Hebrew].

Sheffer, Gabriel. *Moshe Sharett: A Political Biography*. Jerusalem: Carmel, 2015 [Hebrew].

Shiff, Ofer. "Abba Hillel Silver and David Ben-Gurion: A Diaspora Leader Challenges the Revered Status of the 'Founding Father.'" *Studies in Ethnicity and Nationalism* 10, no. 3 (2010): 391–412.

———. *The Defeated Zionist: Abba Hillel Silver and His Attempt to Transcend Jewish Nationalism*. Tel Aviv: Resling, 2010 [Hebrew].

Slater, Leonard. *The Pledge*. Tel Aviv: Ministry of Defense, 1971 [Hebrew].

Slonim, Shlomo. "The 1948 American Embargo on Arms to Palestine." *Political Science Quarterly* 94, no. 3 (1979): 495–514.

Slutsky, Yehuda. *History of the Haganah*. Vol. 3, Part 2. Tel Aviv: Maarachot, 1973 [Hebrew].

Snetsinger, John. *Truman, the Jewish Vote and the Creation of Israel*. Stanford, CA: Hoover Institution Press, 1974.

Solomon, Abba A. *The Speech, and Its Context: Jacob Blaustein's Speech "The Meaning of Palestine Partitions to American Jews," Given to the Baltimore Chapter, American Jewish Committee, February 15, 1948*. Self-published, Lulu Press, 2011.

Sprinzak, Yosef. *Letters*. Edited by Yosef Shapira. Vol. 3. Tel Aviv: Ayanot, 1969 [Hebrew].

Stern, Anat. "A Party under Trial: The Freedom Fighters of Israel's 'Warriors List' in the Elections to the Constituent Assembly." In *Politics in Wartime: Studies on the Civilian Society during the Israeli War of Independence*, edited by Mordechai Bar-On and Meir Chazan, 411–449. Jerusalem: Yad Izhak Ben-Zvi, 2014 [Hebrew].

Tal, David. "Israel's War of Independence: David Ben-Gurion's War." *Iyunim Bitkumat Israel* 13 (2003): 115–138 [Hebrew].

———. *War in Palestine*. London: Routledge, 2004.

Tal, Izhar. "Declaration of Independence: A Historical-Interpretive Examination." *Mishpat Umimshal* 6, no. 2 (2003): 551–590 [Hebrew].

Tauber, Eliezer. *Deir Yassin: The End of the Myth*. Or Yehuda, Israel: Kinneret, 2017 [Hebrew].

Teveth, Shabtai. *Kin'at David*. Vols. 3–4. Jerusalem and Tel Aviv: Schocken, 1987, 2004 [Hebrew].

———. *HaDerech LeIyar*. Tel Aviv: Ministry of Defense, 1986 [Hebrew].

Tsoref, Hagai, ed. *Zalman Shazar: Israel's Third President, Selected Documents, 1889–1974*. Jerusalem: Israel State Archives, 2008 [Hebrew].

Tzahor, Zeev. "The First Elections Campaigns and the Political Map." In *The First Decade: 1948–1958*, edited by Zvi Zameret and Hana Yablonka, 27–40. Jerusalem: Yad Izhak Ben-Zvi, 1998 [Hebrew].

———. *Israel's Political Roots*. Tel Aviv: Hakibbutz Hameuchad, 1987 [Hebrew].

———. "Mapai, Mapam, and the Formation of the First Israeli Government." *Iyunim Bitkumat Israel* 4 (1994): 378–426 [Hebrew].

———. *Vision and Reckoning: Ben-Gurion—Ideology and Politics*. Tel Aviv: Miskal and Sifriat Poalim, 1994 [Hebrew].

Tzur, Eli. "The Exodus Began and What Did the Pioneers Contribute to It?" *Iyunim Bitkumat Israel* 9 (1999): 316–337 [Hebrew].

Warhaftig, Zorach. *A Constitution for Israel: Religion and State*. Jerusalem: Mesilot, 1988 [Hebrew].

Weisgal, Meyer W. . . . *So Far: An Autobiography*. London: Weidenfeld and Nicolson together with Ma'ariv Book Guild, 1971.

Weisgal, Meyer W., and Joel Carmichael, eds. *Chaim Weizmann: A Biography by Several Hands*. London: Weidenfeld and Nicolson, 1964.

Weitz, Yechiam. *From Underground to Political Party: The Foundation of the Herut Movement, 1947–1949*. Sde Boqer, Israel: Ben Gurion Research Institute, 2003 [Hebrew].

Weizmann, Chaim. *The Letters and Papers of Chaim Weizmann*. Vol. 22, May 1945–July 1947. Edited by Joseph Heller. Jerusalem: Transaction, 1979.

———. *The Letters and Papers of Chaim Weizmann*. Vol. 23, August 1947–June 1952. Edited by Aaron Klieman. Jerusalem: Transaction, 1980.

———. "Plea to Accept Partition Plan," Address to Twentieth Zionist Congress, Zurich, 4 August 1937. In *The Letters and Papers of Chaim Weizmann*. Vol. II, Series B, edited by Barnet Litvinoff. New Brunswick. Canada: Transaction, 1984.

———. *Trial and Error: The Autobiography of Chaim Weizmann*. London: Hamish Hamilton, 1949.

Weizmann, Vera. *The Impossible Takes Longer: The Memoirs of Vera Weizmann as Told to David Tutaev.* London: Hamish Hamilton, 1967.

Yadin, Uri. "The Transition Law for a Constituent Assembly, 17 January 1949." In *In Memoriam: Uri Yadin*, edited by Aharon Barak and Tana Spanic, 79–82. Jerusalem: Bursi [Hebrew].

Yogev, Gedalia, ed. *Political and Diplomatic Documents, December 1947– May 1948.* Jerusalem: Israel Government Press, 1979 [Hebrew].

Yosef, Goldie. *Memoirs, Diaries, Letters, and Stories.* Jerusalem: Reuven Mass, 1979 [Hebrew].

Zionist Organization and Jewish Agency. *The Twentieth Zionist Congress and the Fifth Session of the Jewish Agency Council, Zurich, 3–21 August 1937.* Jerusalem: Zionist Organization Executive and Jewish Agency Executive, 1937 [Hebrew].

INDEX

MEIR CHAZAN is Associate Professor in the Department of Jewish History at Tel Aviv University. He is author (in Hebrew) of *Moderation: The Moderate View in Hapo'el hatza'ir and Mapai, 1905–1945* and *The Modest Revolution: Women and Defense in Palestine, 1907–1945.*

For Indiana University Press

Tony Brewer, *Artist and Book Designer*

Brian Carroll, *Rights Manager*

Gary Dunham, *Acquisitions Editor and Director*

Anna Francis, *Assistant Acquisitions Editor*

Brenna Hosman, *Production Coordinator*

Katie Huggins, *Production Manager*

Nancy Lightfoot, *Project Editor and Manager*

Dan Pyle, *Online Publishing Manager*

Leyla Salamova, *Senior Artist and Book Designer*

Stephen Williams, *Marketing and Publicity Manager*

www.ingramcontent.com/pod-product-compliance
Lightning Source LLC
Chambersburg PA
CBHW031127270326
41929CB00011B/1529